ARTMACHINES

ARTMACHINES

Deleuze, Guattari, Simondon

Anne Sauvagnargues

Translated by Suzanne Verderber with Eugene W. Holland

Introduction by Gregory Flaxman

EDINBURGH
University Press

Edinburgh University Press is one of the leading university presses in the UK. We publish academic books and journals in our selected subject areas across the humanities and social sciences, combining cutting-edge scholarship with high editorial and production values to produce academic works of lasting importance. For more information visit our website: www.edinburghuniversitypress.com

© Anne Sauvagnargues, 2016
Preface and English translation © Suzanne Verderber and Eugene W. Holland, 2016
Introduction © Gregory Flaxman, 2016

Edinburgh University Press Ltd
The Tun – Holyrood Road, 12(2f) Jackson's Entry, Edinburgh EH8 8PJ

Typeset in 10.5/13pt Sabon
by Iolaire Typesetting, Newtonmore, and
printed and bound in Great Britain by
CPI Group (UK) Ltd, Croydon CR0 4YY

A CIP record for this book is available from the British Library

ISBN 978 1 4744 0253 8 (hardback)
ISBN 978 1 4744 0255 2 (webready PDF)
ISBN 978 1 4744 0254 5 (paperback)
ISBN 978 1 4744 0256 9 (epub)

Contents

Acknowledgements

Chapter 1

'Deleuze et les cartographies du style', *Les styles de Deleuze*, ed. Adnen Jdey (Brussels: Les impressions nouvelles, 2011), 157–82. The English translation included in this volume originally appeared as: 'Cartographies of Style: Asignifying, Intensive, Impersonal', *Qui Parle* 23:1 (Fall/Winter 2014), 213–38. Reproduced by permission of the University of Nebraska Press.

Chapter 2

'Diagnostic et construction de Concepts', *La géophilosophie de Gilles Deleuze, entre esthétiques et politiques*, ed. M. Carbone, P. Broggi and L. Turarbek (Milan and Paris: Mimesis, Vrin, 2012), 27–46.

Chapter 3

'Ecologie des images et machines d'art', *Pourparlers: Deleuze entre art et philosophie*, ed. Fabrice Bourlez and Vinciguerra Lorenzo (Rheims: Presses Universitaires de Rheims, 2013), 165–82.

Chapter 4

'Le concept de modulation chez Gilles Deleuze et l'apport de Simondon à l'esthétique deleuzienne', *Concepts* (January 2002), 165–99, Special Issue on Deleuze. Reproduced with thanks to Sils Maria.

Chapter 5

'L'image, Deleuze, Bergson et le cinéma', *L'image*, ed. Alexander Schnell (Paris: Vrin, 2007), 157–76. 'Le sujet cinématographique, de l'arc senso-rimoteur à la voyance', *CINéMAS, Revue d'études cinématographiques/Journal of Film Studies* 16:2–3 (2006), 96–114. Reproduced by permission of Vrin publishers, Paris.

Chapter 6
'La table des catégories comme table de montage', *Gilles Deleuze et les images*, ed. François Dosse and Jean-Michel Frodon (Paris: Cahiers du Cinéma, INA, 2008), 117–28.

Chapter 7
'Ritournelles des temps', *Chimeres* 79 (July 2013), 44–59.

Chapter 8
'Guattari: Un cavalier schizoanalytique sur le plateau du jeu d'échecs politique', *Multitudes* 34, 'L'effet Guattari' (2008), 30–40. Previous English translation: 'A Schizoanalytic Knight on the Chessboard of Politics', *The Guattari Effect*, ed. Éric Alliez and Andrew Goffey (London and New York: Continuum, an imprint of Bloomsbury Publishing, 2011), 172–85.

Chapter 9
'Les symptômes sont des oiseaux qui cognent du bec contre la fenêtre', *Chimeres* 72 (2010), 99–113.

Chapter 10
Previously unpublished.

Chapter 11
'Machines, comment ça marche?' *Chimères* 77 (2012), 35–46.

Chapter 12
'Machines désirantes, 5 articles', published online in 2007, at http://jean-cletmartin.blog.fr

Chapter 13
'Visiagéité, 3 articles', published online in 2007, at http://jeancletmartin.blog.fr

Abbreviations

Works by Gilles Deleuze and Félix Guattari

AO	*Anti-Oedipus: Capitalism and Schizophrenia, Volume 1*
K	*Kafka: Toward a Minor Literature*
TP	*A Thousand Plateaus: Capitalism and Schizophrenia, Volume 2*
WP	*What is Philosophy?*

Works by Gilles Deleuze

C1	*Cinema 1: The Movement-Image*
C2	*Cinema 2: The Time-Image*
CC	*Essays Critical and Clinical*
D	*Dialogues*
DI	*Desert Islands*
DR	*Difference and Repetition*
EP	*Expressionism in Philosophy: Spinoza*
F	*Foucault*
FB	*Francis Bacon: The Logic of Sensation*
FLB	*The Fold: Leibniz and the Baroque*
LS	*The Logic of Sense*
N	*Negotiations*
PS	*Proust and Signs*
SPP	*Spinoza: Practical Philosophy*
TRM	*Two Regimes of Madness*

Works by Félix Guattari

C	*Chaosmosis*
MRB	*Molecular Revolution in Brazil*
MU	*The Machinic Unconscious*
PT	*Psychanalyse et transversalité*
RM	*La révolution moléculaire*
TE	*The Three Ecologies*

Translator's Preface

Artmachines: Deleuze, Guattari, Simondon contains thirteen essays by French philosopher Anne Sauvagnargues, only two of which have previously appeared in English. Unlike Sauvagnargues's previous collection, *Deleuze and Art*, published in France in 2005 and in English in 2013, *Artmachines* is not a translation of a collection first published in France. This unique collection came about through my fortuitous encounter with Sauvagnargues in Lisbon, at a Deleuze Studies conference and seminar. Listening to Sauvagnargues teach, I realised that her work addressed a philosophical problem I had faced in my own historical research on medieval subjectivity: how do we analyse individuated forms of subjectivity without simultaneously presupposing the existence of an individual, in other words, without presupposing the existence of that which we are purporting to explain? How do we speak of the emergence of any individualised entity as a process, rather than as a *fait accompli* or as a substance endowed with essence? In a sort of flash of regret coupled with excitement (I had already published my study) I realised that Sauvagnargues was creating the philosophy I needed for the historical questions I was trying to pose. Through a redeployment and transformation of the concepts of Deleuze, Guattari, Simondon, and those of a wide range of other thinkers, Sauvagnargues positions any individuation, human or otherwise, as transitory and as occurring on a plane of actualisation that is always set in relation to a virtual plane of immanence. This has the implication of making us see that any individuation is dynamic, provisional and subject to time and becoming. Perceiving the originality and usefulness of this approach, I expressed as much to Sauvagnargues, along with the offer to translate her work into English to make it more widely available. Within weeks she had sent me at least twenty essays, from which we selected the thirteen contained in the present volume.

Be forewarned. *Artmachines* begins *in medias res*. In the three essays contained in Part I, 'Individuation on Three Planes: Literature, Philosophy, Art', Sauvagnargues projects us immediately onto the plane of immanence and shows how this repositioning transforms basic assumptions about literature, language, art, history and philosophy. The most immediate effect of this change in position is the falling away of habitual anchors of thought: in literature and art, that of the human author or artist viewed as a genius standing behind a work that in turn is seen to be a representation of reality; in philosophy and history, the assumption that a cause floating above historical and social conditions teleologically orients development; and again in art, the assumption that art exists on a spiritual plane separate from biological and technical modes of production.

In literature (Chapter 1), this displacement of perspective to the actual and virtual planes of production changes how we define literary style: no longer the production of an exceptional author whose use of language stands out from usage considered normal or average, style here is defined as a singularity, event, or haecceity emerging on the plane of actualisation (the author's name instead becomes a name for the event, the effect of style). This analysis fulfils the promise of Foucault's 'What is an Author?' to dispense with the notion of the human author as agent and see the author instead as a historicised function of discourse, a position given lip service in American literature departments that still largely organise themselves in terms of great authors, biographical criticism, historical periods and nation-states. Sauvagnargues follows the analysis through: if language itself is always in a state of constant variation and cannot be reduced to an abstract structure or norm, then couldn't any utterance, by any speaker, be classified as an effect of style? A constant theme that recurs in these essays is the rejection of the concept of structure and the presuppositions of structuralism, because these assume that there is an ideal system that can be abstracted from empirical reality. Structuralism adds a transcendent, universalising, or normalising dimension to empirical reality that Deleuze and Guattari always refuse. The concept of structure is replaced by that of the collective assemblage of enunciation or the machine, in which language is embedded in a complex, constantly changing, non-linguistic reality from which no ideal structure can be abstracted.

But, Sauvagnargues asks, if there is no linguistic norm, how do we define style? Can't any speaker then be considered a poet because all language is in a state of perpetual variation? 'Stylistic variation thus comes to be understood as creativity, an intensive placing-into-variation of the stratified forms of language.' While language does not possess an abstract norm or ideal structure, it does have 'stratified forms', that is, as I understand it, 'the way people talk in general', often unbearable because so predictable, so laden with clichés and 'common sense' (as Flaubert still continues to teach us). The singularities that now define style affect us because of their strangeness or intensity, a haunting or disturbing quality that distinguishes them from the language we are used to hearing in everyday life, blaring from our technical devices and from people determined to uphold social norms. Sauvagnargues's repetition of Federico García Lorca's haunting line, *at five o'clock in the afternoon*, with no author's name attached, becomes a talisman that helps us remember that style is a singularity or event of language that produces a mood, an affect, that makes the 'stratified' forms of language tremble and crack.

In Chapter 2, we shift from literature to philosophy. But historians should take note as well: Sauvagnargues emphasises that Deleuze and Guattari's redefinition of philosophy as 'geophilosophy' requires the elaboration of a new model of history to account for the relationship between a philosophy and its social and historical conditions of emergence, one that does not locate philosophy on a superstructure determined by an infrastructure, or that relinquishes philosophy's internal consistency across time. First and foremost, it is necessary to no longer see the activity of philosophy as the search for an already constituted truth, but instead as the encounter between thought and a problem (a view Deleuze derives, as Sauvagnargues shows at various points in *Artmachines*, from Bergson, Simondon *and* Proust). It is this encounter between thought and a problem that gives philosophy its relevance, its purchase on historical actuality. In order for thought to encounter a new problem, the problems of our time or of any time, philosophy must be seen to be constructivist: it diagnoses the problem and simultaneously creates a pre-philosophical plane and a conceptual persona that will function as the field of operations and the operator for dealing with the problem. The history of philosophy comes into play here as the collection of concepts that have already been created in past philosophies, that are set to work on a new plane of immanence to address the new problem, and are therefore replayed and reinvented. This redeployment of concepts constitutes the endogenous, virtual consistency of philosophy.

We are thereby led to think about history in a completely different way. In traditional history, a false continuity or causality is imposed upon events that are in actuality contingent and which have the label of inevitability applied to them retroactively. In this sense, Sauvagnargues reminds us that one of the strategies of capitalism has been to impose a universal history upon the past that makes its own contingent emergence appear inevitable. Instead, history consists of the actualisation of virtual possibilities, a view which grants history a necessity that results only from prior contingencies, not from an externally imposed fate or divine will. In my view, a question that emerges from this is, how would rejection of capitalism's universalising narrative on the one hand, and the integration of the concepts of actual and virtual on the other, radically change the way we write history, as well as expand our capacity to envision alternate futures?

In Chapter 3, Sauvagnargues redefines art as an 'artmachine', coining the term that gives the present book its title. Of what, precisely, does an *artmachine* consist? This chapter redefines the image and the sign to thwart our tendency to see both as duplicates of something more real or authentic (and that therefore require interpretation to get to the kernel of truth they contain and conceal) or as projections of the human mind. Instead, both the image and the sign are, on the one hand, considered as instances of real production, and, on the other, as sundered from any human source. They are considered only in relation to other signs and images, situated in 'rhizomes' and 'ecologies' that should be approached through ethology and experimentation rather than through interpretation. Sauvagnargues in part derives this insight from Deleuze's studies of cinema, which drew on both Simondon and Bergson to think the image not in terms of mimesis, but as a process of real individuation occurring within matter (this is addressed in detail in Part II). Equating the image and the sign in that both are singularities or haecceities on a plane of actualisation, Sauvagnargues opens Deleuze's analysis of the cinematic image to Guattari's thought on the sign, semiotics, ritornellos, ecology and ethology. As she does throughout her *oeuvre*, Sauvagnargues traces an original line between the thought of the two authors, whose close identification ('deleuzeandguattari') often seems to preclude the operation of distinguishing and then reconnecting them. We now think of images as individuations embedded in an ecology of images, always in a state of becoming. In the context of this collection, this chapter can be viewed as a crossroads at which many of the subsequent chapters converge to elaborate an entirely new conception of art. If Deleuze brings together the thought of Bergson and Simondon to elaborate a new philosophy of the image, Sauvagnargues effects a surprising suture between Deleuze and Guattari's individual work (Deleuze on cinema and Guattari on the sign) to create a new concept of the image and of art.

Just as in a Greek tragedy that starts *in medias res* there is always a 'backstory', or more accurately, significant 'past' events that are virtually present in the actual events unfolding onstage (Medea's theft of the golden fleece for Jason; Antigone's brothers fighting for control of Thebes), in *Artmachines*, the analyses of individuation and the plane of immanence in Part I are developed in the earlier essays by Sauvagnargues contained in Part II, 'Deleuze: Aesthetics and the Image'. These demonstrate how Simondon and Bergson are decisive for Deleuze's conception of individuation, difference and the plane of immanence (for Simondon, see Chapters 4 and 5; for Bergson see Chapter 5). We can see how Sauvagnargues's concept of the artmachine and the ecology of images emerges in part from a rigorous construction of Deleuze's engagement with Simondon on the one hand, and of his work on cinema on the other. Chapter 4 provides a nuanced evaluation of Deleuze's encounter with Simondon's thought, notably the latter's largely uncited but significant contribution to *Difference and Repetition* with his concept of problematic disparation, which enabled Deleuze to conceive of difference in terms of creation or construction in response to tension between disparate entities in a milieu, rather than difference conceived of in terms of dialectical negation and synthesis. In addition, Simondon's concept of modulation, which dispenses with the explanation of production as the imposition of form upon matter, and instead explains production as a continuous play of forces between entities, powerfully influenced Deleuzian aesthetics and the redefinition of art as a capture of forces and a production of affects and sensations.

In Chapter 5, Sauvagnargues contends with the contributions of both Simondon and Bergson to Deleuze's philosophy of cinema and the invention of the concepts of the movement-image and time-image, both of which are situated on a circuit between virtual and actual planes. If we begin with the virtual plane of immanence defined as a 'universe of universal variation', it is possible for a slowing down or delay to occur (a change in longitude in the play of forces) between an action received and reaction effectuated. In Deleuze's analysis of cinema, this temporal delay is necessary for an individuation to be produced, for actualisation to occur. What occurs during the delay between an action received and the movement effectuated in response? Here, the image, rather than dissipating a perception or an action immediately into a reaction or movement, experiences its own power to affect and be affected (latitude). The image develops a 'sensitive membrane' or a zone of affection and carves out a zone that includes only that which is of interest to it, enacting a sort of 'vital framing'. The image becomes a provisional, transitory centre of determination through the subtraction of all that does not interest it. This is Deleuze's elegant, economic and non-substantial definition of the subject – subjectivity defined as a provisional instance of framing – and an explanation of how perception is derived from movement rather than presupposed to be an aspect of human consciousness. Sauvagnargues calls attention to the fact that the cleavage of perception from human consciousness is facilitated by the technical nature of cinema, which de-anthropomorphises perception by situating it on the plane of matter itself, thereby gaining access to images inaccessible to human perception.

In Part II, Sauvagnargues traces out a line of transformation running through Deleuze's work from the 1960s to the 1980s, one concerning the transvaluation of the image: from its negative formulation in the 'Image of thought' of the 1960s, the image is affirmed as an anti-mimetic, impersonal individuation in a state of becoming in the work on cinema in the 1980s. In Chapter 6, Sauvagnargues harks back to Deleuze's pejorative defini-tion of the image, in the concept of the Image of thought, in *Difference and Repetition*, to demonstrate how his work on cinema opened the way for an affirmative treatment of the image in relation to thought. She demonstrates the implications of Deleuze's engagement with cinema for philosophy, opening the possibility for the invention of a new image of thought appropriate to the contemporary (as opposed to the ancient and pre-modern) era. In this new image of thought, Kant's 'table of categories', which presupposes a transcendental, knowing subject, is transformed into a 'table of montage', the framing of a provisional perspective on a plane of immanence through cutting and connecting, the operations proper to montage. Cinema itself supplies us with a new image of thought that is creative rather than reductive, is de-anthropomorphised (not derived from human consciousness), and that is suitable to modern rather than classical conceptions of time, space and motion.

In Part III, 'Schizoanalysis: Territory, Ecology and the Ritornello', *Artmachines* branches like a medieval romance, following the adventure of another knight, Guattari, in his elaboration of schizoanalysis. Throughout the collection, Sauvagnargues painstakingly untangles the thought of Guattari from that of Deleuze, in turn revealing previously unspecified points of connection and collusion. She shows us how with Guattari we are in the midst of a drawn-out battle, one with an opponent who is familiar and who, in certain circumstances, is not an opponent at all, but rather an interlocutor who relies upon concepts nevertheless deemed transcend-ent and universalising: namely, Lacan and his linguistic model of the unconscious. For Guattari, while this model, by insisting upon its linguistic structure, has the merit of conceptualising the unconscious in terms of the social field rather than a personal individual, it merely trades one universal (Freud's Oedipus complex) for another (the phallus and castration), both of which he claims obscure the productive, machinic nature of the uncon-scious. Even worse, the definition of the unconscious in terms of structural linguistics excludes non-linguistic components and historical actuality. I would add here that in my years teaching Lacanian theory at an American art school, the greatest resistance my students express to Lacan concerns this insistence upon the absolute centrality of language to the unconscious. How can this be so, in our era, which is witnessing the waning of the printed word and in which the image and visual media dominate?

Guattari shifts the focus of psychoanalysis away from interpretation toward experimentation, and his concept of the 'ritornello', the focus of Chapter 7, in effect explains how all creatures, not just humans, change through experimentation, through an alternation between territorialisation and deterritorialisation. As part of the shift away from an anthropomorphic perspective, Sauvagnargues demonstrates how both Deleuze and Guattari deploy modes of thought (e.g., ethology and the Markov chain) that eradicate differences between the human, biological and technical levels of existence. All living beings strive to configure a territory through the arrangement and consolidation of expressive signs, both linguistic and non-linguistic (the child whistling in the dark, the bird configuring its territory). Presenting a new, ethological version of individuation, the ritornello refers to a procedure of vital framing or a provisional centring through the repetition of signs and habits in response to a situation that has become too chaotic to bear (the child whistling in the dark to ward off fear, to create a provisional centre), recalling Deleuze's definition of the subject as a provisional centring on the plane of actualisation (Part II). Thinking existence in terms of the ritornello offers an appealing alternative to Freudian psychoanalysis, which importantly focuses on the symptom and the repressed traumas it condenses, but which remains vague on the question of how to creatively deploy repetition and the symptom to create a different future (I would add that in the 1970s, with the conceptualisation of the 'sinthome', Lacan presents the work of the symptom as a creative process – Joyce's experiments with language being a privileged example – but he maintains the triad of the Real-Symbolic-Imaginary, inherently problematic to Guattari).

Chapter 9 deals specifically with the need to rethink the symptom in light of Guattari's work: 'We should not translate the symptom as a map of the past in accordance with the reductionist modelling of psychoanalysis, but instead make use of it to experiment with *becomings*, to explore cartographies of a *possible* future.' Like style, like the philosophical concept, and like the image, the symptom is situated on a circuit between actual and virtual planes. Seen in this way, the symptom is treated affirmatively, standing for the possibility of becoming or a change in actual circumstances, rather than as an indicator of a personal, repressed trauma to be deciphered and neutralised through interpretation. Like the ritornello, the symptom that becomes actualised may or may not gain consistency and create lasting change; it instead offers a site for experimentation: 'The symptom is always plural and as such it is assemblage, a kinetic fragment, a point of view that opens the way to a reconfiguration of territory.' Two key points of disagreement Guattari has with Freudian and Lacanian psychoanalysis, then, concern not whether the symptom is important, but, on the one hand, what to do with it (to experiment with it or to interpret it), and on the other, to whom it refers (a collective unconscious complex open to historical actuality or a personal unconscious formed within the confines of the Oedipal complex).

A pitched battle between Lacan and Guattari, between the master and his old student, takes place at the site of the signifier. Lacan himself broke away from his master, Freud, through his original work on psychosis. Already enacting his return to Freud through the introduction of structural linguistics on the plane of Freudian thought in his work with psychotics, Lacan made the important discovery that the distinction between the neurotic and the psychotic occurs at the level of the structure of the unconscious, and concerns the foreclosure of the paternal function, the name Lacan gives to the transcendent entity, the 'quilting point', that confers meaning upon the signifying chain (Chapter 8). Diagnosing the transcendent character of this concept, as well as the idealisation that always accompanies structure, Guattari replaced Lacan's paternal function as the organiser of discourse and meaning with the desiring machine. While, like Lacan, he accepted that the unconscious undergoes a process of coding, he proposed a mode of coding that was not exclusively linguistic and that took historical actuality into account. This marked Guattari's important shift from the concept of structure to that of the machine, in this case the conception of the unconscious as a desiring machine, predicated upon connectivity and production and not bounded by individual or familial boundaries or representations.

I felt it important to include Chapter 10 in *Artmachines* to supplement the scant material available in English about Fernand Deligny, whose life's work addressed the controversial topics of childhood and autism. Deligny's collective works have only recently been published in France (in 2007 and 2008), and, as the essay points out, he eludes easy disciplinary categorisation, the labels writer, artist, therapist, filmmaker and philosopher all resonating while remaining insufficient. Sauvagnargues navigates his massive and diverse *oeuvre* to extract a perspective that gives us an orientation point, one concerning Deligny's resistance to definitions of the human in terms of language. For Deligny, the human needs to be defined in terms of ethology, not linguistics. One problem with language, with its subject-predicate structure, is that it creates the illusion of human will or intention and of notions of cause and effect (here, Deligny follows Spinoza). His work also recalls Foucault's insight that knowledge is a relay of power (in this case, the production of the abstract child as an object of knowledge). Deligny's concept of the *arachnéen* (the French term that denotes 'spider-like qualities') involves an 'ecological competence' and a strategic mode of operating that resists established institutions, experimenting with existing elements in the surrounding milieu, thereby recalling Guattari's concept of transversality. The *arachnéen* takes advantage of what it finds at hand and of its ability to insinuate itself in the nooks and crannies of institutions, just as a spider spins its transitory web wherever conditions are available and advantageous. The focus is on experimentation and chance in a lived milieu, evoking a kind of chaosmic submersion into the virtual cloud and the retrieval of a differentiated complexion, recalling Guattari's concept of the symptom (Chapter 9). Sauvagnargues implicitly shows us how Deligny's experiments embody some of Deleuze and Guattari's key concepts – cartography, lines of flight, territory – in a startlingly tactile way.

An insistent 'ritornello' in this book is the replacement of the concept of structure with that of the machine, which is the focus of Part IV, 'Machines and Assemblages'. Structure always drags along with it the notion that any real thing is doubled by an ideal or normative model, whereas the machine, whose definition is expanded far beyond our common-sense 'mechanical' definition, offers a purely immanent and open concept for analysing complex social realities, including all manner of heterogeneous elements including language, non-linguistic signs, images, technology, desire and the unconscious, without resorting to ideals or normative structures. The machine encompasses not just the isolated technical object, but also its entire milieu of individuation, which functions as a 'transcendental milieu of possibility' (Chapters 11 and 12). The unconscious and desire are coded under these real conditions, not in terms of Oedipus or the family. Marx and Freud are brought together in unique way, opening the unconscious and desire directly to real social conditions, including the organisation of production, labour, surplus value and language (the collective assemblage of enunciation) that gives a social assemblage its consistency. As in the economic definition of subjectivity as provisional framing or centring on the plane of immanence, here, subjectivity is peripheral, adjacent to the components of the social machine.

The components of the machine are held together not by any transcendent glue, but by an 'abstract machine', the virtual cloud that accompanies any social machine and becomes palpable only at the points where the machine breaks down. Again, we are reminded of the importance of situating any analysis in relation to the actual and virtual planes. The abstract machine, which introduces the possibility of becoming into any social machine (Kafka diagrams these virtual possibilities in his novels), is closely related to the Foucauldian diagram (Chapter 12), which calls for an analysis that reveals the relations of forces that constitute the regimes of power, knowledge and social visibility. 'Preferential nodes of forces' are given the name 'strata' (Chapter 13). Strata 'lock singularities' and oppose vital becoming. In the history of the West, with the emergence of Christianity and capitalism, two strata intersected by chance in a particular way: the strata of significance and of subjectification, making possible the emergence of the abstract machine of faciality, the virtual conditions for the possibility of the face, no longer considered a natural component of the human body. Rather, the face is a molar stratification that is traversed by molecular, deterritorialising forces that offer subjectivity in the West the chance to become something else, something other than the oppressive, colonising, great White Man. Here, Sauvagnargues brilliantly aligns the difficult concept of the abstract machine with Foucault's notion of diagram (via Deleuze's reading of *Foucault*), supplying us with a crucial way of speaking of immanent causality in history, at the same time as she demonstrates how Ruyer's presentation of the Markov chain offered Deleuze and Guattari a means of dispensing with the notion of structure and signification once and for all, instead viewing language as 'jargon' characterised by a collusion between chance and localised determinism.

Sauvagnargues's writing style in French possesses a fluidity, dynamism and elegance that I cannot hope to have fully captured in the translation. At the same time, despite their sophistication, the rigour, logic and clarity of her arguments made the task of translation much easier, a kind of intellectual adventure. In translating these essays, I consulted the English translations of the works to which they refer, and mostly retained the commonest translations of new words and concepts. For example, I have kept the English 'assemblage' for the French 'agencement', even though the French term conveys a sense of action and dynamism than the English 'assemblage' lacks, conveying more of a sense of static heterogeneity without movement. Often, but not always, I translate 'sens' as 'sense' rather than meaning, to recall the status of 'sense' as an event rather than an essential kernel hiding below the surface. A major exception is the French term 'ritornelle', which was translated into English as 'refrain' in *A Thousand Plateaus*, but which I have decided to render as 'ritornello'. I did so because we have a similar word in English, even if it is less familiar. To me, 'refrain' in English has a negative connotation, suggesting dull repetition, whereas 'ritornello' has the affirmative connotation of repetition coupled with transformation and creativity, repetition that offers the possibility of drawing a line of flight, a way out. In addition, the nasal sound of the second syllable of 'refrain' connotes a kind of droning or grinding, whereas the open vowels of 'ritornello' connote openness and possibility.

I am indebted to Eugene Holland for offering his expertise to this project by scrutinising every word of the first draft, making invaluable corrections, polishing rough edges, and supplying more apt phrasings. Any errors that remain are mine, not his. I am also indebted to Gregory Flaxman, who – in addition to writing the introduction, putting Sauvagnargues's work in the context of both her *oeuvre* and the state of contemporary philosophy – offered advice on the translation of terms and the organisation of the essays. Peter Canning provided a crucial critique of this preface. I am also grateful to Carol Macdonald at Edinburgh University Press for her confidence in this project from its inception, and her patience and attention throughout the process.

Finally, Sauvagnargues requested that I to try to avoid words or phrases that promote the fiction of substance or essence. This was my intention, but I will leave it to the reader to judge whether I succeeded. It is important for the reader to know, though, that this was my intention and the author's wish.

Suzanne Verderber

Introduction

Gregory Flaxman

Among Anglophone philosophers, the market for French imports is not what it used to be. Once upon a time, the introduction of structuralism and poststructuralism galvanised an unprecedented demand for what came to be called 'French Theory'. In the 1970s and 1980s, an astonishing array of Francophone philosophers, scholars and theorists were introduced to audiences in the US, UK and elsewhere. Roland Barthes, Jean Baudrillard, Hélène Cixous, Jacques Derrida, Gilles Deleuze, Michel Foucault, René Girard, Luce Irigaray, Jacques Lacan and Jean-François Lyotard were but a few of the French legion whose works were ardently translated and voraciously consumed. More than anything else, French Theory bears witness to a reception history whose enthusiastic and even inflationary excesses are likely to strike us as 'days of wine and roses' – not just ethereal but impossibly remote.[1]

Naturally, a handful of luminaries from this older generation of French philosophers remain (e.g., Alain Badiou, Julia Kristeva, Jean-Luc Nancy and Jacques Rancière), and a smattering of 'younger' philosophers have achieved notoriety in the Anglophone world (e.g., Bernard Stiegler, Catherine Malabou, Quentin Meillassoux). But my point is that the milieu of philosophy, the so-called marketplace of ideas, has undergone a profound transformation. Today, the significance of a philosopher, French or otherwise, seems to have been hitched to the fluctuations of academic vogues and the rapid cycling of intellectual paradigms. The philosophical marketplace is characterised by breathtaking speeds and sudden accelerations which outstrip our powers of comprehension, leaving us with the most impoverished of theoretical measures: is it *trending*? In a sense, what we call theory resembles nothing as much as a futures exchange in which (as most any graduate student can tell you) intellectual investment becomes a matter of speculation. Of course, futures markets were initially developed to manage risk, but the means of hedging one's bets – derivatives – have introduced risks that seem to typify, *mutatis mutandis*, the theory market. Inasmuch as I've suggested that this market increasingly renders intellectual investment speculative, the nature of the wager no longer concerns a philosopher, a theory or a discourse so much as it refers to what economists call the 'underlying', a contract whose value is contingent on the performance of an underlying entity. In a sense, value has been displaced onto market factors to which philosophy is indexed.

No doubt, this is a ruefully nihilistic portrait of our state of affairs, but it's in the context of this cynical calculus that, I think, the importance of Anne Sauvagnargues's work can be appreciated. For those who do not yet know her work, Sauvagnargues is among the most rigorous, creative and wide-ranging continental philosophers working in France, or anywhere else, today. Her philosophical project, especially as we find it in *Artmachines*, offers a singular rejoinder to the marketplace of philosophy: the book before you formulates a style of thinking whose intelligence and humour, joy and vitality, presage a different way of pursuing philosophy and, I would add, a different *modus vivendi*. Not that she is unaware of dangers faced by philosophy today or insensitive to their extent: rather, it seems to me that Sauvagnargues continually manages to make the sad passions visited on philosophy the impetus to affirm the practice of philosophy as both 'critical and clinical', diagnostic and creative. Indeed, one of the great virtues of Sauvagnargues's work is that she demands rigour without sacrificing the living latitude – the wiggle room – within which something new can be created. Her thinking is unfailingly precise but never petty.

A professor at L'Université de Paris Ouest-Nanterre La Défense, Sauvagnargues has written (and co-written) several books of philosophy, edited several more, and authored scores of articles on a stunning variety of subjects. Having said that, she is surely best known for her authoritative and masterful engagements with the work of Gilles Deleuze. Over the course of roughly the last ten years, Sauvagnargues has developed a reading of Deleuze's philosophy that, far from simply determining what he means, insists on the contours of a meticulous and delicate intellectual periodisation. We might call her method telescopic in so far as she is capable of taking any given enunciation, in any given text, and opening it like the compartments of a telescope onto the continuum of a past and the future. With Sauvagnargues, the prospect of anything like hermeneutics is displaced by a cartography composed of so many lines and vectors, trajectories and transversals. There may be no one better at unfurling the history of Deleuze's own philosophical inventions, no one who better understands the complex and shifting landscape, and no one better equipped to resist the reification of concepts (i.e. clichés) to which Deleuze is so often subjected.

Like the late, great François Zourabichvili, Sauvagnargues's capacity to map Deleuze's concepts without sacrificing their intrinsic complexity remains virtually unsurpassed.

Like many, I first encountered Sauvagnargues's work in the course of reading *La philosophie de Deleuze* (2004), a co-authored book that included her fabulous long essay (really, a kind of novella) 'Deleuze, de l'animal à l'art'. While the essay established the coordinates of her own approach – namely, metaphysics, aesthetics and vitalism, though only in so far as each term is defined anew – it also made clear, to anyone who read it, the invention of a singular philosophical voice and a style. This unique combination of rigour and lyricism, precision and invention, was confirmed with the publication of *Deleuze et l'art*, Sauvagnargues's first monograph, the following year. Published in English in 2013, *Deleuze and Art* duly situates Deleuze's philosophy in the domain of aesthetics, but if anything, her contention is that aesthetics ought to be situated at the heart of Deleuze's philosophy. Whether she is meditating on Proust's fiction, or digressing about Ozu's cinema, or reflecting on Michaux's 'pictorial experiments', Sauvagnargues peers beyond the veil of ontology to affirm the genetic and creative dimension of Deleuze's philosophy.[2] To put it another way, philosophy is inextricably related to art *qua* aesthetics, but only in so far as aesthetics itself is understood in light of the affects that we communicate and experience, the modes of existence that we inhabit, the ecology of ideas we nurture. Indeed, Sauvagnargues's project properly recalls the remarkable ambition that Nietzsche formulates in his 'Attempt at Self-Criticism': '*to look at science [Wissenschaft] through the prism of the artist, but also to look at art through the prism of life*'.[3]

Doubtless, this endeavour defines the book for which Sauvagnargues remains best known, *Deleuze, L'empiricism transcendental* (2008). Her title is taken from the definition Deleuze gave his own philosophy, especially in *Difference and Repetition* (1968), and if such a thing is possible, Sauvagnargues succeeds in producing a book commensurate to Deleuze's own. Still, the most fascinating, counterintuitive and perhaps misunderstood aspect of *L'empiricism transcendental* is its author's refusal to privilege *Difference and Repetition* as the *locus classicus* of Deleuze's philosophy. Unlike many of his best readers and worst detractors, Sauvagnargues fundamentally resists this conceit, preferring instead to telescopically locate Deleuze's monograph in the mobile lines of the philosopher's own becoming. And it is along that line that Sauvagnargues exerts the force of her own philosophical predilections, feeling her way into moments of transition, modulation and metamorphosis that bear us into the living thought of Deleuze's philosophy. To my mind, *L'empiricism transcendental* is among the best books ever written about Deleuze, and there is every reason to believe that, once the book is translated, its influence will become even more profound.

In a sense, the great virtue of *Artmachines* is to have confirmed Sauvagnargues as a supreme scholar of Deleuze's philosophy while also correcting the impression that she is, so to speak, a 'Deleuzian'. I have to admit that I have always disliked this term, regarding it as the inelegant expression of particularly bad faith.[4] But if the term is indifferent to the nature of Deleuze's thought, it's no less crude with respect to Sauvagnargues's own philosophy. The essays comprising *Artmachines*, all but one of which were published over the past decade, amply demonstrate the remarkable diversity of Sauvagnargues's work. The collection unfolds a rich menagerie of philosophers, scholars, scientists and artists, and while Deleuze is among the most significant of her 'conceptual personae', *Artmachines* leaves no doubt that Sauvagnargues's philosophical assemblage constitutes a polyvocality of its own. In this respect, one could imagine the subtitle of this collection duly followed by an ellipsis, since readers will discover scintillating discussions of Spinoza or Bergson, Ruyer or Deligny, among a host of others. But what makes *Artmachines* such a brilliant and compelling introduction to Sauvagnargues's philosophy is that it discloses the fundamental coordinates of her own cartography in the triumvirate of Deleuze, Guattari and Simondon.

It should be noted that the essays to follow appear together, in this volume, for the first time, since they have been selected and arranged so dexterously that we might otherwise have the impression that *Artmachines* was conceived *in toto* and written in kind. The ingenuity of Suzanne Verderber's edition is to have brought out the continuities and evolutions, the problems and predilections, which characterise Sauvagnargues's thought. Above all else, the book demonstrates that her philosophy, while committed to Deleuze, is no less engaged with the psychiatrist Félix Guattari and the philosopher Gilbert Simondon; indeed, we might go so far as to say that these are the three axes of Sauvagnargues's philosophy and that her uniqueness consists in having formulated their collective assemblage. To understand as much, we should admit the sense in which this proposition is liable to seem obvious, even redundant. After all, Deleuze and Guattari famously undertook a collaboration that, however intermittent, spanned roughly twenty years, beginning with *Anti-Oedipus* (1972) and concluding with *What is Philosophy?* (1991). The fact remains, however, that when one discusses Deleuze's philosophy, his proper name often implicitly includes (and effaces) Guattari's. Hence, Sauvagnargues is among those scholars who have long sought to counteract this tendency, and in this context we can understand her refusal to canonise *Difference and Repetition* as the paradigmatic expression of Deleuze's thought. After all, that familiar conceit elides the subsequent collaboration with Guattari, no less the broader question of a 'Guattari Effect'.[5]

Thus, *Artmachines* strives to illuminate Guattari's contributions and to underscore the degree to which the psychiatrist, activist and founder of CERFI (Centre d'études, de recherches et de formation institutionelles) transformed the philosopher down to the very concept and expression of his style. Consider, Sauvagnargues says, Deleuze's successive editions of his book on Proust (see Chapter 1). In the 1964 version, 'Deleuze observed that "style is not the man; style is essence itself," and defined this essence, in the 1970 version, as the "formal structure of the work."' But in the 1976 version, where Deleuze says that 'style is never a matter of a man, it is always a matter of essence (nonstyle)', Sauvagnargues reveals how Deleuze actually recasts the 'formal structure' of style according to Guattari's signature concept – transversality. The latter 'marks a decisive break with centred forms of organisation, with vertical hierarchies and their horizontal correspondences, and which torques structure on its machinic diagonals and anarchic connections'. Even more to the point, Sauvagnargues turns to Guattari because his own feverish invention of concepts augurs the deviant path that Deleuze will follow: the very transition of philosophy 'from structure to the machine' derives from Guattari's own psychiatric practice and theory.

Artmachines maps the transversal line that carries style, so to speak, from Deleuze's transcendental empiricism to Guattari's schizological production, but along this line we discover the final aspect of Sauvagnargues's assemblage, and it is with Simondon's philosophy of individuation and ontogenesis that we might appropriately conclude. Gilbert Simondon is likely the least known of her three conceptual personae. Simondon was the subject of intermittent admiration during his life as well as after his death (in 1989), but his work has attracted renewed interest in recent years, and Sauvagnargues is surely among those who have helped to stoke this new readership.[6] Though much of his foundational work, dating back to his dissertation, remains untranslated, Simondon's deeply original philosophy – ranging from evolution to phenomenology, from cybernetics to biology – already inspires a small cottage industry outside of France. In *Artmachines*, though, Simondon's importance consists in extending the concept of style, usually understood as matter of art and aesthetics, into the semiotic machines of philosophy and even science. For Sauvagnargues, 'art, literature, philosophy and science all possess the capacity to produce new individuations, with their personae and their respective modes of experimentation'. While these are distinct fields, they each undertake (*pace* Simondon) 'the creation of such individuations, completely differentiated and new, which consequently do not pre-exist their enunciation or their semiotic effectuation. This is the "transductive" function of style' (Chapter 1).

More than borrowing Simondon's 'felicitous expression', Sauvagnargues configures the concept of style on the basis of a concept, 'transduction', which goes to the very heart of the philosophy of individuation. Simondon describes transduction as 'an individuation in progress' (Chapter 3), which is to say that it consists in an interval, but that the 'interval *is* substance'[7] – the modulation of matter. The process of individuation is uncertain ('metastable'), but Sauvagnargues's point is that, for this reason, it also inventive. 'Transduction provokes a system to enter a new state, an unpredictable change of phase', and on this point she appeals to Simondon's own formulation: invention means that the terms created by dint of 'the operation do not pre-exist this operation' (Chapter 1). In effect, readers will discover that Sauvagnargues's rigorous appropriation of Simondon nevertheless makes him the conduit along which, once more, metaphysics is seen from the perspective of art, and art is seen from the perspective of life. The 'most direct and explosive consequence' of this procedure, she adds, is to be found 'in the movement from representation, from reproduction, in short, from all of the old ontologies of the image that separate and superimpose model and copy, to a philosophy of becoming, of individuation, and of metamorphosis' (Chapter 3). With *Artmachines*, Sauvagnargues gives us precisely such a philosophy.

NOTES

1. See, for instance, François Cusset, *French Theory: How Foucault, Derrida, Deleuze & Co. Transformed the Intellectual Life of the United States*, trans. Jeff Fort (Minneapolis: University of Minnesota Press, 2008). While I take 'French Theory' to designate the invention of a reception history, this is not to deny the history of modern French philosophy. For an account of this history (if not a particularly sympathetic one) see Vincent Descombes, *Modern French Philosophy*, trans. L. Scott-Fox and J. M. Harding (Cambridge: Cambridge University Press, 1980).

2. It's worth noting that, among many other things, Sauvagnargues has produced some of the most remarkable pages ever written on Oscar Michaux. See, in particular, her chapter on 'The Violence of Sensation', in *Deleuze and Art*, especially pages 136ff.

3. Friedrich Nietzsche, *The Birth of Tragedy*, ed. Raymond Geuss and Ronald Speirs (Cambridge: Cambridge University Press, 1999), 5.

4. Of course, Deleuze had a great deal to say about proper nouns and the possibilities they retain for the creation of singular modifiers – the way, for instance, a name can evoke the characteristic features and movements of thought apart from any determinate subjectivity (for instance, 'Kafkaesque'). Still, there is a difference between the mobilisation of the name for this operation and the baptism of a name for the purpose of affiliation: while a philosophical gesture can be Platonic, Cartesian or

Kantian, this ought not to be conflated with what it means to call someone *a* Platonist, Cartesian or Kantian. The latter makes the proper name the object of belonging, as if we had strayed from philosophy into politics or theology: can one be identified with a philosopher in the same way that one is called a Marxist or a Reaganite, a Catholic or a Mooney? The predilection seems run to against the grain of Deleuze's notorious affinity for a life 'without qualities', for 'becoming imperceptible', and for 'forgetting oneself'. Only on the basis of this ascesis, he insists, does philosophy open itself to the habitation of new ways of thinking: affiliation with a philosopher, any philosopher, contradicts the premise and practice of philosophy itself – to 'think otherwise'.

5. I've borrowed this line from Éric Alliez and Andrew Goffey's fine collection, *The Guattari Effect* (London: Bloomsbury, 2011). Notably, Sauvagnargues's own essay in that collection, 'A Schizoanalytic Knight on a Political Chessboard', has been included in this volume.

6. Among other things, see the special volume of *Pli* from 2012 dedicated to 'Deleuze and Simondon'.

7. Deleuze and Guattari, *A Thousand Plateaus*, 478. Notably, Sauvagnargues elaborates this point by drawing on Bergson's *Matter and Memory* and Deleuze's two books on the cinema.

PART I: INDIVIDUATION ON THREE PLANES: LITERATURE, PHILOSOPHY, ART

1. *Cartographies of Style*

Style sweeps away, infiltrates and overturns the signifying components of language, producing new percepts, surprising and splendid individuations, *at five in the afternoon, an afternoon in the steppe.*[1] Taking this position, Gilles Deleuze and Félix Guattari counter the tendency in art and literature to turn style into an operator of identity. No longer treating style as the marker of a unitary signification, of a personal origin, or of a defined genre, they redefine it as asignifying, impersonal and intensive. Nevertheless, there is nothing uncertain or reactive about these subtractive formulations, whose critical impact ignites a creative explosion.

Indeed, of what does style consist? In literature or in art history, style usually exercises a personological, identifying and signifying function, sorting exceptional works from unimpressive or minor ones. Style is the hallmark of a habit that surpasses the average level of language usage or of art production, and personifies the genius artist in possession of a unique, transcendental ego who, in the classic version, deploys the norm in an exceptional way, or, in the Romantic version, creates the norm. Exemplarity or exception: the normative strategy of style reveals itself in this process of distinguishing major works from minor ones. Even if we ignore its tendency to establish hierarchies and consider only its descriptive function, style establishes a repertoire of morphological forms and classifies by subsuming and identifying a plurality of objects under a common label. Any application of a label is part and parcel of this double movement of affiliation and exclusion; in this case as well, style serves to identify a difference, but a difference only as a form of identity.

Style thus depends entirely upon a political epistemology of normativity: a principle of identification, it acts as a unifying form, moulding creation, regulating the production of works and of their statuses in the genealogical and capitalist mode of appropriation, filiation and inheritance, reproducing the logic of persons and goods. The history of style constitutes a veritable policing of attribution and authentication, one that functions vertically, through the ordering of a hierarchy of works, genres and epochs, as well as horizontally, through the designation of a zone of spatiotemporal placement, of inclusion and of material transmission. Style is thus caught up in a theory of individuation, politically and theoretically favouring the personal, the unitary, the stable norm, the established trait. Beyond its function of classification and attribution, it judges the quality of works in order to exclude or to condemn, to disqualify or to normalise: style is an archetype factory.[2]

Deleuze and Guattari completely transform the question of style by reexamining style from two points of view: the individuation of any enunciation whatsoever and individuation in creation. Style does indeed engage in a process of individuation, but it does not function according to the model of an author who is the original, proprietary owner of his or her traits, organically centred on his or her ego.[3] Throughout his work, including that done in collaboration with Guattari, Deleuze favours a different model of individuation, one that is modal rather than substantial and that is defined not as a body, a subject, a form or an organ, but rather as an event, what he terms a 'haecceity'. These modal individuations of the type *at five in the afternoon* are defined by their capacity to affect and to be affected, that is, as longitudes or compositions of relations of force, complex relations of variable speeds (speeding up and slowing down), but also as latitudes, variations in power and vicissitudes of affects.

This new politics of individuation transforms stylistics and reverberates in linguistics, literature and in all fields of art. It also explains why Deleuze often speaks of *non-style* in order to emphasise the polemical aspect of an 'absence of style' that he defines as 'the inspired power of a new literature' (PS 165): 'but you have to be careful with people who supposedly "have no style"; as Proust noted, they're often the greatest stylists of all' (N 165). Of what, then, does this non-style consist? Didn't the Romantics already execute this pirouette by defining style as a variation of the genre, as a genius anomaly that simply reverses the formula of allegiance to the norm, at the cost of a symmetrical and shameful conformity? Deleuze's affirmation of minor non-style does not prevent him (or Guattari, for that matter) from privileging Artaud or Beckett, Michaux or Kafka, or from multiplying arbitrary lists: Kleist but not Goethe, Artaud instead of Carroll. This is the paradox of the minor: to proclaim that great style entails the minorisation of the norm immediately raises the minor to the status of the major. The challenge is thus to explain the atypical success without normalising it. Style thereby opens the question of singularity, in art and in language, of creation as an event as well as of the mode of explanation appropriate to it.

ASIGNIFYING EFFECT

Of what, then, does style consist? First, it neither lies on a semantic plane nor depends upon a composition of signifieds, even if literature is situated on a discursive plane. Deleuze joins 'authors referred to as "structuralists" by recent practice' (LS 71) in adopting the mutation affecting all systems of signs, including linguistic ones: meaning does not emanate from a consciousness imprinting its signification, but rather from an impersonal production of asignifying elements. The linguistics of Jakobson, the anthropology of Lévi-Strauss and the psychoanalysis of Lacan all effect a displacement from a theory of overarching signification to one of material production, in which signifiers and signifieds do not have meaning in themselves and only gain meaning by reacting to one another. Sense no longer emerges from the depths of consciousness or from the heights of logical essences. Similarly, style operates on the plane of the textual machine, on the plane of syntax and not of discursive significations: it is asignifying.

Deleuze does not simply adopt the structuralist hypothesis, however; he specifies that style, like sense, is a surface effect. He became interested in the structural analysis of literature, such as that associated with the Tel Quel group or exemplified in Jakobson's and Lévi-Strauss's reading of Baudelaire's poem 'Les Chats', which focuses exclusively on the text, not on the biography of the author or on the comparative history of literary ideas.[4] But Deleuze and Guattari quickly broke with structural analyses through their conception of sense. As a secondary, machinic effect, sense is composed on a plane that is not punctured by any transcendent opening exterior to the system. The sign 'chair' functions neither through resemblance nor through denotation: it does not derive its meaning from any exterior reality, but neither does it manifest the psychological state of the speaker's soul or the logical essence of the concept (the 'chair in itself', aimed at by the mind). It functions in an immanent mode, being produced as a position on a surface in the system of language, through a combinatory play of terms that in themselves are asignifying, phonemes and syntagms that become actualised differentially (pronouncing 'chair' instead of 'chore'; specifying 'chair' and not 'couch').

Along with Guattari, Deleuze accepts this structural, epistemological transformation, but only by displacing it: between words and things, a new domain of idealities opens up, collective and unconscious, structured but not transcendent, constrained by empirical realities but not identical to them. Nevertheless, this is not a symbolic plane and it does not function as a closed system, even though it is immanent. These two specifications undermine structuralist positions, rendered all the more destabilising by the Guattarian transition from structure to the machine, which marked the end of Deleuze's interest in structural analysis. At the start of his collaboration with Guattari, Deleuze began to reject energetically any notion of structure as a given ideality, instead proposing that a structure must be produced, and that its ideal relations must be explained in terms of diagrams, not structures. Style depends upon a plane of production of sense endowed, as on a symbolic plane, with a power of internal organisation capable of conferring a relational value to the asignifying elements that it distributes systematically. But it also entails a kind of signature, the singularity of the production of sense, which can be ordinary or exceptional without affecting its definition. The Baroque, the style of an epoch; Anglo-American literature as distinguished from the French novel; a line by Michaux: these are examples of styles on different scales, but they are no less singularised for that reason. Each style must be understood as the individuation of a virtual differentiation, completely shifting the terms of the debate.

Guattari and Deleuze no longer draw distinctions between the Imaginary, Symbolic and Real, concepts following an anthropomorphic logic centred on the psychological split between the Imaginary individual and the collective Symbolic, both in turn separated from the Real. They privilege a new division, one concerning modalities that are connected to but also disjointed from the Real: the present actual and the differential virtual, the two aspects of difference. The Symbolic is transformed into virtual differentiation, into distributions of singularities, and is no longer opposed to the Real, but only to the empirical enunciation that it determines. Style thus consists of a diagram, an operational set of singularities that can be mapped or for which a formula can be specified. Style evokes a signature, such as that of the painter Francis Bacon, who favoured the technique of isolating figures on an abstract background strewn with inchoate perspectives and larval scenery.[5] Nevertheless, there is nothing personal about this map, which depends neither on the artist's fantasy or experience nor on any general property of his syntax. Style, simultaneously real and virtual, signs a work, but in an impersonal mode.

In a second, equally distinct displacement, the system of signs thus diagrammed is no longer seen as a closed system. Of course, deprived of their referents (i.e., their extrinsic signification), and bereft of essence (i.e., their intrinsic signification), the value of the terms in question depends exclusively upon their position in the system. It is no longer a question of discerning relations of resemblance between real things, but of producing a system of differential intervals between terms that have no signification in and of themselves, and which only acquire their sense through this play of positions. Like sense, style is produced in this topological and relational mode. Because it is a function of the position elements occupy in a constrained, combinatory apparatus, style is always the effect of an immanent game, of a machinery, of a machination: of an unconscious, social and collective machinic production.

Nevertheless, adopting Mallarmé's dictum that 'all thought is a throw of the dice!', Deleuze opens the system of signs to the aleatory pulsations of style. Any production of sense proceeds by means of a distribution that shuffles and deals out thought as if in a chance encounter, a shock, a throw of the dice. In such a configuration, sense is no longer given but is actualised in a contingent emission of singularities – the dice that are thrown – and derives no longer from fixed and pre-established sedentary divisions nor from an originary parcelling-out of sense into established meanings. Aleatory and coming afterward, it is produced as a contingent actualisation. While Deleuze had been open to the structuralist approach to literature in 1967, he emphatically rejected it after the beginning of his collaboration with Guattari. Deleuze and Guattari thereby dissociated themselves not only from structuralism and formalism (Jakobson, Ruwet, Ricardou), from hermeneutics and biographical interpretation whether inspired by psychoanalysis or not (Marthe Robert, *Roman des origines et origines du roman*), but also from philosophies of language still inspired by Heidegger, which they find in Blanchot, Foucault and Derrida. No longer proceeding from an already-existent distribution of significations given in a closed system, sense becomes an event. It follows that any singular emission of sense marks the signature of a style.

This consequence, perfectly elaborated in *The Logic of Sense*, is reinforced with the transition from structure to the machine, theoretically elaborated by Guattari and worked out practically in the new collective assemblage, the Deleuze-and-Guattari-writing-machine that explodes any notion of a unitary author. Style opens onto a synthesis, to be sure, but a disjunctive synthesis. It creates differences and not identities, bearing no trace of a distinct formal structure; it is an assemblage, practical and no longer formal, impersonal and no longer identified with a sovereign individual. The authority of style becomes collective, bound up with its real individuation, assembling and plotting its imperfect gestures of formalisation with a kind of joyous impertinence and ludic impropriety. As an assemblage, style no longer possesses the character of experience or of a defined grammaticality: now, it is an event, like sense, cutting across words and things, composing unheard-of individuations through completely new syntactic usages. From this perspective, the only difference between artistic, literary, philosophical and scientific creation concerns what these discourses produce: philosophy strives to create concepts, while literature more often proceeds through provoking the variability of perceptions and the contagiousness of affects. Nevertheless, it is important not to draw these lines too definitively since art, literature, philosophy and science all possess the capacity to produce new individuations, with their personae and their respective modes of experimentation. Style, in art and philosophy and in science as well, lies in the creation of such individuations, completely differentiated and new, which consequently do not pre-exist their enunciation or their semiotic effectuation. This is the 'transductive' function of style, to appropriate Simondon's felicitous expression, for transduction is truly invention in that it provokes a system to enter a new state, an unpredictable change of phase, so that the terms 'achieved by the operation do not pre-exist this operation'.[6] Any style thereby actualises the virtual potentialities of individuation.

To briefly summarise the different stages of this conceptualisation of style, and to mark the decisive importance of the collaboration with Guattari, in the 1964 version of *Proust and Signs*, Deleuze observed that 'style is not the man; style is essence itself' (PS 48), and defined this essence, in the 1970 version, as the 'formal structure of the work' (PS 111). In the 1976 version, 'style is never a matter of a man, it is always a matter of essence (nonstyle)', but this essence or 'formal structure' is henceforth defined as 'transversality', Guattari's signature concept, which marks a decisive break with centred forms of organisation, with vertical hierarchies and their horizontal correspondences, and which torques structure on its machinic diagonals and anarchic connections (PS 167).

In defining style as transversality, Deleuze doesn't merely acknowledge his collaborative writing practice with Guattari; rather, he is integrating this new definition, elaborated in 1975 in *Kafka: Toward a Minor Literature*, into the erudite apparatus of his reading of Proust: 'we believe only in one or more Kafka *machines* that are neither structure nor phantasm' (K 7). Deleuze does not hesitate to depart from a semantic formalism toward a definition of style as a political machine that propels language into a state of continuous variation. Once style is no longer founded on a personal Imaginary or Symbolic generality, it becomes an event, a protocol for experimentation freed from interpretation and meaning. Dispensing with any hermeneutics of meaning or experience, as well as any formal signifying system, Deleuze and Guattari no longer view style as the key to the encoding of the work. It no longer suffices to define the typical (or general) formula of a work; instead, it becomes necessary to extend its functioning outward to the network of social semiotics in order to understand the singularity of a style as an enunciation, as the individuation of a real assemblage of enunciation, and as a performance.

Henceforth, style in language or in art can no longer be viewed as a closed system, while at the same time linguistics loses its position as the unique model of reference for explaining styles, including literary ones. Of course, this is not to claim that structural or semantic traits can no longer be located within literature, or to accuse linguistics of incompetence; instead, linguistics loses its position of dominance once the status of the sign has been transformed, when it ceases to be understood in terms of identity in order to be comprehended as difference. This opening of style to variation follows the logic of the rhizome: connection through heterogeneity, and thereby through multiplicity, and thus through asignifying rupture (without which connections would homogenise difference). This is relevant for all signs, including linguistic signs, which cannot be isolated from other signs with which they establish connections, those codings that are material, biological, social and so forth. The mixed semiotics of the rhizome privileges no one type of sign, instead insisting upon their real interaction, which theory cannot neglect. What is relevant for literature is also relevant for the other arts, whether or not they are discursive. Style connects to its context: as a machine, a collective assemblage of enunciation, it becomes free indirect discourse.

COLLECTIVE ASSEMBLAGE OF ENUNCIATION AND FREE INDIRECT DISCOURSE

Deleuze and Guattari thus call for an elimination of the distinction between stylistics and linguistics, and between high and low uses of language. The disturbance produced by the work of art is due not to its superiority, its ineffable greatness, but to its power of indetermination: what will be retrospectively considered 'great style' is in reality produced 'when the grammatical situation that will become common next does not exist', as Pasolini so aptly puts it.[7] Personological theories that define style in terms of exceptional genius, whose designation of 'pure' genius is politically suspect, are theoretically supported by the hypothesis that a normal, average level of language exists, a dominant norm of spoken or literary language that functions as a correct standard in the midst of which the atypical style carves out its idiolect. Refuting this conception of an average, normal, major grammaticality, Deleuze and Guattari turn style into an experiment in minorisation and elaborate their theory of creation as intensive variation.[8]

Deleuze and Guattari refute the hypothesis of a major norm of language in the 'Postulates of Linguistics', returning to their analyses from *Kafka* and extending them from literary style to linguistics and to the ethology of creation. With the refutation of the postulate that language is organised around a given grammatical standard, linguistics and stylistics can no longer be hierarchised as a theory of speaking and speaking well. The stylistic exception will no longer be considered refined usage, according to the collective theory of free indirect discourse. In proposing that language is composed of minor variations, Deleuze and Guattari demonstrate that a real speaker who actualises a dominant grammatical invariant does not exist, except in order to raise such a figure to the level of a methodological principle in the form of a figure of domination who is, above all, a marker of social power (in embodying the social standard of good usage). They thus refuse the Chomskyian premise that 'language can be scientifically studied only under the conditions of a standard or major language' (TP 100), because 'constants or universals of language' do not exist that would permit it to be defined 'as a homogeneous system' (TP 92). In his studies of idiolects of black English in New York City, Labov demonstrates that the variations between and within them are so plural that they cannot be reduced to a unitary system: we thus must change the very concept of system and relinquish the fiction of language in itself as a closed system, condensed in its formal purity, crystallised in its generative structure. Along with these two postulates, others fall: the internalist postulate of information or communication, whereby language transmits given significations between individualised speakers, and the structural postulate of a language that has no recourse to any extrinsic factor.

Linguistics must not misrecognise its social and pragmatic conditions of existence to the point of representing itself as a homogeneous system, since all languages are continually worked over by a host of forces: political and social fractures; scientific developments; regional, archaic and modernising variations; and appropriations, idiolects, agglutinations and other amalgams. Therefore, the very notion of system must change, taking variation as its constitutive dimension. In opening up the supposedly isolated, closed and unified structure of language to the assemblages that work it over in reality, Deleuze and Guattari take up and extend speech act theory. They do not find it sufficient to say, along with Austin, that 'saying is doing', but instead develop this performative linguistics into a real pragmatics, one that no longer cuts language off from concrete collective assemblages of enunciation. For it is not possible to understand the functioning of language if language is artificially isolated from other material, political and theoretical systems with which it interacts. It is thus necessary to move toward a new theory of the system, as a system in variation.

In refuting the four postulates of major linguistics, all founded on a notion of formal purity, Deleuze and Guattari delineate the semiotic conditions of minor style: every style is mixed and heterogeneous, because we no longer seek to reduce style to a constitutive matrix or a closed, unitary structure, or to reduce its singular signature to a formal encoding, whose generative formula we could determine once and for all. To do so would be to confuse style with a principle of repetition. No style is identical to itself or in any way homogeneous: discursive style is never purely about language (nothing in language is) and cannot be separated from its context of enunciation and reception, its real assemblage. Style should not be represented as circulating or transmitting lofty meanings, specific information or literal communications. Style 'en-signs', like language, constituting its repertoire of sense with asignifying materials, violently imposing its order words on ordinary language, which it twists following its conception of good usage (first postulate). No more than a language, a style does not consist of a closed, structurally pure system of signs that would adhere to an isolationist and archaic conception of identity (second postulate). No identity can be defined in a purely internal mode. The machine of language always extends out to political actuality, and this is true of style as well. From this it follows that (third postulate) style cannot be reduced to a petrified axiomatic wherein constants of any kind allow for the extraction of a consistent core of generative rules. This observation does not amount to a call for a renunciation of science (fourth postulate), just of the weak and contested concept of formalisation that identifies the logic of truth with a closed system and postulates that one can only know a given grammaticality as a homogeneous system. Such a conception of language or of style seeks a generative, structural invariant, and derives it, as does Chomsky, from the mental structure of the subject. Despite its imposing formal apparatus, this concept nevertheless boils down to a truism: the major is that which a dominant or authorised speaker deems major. Looked at this way, any attempt to isolate a style, even in the case of a Rimbaud, degenerates into the validation of a correct standard, which in turn imposes itself as the new dominant norm.

Stylistic variation thus comes to be understood as creativity, an intensive placing-into-variation of the stratified forms of language. It no longer crystallises around an internal axiomatic, but can be defined as an operation, a mixing, a hybridisation at the border. Such variation is not the prerogative of great artists or stylists, but constantly affects the most ordinary uses of languages. Style must therefore be understood in its thickness and polytonality as free indirect discourse, discourse within discourse.

The analysis of free indirect discourse, initiated by Bakhtin and taken up by Pasolini, inspired Deleuze and Guattari to define style as variation. Following Bakhtin, Pasolini privileged indirect expression because it allowed for the dynamic interaction of heterogeneous discursive dimensions. Free indirect discourse refers to a layered enunciation in which the discourse to be transmitted and that which serves as the means of transmission are simultaneously present and distinguished: it is a discourse within a discourse. Bakhtin considered it to be of exceptional methodological interest but also wrongly neglected, because it includes the sociological axis of speech in its enunciation, and through this fact demonstrates the collective character of speech.[9] Free indirect discourse, which demonstrates the real sociological thickness of discourse in its polytonality, paves the way for Guattari's concept of the collective assemblage of enunciation. This polytonality allows us to comprehend creativity within languages: 'inventing words, breaking up syntaxes, inflecting significations, producing new connotations', (MU 25, with modification) – these are not just the prerogative of a major poet, but also of any everyday speaker of the language. Accordingly, style transcends the distinction between minor and major, between ordinary speech and extraordinary style, and therefore between linguistics and stylistics, because we must account for the ordinary as well as the exceptional in order to be able to explain the passage between them without resorting to the argument of authority, which establishes poetic licence as a new major norm. Indeed, what needs to be explained is minorisation, the production of a singularity. Pasolini, the poet, points out that the infinitive of narration, for example, serves as a modest, collective, sociological, epic form, one that humbles language and brings poetry closer to prose: in this way he defines the conditions of an enunciation that precede its grammatical conditions.[10] There is nothing mysterious about this overtaking of the norm by style. Free indirect discourse allows those who do not yet speak to speak, sociologically assuming a revolutionary short-circuit between allegedly elevated language and the ordinary vernacular. As Pasolini explains, Cantos XXV and XXVI of Dante's *Inferno* vibrate with this invention of a language, soldering theological Latin to the Italian of the Florentine bourgeoisie to create a completely new mode of expression.[11] It is not only a question of varying the minor and major thresholds of a language to show how syntactic invention expresses the intolerable, the visionary pathos of existing social modes. It is also a question of insisting that creation occurs on the fringes of the minorisation of the major. Deleuze, in *Cinema 2*, echoes these analyses in calling for a people who are missing (C2 216–17). It is a question of writing or creating not in order to represent a people to come or a hypothetical future in the style of the *avant-gardes*, not to speak in the *place of*, but rather *before* or *in favour of* the aphasic minors, those who cannot be heard, the imperceptible people 'to come', the insignificant, the negligible, 'the animal who knows how to die' (CC 2): to speak in the name of impersonal, asignifying becomings.[12]

If language in general is an exercise in minorisation, it does not follow that every speaker is a poet: stylistic success broaches the ordinary habits of speech without appealing to any factor that transcends the linguistic fact. Here also Deleuze and Guattari reconnect with Pasolini's fine linguistic analyses: free indirect discourse, through its function of depersonalising the utterance and in conjunction with its diagnostic capacity, becomes a syntactic mode of transformation initiated by literature. Current lexical or poetic creations do not depart from an average or correct language, but emerge from the collusion between different social levels of expression and through elision of the level assumed to be average. The epistemological fiction of grammaticality in Chomsky's scheme reveals its status as a concrete operator of real domination, one that proscribes deviant uses by imposing a dominant norm, that of speaking well. This is why the analysis of style is so tricky: our admiration tends to elevate any minor variation to a dominant norm. By contrast, as soon as the average, grammatical level of a major language is elided, phenomena of minorisation propagate within all linguistic usages and prevent us from isolating literary creation in its own separate sector, without at the same time confusing it with current usage.

Style is thus neither constructed on a median nor on a superior level of linguistic usage, but rather shatters the humble and the refined, the low and the high, and good and bad usage, in all directions, according to the different mannerisms that are connected and co-present in every language. Whether these mannerisms function through sobriety and subtraction or by expressive proliferation, all variations are welcome and none is *a priori* preferable. To label a 'poor' language as 'poor' or 'excessive' only stems from a certain malevolence of linguists; in reality, to subtract, to cut out, to overload or to place in variation are all aspects of one and the same operation: minorisation. What is essential is neither in the minor language nor in the standard or major language, but 'in language X which is nothing other than language A in the process of really becoming language B'.[13] This is the definition of style: all style operates through mannerism, that is, through variation.

The theory of free indirect discourse and that of a sober mannerism leads us to reassess the distinction between minor style and major style, a distinction that remains pertinent but only relative, and which can be deceptive if it validates any major or minor state in itself. It is essential to avoid uselessly reifying these statuses as if they concern two styles, or even two usages of style. In reality, what is at issue is the coexistence of two epistemological regimes, two opposed politics of language, which do or do not hypostasise the capacity of the norm to be reified into a social marker, but which only a preference for maintaining the major/minor binary can concretise into a real opposition. No major style exists outside of these very real phenomena of domination, which elevate a minor style of whatever kind to the provisional status of a dominant norm, all the while impoverishing it through scholarly redundancy. Deleuze and Guattari can thus simultaneously hold, first, that all real becomings are becomings-minor, and second, that it is necessary to struggle against the very real phenomena of domination of the major. The dual couple major/minor might allow us to think that styles are either ordinary or exceptional, and in essence dominant or subaltern in themselves, but this is another trap. Instead, the concrete oscillation between minor and major demonstrates the necessity of acknowledging the continuous variation that produces both of them as adverse and variable poles, as tensors. Any empirical style can be considered remarkable or ordinary, major or minor, according to circumstances, not because the appreciation of style is relative, but because, in matters of style, 'fluctuation of the norm replaces the permanence of a law' (FLB 19). Style becomes mannerist rather than essentialist: it is an event that generates its remarkable singularity in a minor mode, and becomes ordinary when it is imposed as a major norm. Carmelo Bene, in his *Richard III*, shows that in order to render homage to a great author like Shakespeare, one must set his formulae in variation, lest they be reduced to cultural ornaments, fetishes. Otherwise, 'we pretend to recognize and admire, but in fact we normalize'.[14]

This is the paradox of style: it is impossible to love and admire works or authors without immediately reducing them to impaled figurines arranged on the patrimonial shelves of the cultural canon. It should not be surprising, then, if style violently lays claim to a theory of amputation, deformity and creative anomie. All creation is subtractive.

INTENSIVE VARIATION AND IMPERSONAL POWER

Henceforth, style will be defined as placing language in intensive variation. This is why it is always defined as a line of flight implying intensive variation, an agrammatical, becoming-minor or becoming-animal of language, in other words, a creative transformation of syntactical materials and of conditions of enunciation. Now style becomes a tension that puts language into relation with its intensive border: unformed matter, musical sound, or asignifying cry, in other words, the deterritorialisation of sense that carries language to its limits. For Deleuze, the limit is never the place where language stops; rather, the limit is situated at the point of the disjunctive bifurcation from which an individuation proceeds: this is where one encounters the body without organs of language, where literature imposes its asignifying power and semiotic efficacity.

The minor affects the intensive border of phonetics and the political boundary of accepted grammatical usage, as for instance when Kafka imposes a Yiddish mannerism upon Goethe's German, as well as a Czech idiom that torques German, not toward the superfluity of Meyrink's baroque mannerism, but toward a poverty, an aridity, an intense sobriety. Creation is always subtractive: style culls from language its conventional conditions of equilibrium in order to try out a new assemblage, imposing a becoming-minor upon language.

This becoming allows us to define style intensively, as agrammatical stuttering and as foreign language, and which strives to attain the limit of a becoming-minor, a becoming-animal, a body without organs with regard to the rhythm of speech, the linguistic organisation, and strangeness (*l'étrangeté du style*). In all cases, language is transported to a plateau of variable intensity. Style is defined as a placing of language into variation at the very heart of speech, in accordance with the Proustian maxim, 'Great works of literature are written in a kind of foreign language', the formula to which Deleuze refers throughout his work and which serves as a kind of epigraph to *Essays Critical and Clinical*, Deleuze's final work devoted to literature. This asyntactic, agrammatical stuttering, this foreign language, should not be confused with an affectation of speech, as if what is at stake in style were the imitation of a disorganisation of language or the abuse of a cliché in order to gain creative inspiration. It is not a question of imposing a rule of bad usage of speech, but of carving out within language a minor usage that removes its elements of power and domination, and which reorganises all of language according to a virtual tension, which must be traced on its asyntactical borders precisely because it does not already exist.

If Kafka's work is exceptional, it is because the newness of his style is one with its original investigation (and this an investigation that is not 'literary' in the sense of a quest for conformity with the major codes of literature) into the real tissue of the social. Literature becomes a physics of affects, a social ethology. The writer is not defined by his or her predilections in modifying the arbitrary and subjective rules of the literary code, or even by his or her designation as minor in a linguistic or socio-cultural sense. In this latter sense, it would suffice to adopt a minor pose in order to be guaranteed to produce a work of art, which would once again only transform the minor into a major prescription. Despite these caveats, style is not undefinable; it is rather unpredictable and immanent, irreversible and improbable, assuming the traits of the event.[15] It can be characterised by its lack of affectation, its urgency, its affective power, and by the contagious virulence of its capacity to depict the way it is affected by the social physics of time.

The analysis of style thus offers a decisive confirmation of the critique of personal individuations. No primordial 'I', no substantial *cogito* possessing the power to initiate a discourse, lurks beneath the enunciation. The subject-position is produced by the enunciation itself, and when the subject of the enunciation, he or she who speaks, is arbitrarily distinguished from the act of enunciation, when he or she is accorded the status of transcendent cause of the subject of enunciation, of the pronoun that he or she utters, this occurs by means of a linguistic fiction in the service of a political strategy. In reality, the extraction of the *I* that speaks and the psychological ego hinders the immanent analysis of discourse in terms of enunciations, and makes the comprehension of style as a fact of language impossible. In order to explain an effect of style without deriving it from an originary *I*, Deleuze insists upon the necessity of refusing Jakobson's linguistic theory of shifters or Benveniste's of auto-referentiality, demonstrating the complicity between these linguistic analyses and a kind of hermeneutical phenomenology, whether this be centred on the *I* or the *You*. It is not that the individuated human subject is an illusory form, but rather that, like any form, it is derivative. There are thus subjects, and even a variety of types of subjects, but they are not the origin of discourse, and are instead produced by discourse as a place within it. Subject positions thus do not appear as figures of an originary *I* that would be the source of the enunciation, but are the products of the enunciation in that they must be situated in the 'thickness of the anonymous murmur' and transformed into an 'it' or a 'one', an 'it speaks' or a 'one speaks', impersonal instances of the productivity of language, modes of impersonal subjectivation (F 7).[16]

Benveniste's personological linguistics, which derives language from an originary *I*, positioned as the initiator of discourse, in reality relies upon the linguistic fiction of the pronoun, which alone makes the subject, the person, the origin of discourse. But from 1963 on, Deleuze insists: 'The question "*who?*" does not refer to persons, but to forces and wills' (CC 99).[17] Following a procedure that Deleuze deploys in all of his literary studies, stylistic analysis corrects false theoretical positions that in reality reinforce dogmatic subaltern positions: Proust, Sacher-Masoch, Artaud, Kafka, Beckett and Blanchot each in his turn offers support to theoretical thought.

Rather than being a site of an autotelic redoubling, modern literature, Blanchot's in particular, is marked by the dispersion of language, deploying language's pure exteriority. Foucault expressed this perfectly in the precise analyses that he devoted to literature, and Deleuze read his homage to Blanchot, 'The Thought from Outside', with great care. Literature is not an operation of 'language approaching itself until it reaches the point of its fiery manifestation', but instead of 'language getting as far away from itself as possible', a 'banishment from itself', which Blanchot both theorises and practices: it is indeed literature that produces this surface of exteriority that exhibits thought from the outside, language deprived of its sovereign interiority.[18] This allows us to grasp the importance of literature to Deleuze; for him, literature is a clinical exteriority that does not refer to any originary experience of a phenomenological subject. A neutral experiment, an exteriority in the third or even the 'fourth person' to use Ferlinghetti's wonderful phrase, literature substitutes for lived experience and definitively disavows any identification with the experience of a person, of the *I-You* of enunciation, in favour of an impersonal assemblage of enunciation.

This impersonal assemblage indicates how style as signature (or proper name) is acquired only at the cost of a severe exercise of depersonalisation, as Deleuze so often insists in relying upon Blanchot's superb analyses of Kafka. It was, Kafka said, the day he became capable of no longer writing *I* but *He*, that he became a writer:

> It is thus not enough for me to write: *I* am sad. When this is all I write, I am too close to myself, too close to my sadness, for this sadness to truly become mine in the mode of language: I am still not truly sad. It is only beginning at the moment when I happen upon this strange substitution: *He* is sad, that language begins to constitute itself into a sad language for me, to trace out and slowly project the world of sadness as it realizes it in itself.[19]

This impersonal becoming in writing in no way implies a renunciation of the self; on the contrary, it creates the opportunity to infuse language with the real breath of the event. It does not constitute a mystical mortification, a deadly dispossession, but enables a violent and passionate construction that carries language to its limit, to a point of tension where defined individuations, modes of social subjectivation, form within it. For Kafka and Blanchot, as well as for Deleuze, the problem is not that of renouncing the *I*, but rather of showing how the *I* is produced by an indefinite neutral, a *He* which is no longer a person, but which constructs a virtual line of flight. This *He* carries language to the point of its disequilibrium, but also to the point of creativity, because it does not represent a substantial subject, but instead tries to map a new individuation. The 'ONE and the HE – *one* is dying, *he* is unhappy – in no way take the place of a subject, but instead do away with any subject in favor of an assemblage of the haecceity type', as Deleuze and Guattari explain (TP 265). That is a style: not to reterritorialise statements onto persons, centring language upon an alleged, abstract point of origin, a transcendental *I* given as a substantial subject, but, on the contrary, to elongate syntax in order to allow it to be traversed, to carry it to its exteriority, which is not an extension but an extreme point of transformation, a threshold of metamorphoses.

Deleuze and Guattari thus propose a grammar of haecceity, an impersonal syntax that corresponds to this intensive individuation and that opposes Aristotelian logic characterised by its propositional model of judgement (a substantial subject + the copula 'to be' + an accidental predicate [e.g., 'Socrates is bald']). A semiotics freed from these models of structural signification and personal subjectivations can take the form of an intensive proposition wherein the indefinite article and the proper name replace the substantial subject, and the infinitive form of the verb replaces the copula and its predicate. This is the semiotics that Deleuze and Guattari propose in *A Thousand Plateaus*: '*indefinite article + proper name + infinitive verb*' (TP 263). The indefinite, the proper name, the infinitive and the conjunction make up this telegraphic, intensive, asyntactical style, which defines the polytonality of style and its capacity to capture haecceities, events, *at five in the afternoon, an afternoon in the steppe*.

Haecceities carve out individuations that are unexpected but not at all imperfect, individuations composed of variations in speed (speeding up and slowing down) and variations in power, and which do not have a substantial *I* for an origin. Everything depends upon this philosophical decision: Will the statement individuate itself in the manner of an event or of a subject? For Deleuze, as for Guattari, it is the definite article and the verb conjugated in the first person that suffer from indeterminability, because they do not pertain to real processes but only to those that occur in name only. The indefinite article and the infinitive of the verb do not lack determination; rather they reveal the impersonal power of individuation, which in turn reveals the ability to neutralise the indetermination of the socially fabricated person, to replace this dogmatic artifact with a creative individuation, which determines the singular.[20]

Such is the transductive function of art: to infuse syntax with intensity, to disturb and minorise stable, normative structures and strata; to reintroduce the aleatory into cultural codes by tracing a virtual line of flight that does not pre-exist its operation. Vaporising already-constructed identities, the indefinite infuses language with the power of the event and bears witness to the fact that its purpose is not to represent socially defined persons, social redundancies, or the familiar cast from our pre-school alphabet books, but instead to capture new existences in order to topple syntax and expand its power to make us experience new affects.

Just as the pronoun refers to an impersonal individuation, the infinitive form of the verb refers to the undivided time of becoming, accelerations and decelerations themselves independent of the chronological or chronometric modes that time adopts elsewhere, this very division corresponding to the Stoic distinction between Chronos and Aion. The infinitive is becoming, eluding the present of Chronos and flowing into the disjunctive time of Aion, a past-future that does not become stabilised in a subject. As Bréhier has demonstrated, the Stoics struggled against Aristotelian logic, understanding the attributes of beings not as epithets that marked their property, but as verbs that indicate their becomings.[21] As soon as we come to think of individuation as haecceity and not as a personal subject, the verb expresses itself in the infinitive, slides to the participle, and in a way includes its mode of individuation in its actualisation.[22] The mannerism of variation (And) replaces the essentialism of predicative logic (Is): the point is not to target the essence of Being but to unfold the variation of becomings. Language no longer states that the accident is a property of the subject, but rather heralds intensive variation as impersonal production of subjectivity, as a perspective that produces together, in language, the places of the object and subject that did not pre-exist their formulation. The grammar of the haecceity thus prefers the impersonal adjective to the personal pronoun, replaces the definite article by indefinite power. This is the meaning of the enigmatic formula, 'Immanence? . . . a life . . .', which substitutes for the predicative copula 'is' the iterative conjunction 'and': a life contains nothing but the singularities that it actualises in this iterative mode. These paradoxical antidotes are required to infuse language with the capacity to capture new individuations and events.

Here, the theory of the proper name receives its definitive articulation and allows us to come to a conclusion concerning the singularity of style as a signature: style-as-signature does not designate a personal subject, but the mode of individuation of a haecceity, a complex relation of variable speeds and variations of power. This theory of proper names was already implicit in the theory of minor style and the becoming-impersonal of the author. This is what signs style as intensive singularity, and consequently as individuation within language, not in the mode of a personal individual, but as an instance, an event. This is why the proper name is not a subject of a tense but the agent of an infinitive: it traces the new coordinates for a cartography of bodies. Far from functioning as a label for a pre-existing entity, it invents a capture of force that produces a new individuation as a becoming or a process (D 92; TP 264).

The proper name designates this singular capacity of existence, a power that does not refer to an already-given human subject but to a bundle of forces (a symptom, as Deleuze will call it in the era of Sacher-Masoch), which refers neither to the permanence of a knowledge nor to the identity of a substance. It opens the generality of a word onto the singularity of its act of enunciation, revealing the singularity of any linguistic act. Singularity is not the individual, and the proper name is neither a generic term nor a symbolic articulation of an empirical reality, but is rather an effect, not in a causal sense, but in the sense of a perceptive effect: the proper name Roberte in Klossowski's work first of all indicates a difference in intensity before referring to a person, marking the impersonal bundling of a singular haecceity, of a potential of singularity. These effects are designated by a proper name; they arrange a typology of powers and turn the history of literature into a table of symptoms: the 'Kafka effect'; the 'Carroll effect' (LS 70; D 92).

The proper name is thus a symptomalogical composite that refers to a typology of forces. It does not require a support in any personal identity, and implies a depersonalisation that opens out onto the multiplicities that traverse it (latitude) and the intensities that wander across it (longitude). Agrammatical and telegraphic style must then be seen as a positive means of saying haecceity, and not as a result of psychic disorganisation or of a process of decomposition.

By refusing to reduce style to a personal biographical composite, imaginary or symbolic, or to identify the author with personal experience, Deleuze does not thereby intend to abandon the concept of the author, but rather to transform it. The name of the author no longer refers to a personal interiority, an individuated ego, but is, as Deleuze repeats in formulas that he takes up again and again, the nexus of an effect, of a proper name, which itself entails a process of depersonalisation. It is precisely this operation of depersonalisation that I have sought to explain here, to demonstrate that its collective, impersonal, imperceptible and intensive modes form a rigorous chain of connections. For Deleuze, the success of a style does not depend on the exceptional personality, but on the special power of attaining to the impersonal: a constructed, potential and joyous impersonality that does not return us to the bloody procedure of abolishing our little egos, but rather introduces us to the experience of the vehement, augmentative power of its metamorphoses.

NOTES

1. 'At five in the afternoon' is the iterative verse from Federico García Lorca's poem 'Lament for Ignacio Sánchez Mejías'; 'an afternoon in the steppe' evokes one of Leopold von Sacher-Masoch's preferred settings. Translator's note.

2. Even today, this conception of literary history continues to norm discourses on literature and its history, as well as the way it is taught, organised into national or comparative divisions that imply a history of 'great men', 'great works' or 'great authors' (usually men). Criticised in literature by Proust (*Contre Saint-Beuve*) and in the epistemology of history by the historians of the Annales School (Marc Bloch, Lucien Febvre, Fernand Braudel), it remains entrenched in literary studies (e.g., Erich Auerbach, *Mimesis*). In this sense, Deleuze and Guattari's work may be read as a war against interpretation, hermeneutics and allegory, implying a new definition of literature as experimentation, not as interpretation, as I argue in *Deleuze and Art*.

3. Deleuze and Guattari rely on Michel Foucault's well-known presentation 'Qu'est-ce qu'un auteur?', which concerns the socio-historical existence of the figure of the author in the culture industry, but they also displace it, shifting the focus toward a theory of individuation, pushing Foucault's analysis toward a new theory of subjectivity and a theory of the book as an assemblage, which they present in *Rhizome* (1976). Foucault's

presentation was originally given at the French Society of Philosophy in 1969, published in the *Bulletin de la Société française de philosophie* 63.3 (1969), 73–104. The English translation, 'What is an Author?' can be found in *The Essential Foucault*, 377–91, and in Foucault, *Aesthetics, Method, and Epistemology*, 205–22.

4. Jakobson and Lévi-Strauss, '"Les Chats" de Charles Baudelaire', *L'Homme* 2.1 (1962): 5–21.

5. See Deleuze, *Francis Bacon: The Logic of Sensation*.

6. Simondon, *L'individuation à la lumière des notions de forme et d'information*, 33. My translation.

7. Pasolini, *Heretical Empiricism*, 83.

8. For a fuller development of this notion, see Sauvagnargues, *Deleuze and Art*, Chapter 6: 'Minor Art'.

9. Bakhtin, *Le marxisme et la philosophie du langage: essai d'application de la méthode sociologique en linguistique*, 159–66.

10. Pasolini, *Heretical Empiricism*, 79–80.

11. Pasolini, *Heretical Empiricism*, 82–3.

12. A more complete development of becoming-animal as an intensive power may be found in Sauvagnargues, 'Deleuze: De l'animal à l'art', in Sauvagnargues, Zourabichvili and Marrati, *La philosophie de Deleuze*, 121–227.

13. Deleuze and Guattari, *A Thousand Plateaus*, 106; Pasolini, *Heretical Empiricism*, 98.

14. Bene and Deleuze, *Superpositions*, 97. My translation.

15. See the elegant analysis of François Zourabichvili, *Le vocabulaire de Deleuze*, 40, and his excellent article, 'La question de la littéralité', in *Deleuze et les écrivains: littérature et philosophie*, 531–44.

16. See also Foucault, *L'Ordre du discours*; Blanchot, *La part du feu*, 29.

17. Deleuze, 'Mystère d'Ariane (sur Nietzsche)', 12–15. The article was reedited in *Philosophie* 17 (1987): 67–72. It was taken up again after revision in *Magazine littéraire* 289 (1992): 21–4, and the revised version was published in *Essays Critical and Clinical*, 99–106.

18. Foucault, 'La pensée du dehors', in *Dits et écrits*, vol. 1, 548. My translation. This text has been translated into English as *Maurice Blanchot: The Thought from Outside*. See also Deleuze and Guattari, *A Thousand Plateaus*, 265.

19. Blanchot, *La part du feu*, 29. My translation.

20. Deleuze, 'L'immanence: une vie . . .', 3–7. The last text published by Deleuze, reedited in *Two Regimes of Madness*, 388–93. It has also been translated into English as 'Immanence . . . A Life' by Anne Boyman in Deleuze, *Pure Immanence: Essays on A Life*, 25–33.

21. Brehier, *La théorie des incorporels dans l'ancien stoïcisme*, 19.

22. Guillaume, *Temps et Verbe*.

2. Diagnosis and Construction of Concepts

According to Deleuze and Guattari, geophilosophy addresses the following decisive question directly: how do we think philosophy in its historicity, without maintaining the illusion of a rationality that was born in Greece and assumed Europe as its eternal seat, and, at the same time, without reducing the concept through a geographic and sociological determinism?

This question first requires a political critique of the way philosophies represent their own history. The concept of geophilosophy – with its cutting edge and extreme position – serves this purpose. While still attributing the complete and endogenous consistency of the concept to philosophy (philosophy is the creation of the concept – 'the concept belongs to philosophy and only to philosophy' [WP 34]) – geophilosophy also links Western philosophy to the rise of Europe and its pretension to define man in general, as well as to the development of capitalism.

The concept of geophilosophy is thus strategic, destabilising historical constructions of philosophy that support the colonial ambition of Western thought, a thought that positions itself as the crown jewel of rationality and as the parental figure of Reason, while violently suppressing unfamiliar knowledges emanating from non-European continents. Just as the thinker is ostensibly gendered male, it is no surprise that philosophy, beginning in the Renaissance, lists English, German and French names, with the notable exceptions of a Jew of Portuguese origin who emigrated to Amsterdam and a Scandinavian. Today, even if philosophy is taught globally in most universities and flourishes in America and Asia, following the pathways of technics and science, it still embraces the fiction of its mythic origin, emerging fully-armed in the happy Greek moment, a miracle contemporaneous with the emergence of the city-state, mathematics and art, in short, with the emergence of civilisation according to its European definition.

It is through its insistence on the historicity of philosophy that geophilosophy produces a political critique of the concept of 'history', substituting for the universal history of Reason a transcendental critique of the geopolitical conditions of the emergence of the concept, comprehended as creation and construction. The contingency of the emergence of systems deemed philosophical is therefore understood geographically in terms of the contingency of their ethos, the ecology of a territory, which includes its multiple components and the diverse relations it forges with its outside: neighbouring territories or universes of prior or current values, in accordance with an empirical and fluctuating ethology. It is not a question of relinquishing the temporal density of history while returning philosophy to the static simultaneity of a geography of the present. Instead, it is a question of establishing a relation between philosophy and its planetary situation – between philosophy and the Earth – instead of territorialising philosophy exclusively upon the linear succession of a history of (Western) Reason. Defining philosophy as the construction of concepts, while also taking into account the historical circumstances of its emergence in Greece and its reemergence in Europe, entails a confrontation between philosophy and its own tradition, but with the caveat that the concept of history itself must be transformed. It is paradoxically in the name of the irreducible historicity of philosophy that geophilosophy proposes a new version of its own necessity. Geophilosophy doubles the concept of history with that of becoming, which permits philosophy to be thought not in terms of universality, but in terms of contingency, as the construction of concepts and as creation.

In this way, Deleuze and Guattari open the constructive moment of the system to its historicity, which is entwined with the empirical and political actuality of its social assemblage. Defining philosophy entails explaining what a concept is: a creation. But, reciprocally, defining the concept entails proposing a new conception of philosophy, which in turn requires a new version of its history, the history of the succession of its systems. But its history – the real succession of its systems – cannot be explained within the context of rationality, that of a sole, unitary and all-powerful Reason; nor can it be explained within the framework of habitual conceptions of history. In order to account for the existing and unpredictable conditions of philosophy's diverse articulations, it is therefore necessary to transform our way of conceiving of history.

In other words, philosophy is founded upon this new, critical conception of history as becoming, and in no way upon a denial of its historicity. This is the diagnostic function of philosophy and constitutes its foothold upon actuality, a foothold that is resolutely political.

WHAT IS PHILOSOPHY?

To ask what philosophy is entails the interrogation of the historicity of this type of discourse, as well as its resilient capacity to unify itself under the label of *a* history of philosophy, despite the disparate and enduring variety of its different figures. The conceptual consistency of philosophy poses the historical-political problem of the emergence of European rationality, with its all-powerful universality, as well as the problem of its persistence despite the heterogeneity of its systems. This persistence has authorised every philosophy, at least since Descartes, to position itself as a new point of departure without renouncing the principle of a specific rational tradition. It is precisely in order to bind philosophy to the problem of its history that Deleuze and Guattari followed their collective work, subtitled 'Capitalism and Schizophrenia', by *What is Philosophy?* This work links philosophical consistency to a politics of the concept and to the concrete history of the emergence of capitalism as the condition – necessary, but not sufficient – of the emergence of a unified Reason. This Reason thinks itself as universal even while universality promotes the pragmatic imperative of political domination. Deleuze and Guattari thus rehearse the standard gesture enacted by every philosophy since Descartes by proposing a new departure that redistributes and transforms the history of prior systems. They do not make this gesture, however, in the name of a universal History or a pursuit of truth, but in the name of a geopolitics of the concept as construction and diagnosis.

It is crucial to avoid three misinterpretations here, which in turn correspond to the different moments of this chapter. First, to ask what philosophy is, what it makes, does not amount to asking what its essence is. Neither does it amount to inscribing philosophy into a rational logic of the promotion of truth in accordance with an erroneous conception of the history of systems as a teleology of Reason. This is why Deleuze and Guattari link the endogenous formal consistency of the concept to its conceptual persona and to the unpredictable history of its construction (creation).

Second, thinking the historicity of philosophy does not in any way imply a linear causality between the socio-economic and the cognitive, which a certain kind of Marxist literature might promote as an explanatory scheme: there is no determination of the superstructure by the infrastructure. Instead, the consistency of the concept, adjacent to conditions of historical determinations, operates in a detached way and produces its own virtual temporality, one that is insistent but not eternal, and that is irreducible to the linear unfolding of historical succession. In the absence of this condition, the unpredictable creation of the concept would be replaced by a teleological development.

Third, the shift from a scientific paradigm, in solidarity with a history of the Western telos, to an aesthetic paradigm, which notably defines thought as creation, does not amount to an alignment of philosophy with art. This shift instead requires that we transform the concept of history, including the history of the concept, from one that is retroactive and pre-existing into a prospective geography, conscious of both its duration and of its pragmatic precariousness.

Let us examine the first difficulty. To ask what is philosophy is not to revive the old question of essence, 'what is?' Deleuze formulates the definitive critique of this in 1967, under the rubric of the 'dramatisation of the Idea', one of the initial moments of this debate.[1] He rejects a list of categories centred on the ontological consistency of substance ('what is it?'), and substitutes for it the Nietzschean ethology of the question 'who?', which refers to a clinic of thought, to a typology of thinkers. Such is the search for truth, which exemplifies most flagrantly the manner in which a philosophy, in defining itself, acts as the unifying principle of its prior history as tradition or as a succession of systems. This search for truth does not lead to a unanimous definition but rather diverges into distinct and concurrent dramaturgies, such as doubt (Descartes), inquiry (Hume) and tribunal (Kant). The procedures by which thought tracks down truth are differential and irreconcilable, and propose disparate configurations that are inscribed in distinct scenographies for which a typology can be traced out: the Inquirer (Hume), the Lawyer (Leibniz) or the Judge (Kant). Philosophising never consists in obtaining an already-constituted truth, nor in pursuing it to its limit by means of a procedure defined by a universal method, but rather in describing the gestural choreography of the encounter between thought and a problem, which produces an entire kinematics of thought for a thinker. It is precisely in this sense that a concept is signed, in accordance with the formula that Deleuze and Guattari maintain in *What is Philosophy?*

The question 'who?' is taken up in the figure of the conceptual persona, which should not be confused with a representation of the thinker. The concept is signed in terms of its individual historicity, but Deleuze and Guattari reverse the process by which the work is habitually assimilated to the author, while simultaneously distancing themselves from phenomenology and Marxism. It is the signature that individuates, not the 'I think' or historical conditions of a psycho-social type. Thus, any concept, in the elaboration of its multiple, formal components, liberates a certain image of thought (simultaneously thought and being) that determines a certain conceptual persona. This is an impersonal condition of thought, one which is not empirical but still singular, in that it responds to a new problem, which defines at the same time its task and the experience to which it refers.

The conceptual persona that doubts is not Descartes' psychological ego, but rather an unknown, which remains to be determined. We construct it from the components of the concept of the *cogito*, such as 'to think', 'to doubt' or 'to exist'. These are distinct components – heterogeneous but not separable – that lay out the profile of a concept, the manner in which it attacks prior or adjacent problems by reconstructing them. The conceptual persona, presupposed by the relation between concepts (always characterised by a multiple consistency) and by the diagrammatic plane of the problem (the abstract machine) that they deploy and that contributes to their definition, is thus neither an emanation of René Descartes, nor a transcendent philosophical consciousness given for all eternity in the history of philosophy.

Applying an analysis to philosophy that has been perfectly clarified with respect to art, Deleuze and Guattari demonstrate that the proper name of a philosophy is its signature, in the sense in which it has been defined semiotically in the analysis of the ritornello in *A Thousand Plateaus*: as an individuating material of expression (and thus historically specified *hic et nunc*), but one that is impersonal because it does not presuppose any individual subject given in advance. On the contrary, it is the signature that individuates philosophical thought and gives consistency to its author, permitting this group of writings to be distinguished in the production of an epoch as a new philosophical dealing out (*donne*) 'signed René Descartes'. Deterritorialising prior or adjacent (*limitrophe*) concepts that it replays in recomposing, the signature turns thought into an act of territorialisation, one which does not depend upon any transcendental subjectivity that would serve as its origin, but that rather falls back on the person of the author that it differentiates and actualises. Three distinct levels should thus not be confused: the conceptual persona of the Doubter or the Dancer; the psycho-social type of the French soldier marching in the Europe of the seventeenth century or that of the walker of Sils Maria; and finally the individuals René Descartes and Friedrich Nietzsche, determined by the thought that they inaugurate. The conceptual persona is not identical with the psychology – even the transcendental psychology – of the writer (*scripteur*) or with a psycho-social type determined in accordance with historical materialism. But it is nevertheless the conceptual persona that individuates Descartes as a philosopher, in alignment with the psycho-social traits of his time but without being determined by them (if this were the case, all French soldiers would have written *Discourse on Method*). The conceptual persona, distinct from the psycho-social type, is not independent of the latter and is not ahistorical. It is constructed in an imperceptible way as a condition for the determination of a concept but does not pre-exist it, any more than it is caused by it: it functions as its transcendental virtual condition, one which is not pre-existent, but rather constructed, as a diagnosis.

The conceptual persona thereby turns out to be the agent of enunciation, the one who says 'I' in philosophy (WP 64–5): this 'I' is not originary (phenomenological) or determined (sociological Marxism), but rather 'invented', constructed and presupposed at the same time that a concept is created and a pre-philosophical plane is laid out. The philosophical enunciation is thus not exclusively discursive, grammatical or propositional, but instead on the order of the construction of the concept: one does not think in saying (or in producing a linguistic enunciation) but in constructing a multiple concept, which requires the institution of a pre-philosophical plane (a plane of immanence) and the logical ordination (*ordination logique*) of the components of the concept. This is the formula of constructivism: creating concepts as the laying out of the pre-philosophical plane of the problem. The philosophical persona functions as a shifter between the phases of the created concept and the problem that has been laid out, creating a new formula for the individuation of thought.

This 'I think' – in conformity with Deleuze's work since he took up Simondon (1964), as well as with Guattari's writings on the assemblage of enunciation (1965) – is produced by impersonal and singular individuation, in conformity with the way that Deleuze and Guattari define individuation in *A Thousand Plateaus*: as becoming. The act of positing a concept in philosophy individuates its thinker (contrary to how we habitually think about it) and also explains the link between the concept and its pre-philosophical plane, the plane of immanence that should not be confused with an assemblage of enunciation or with a domain of eternal, virtual idealities. It is not the plane of immanence that produces the concept (any more than the assemblage, for that matter), even if they are in a relationship of reciprocal presupposition.

Are we now in a better position to define the conceptual persona more precisely? Neither an individual figure nor a conscious creation of the philosopher, it is the result of the new individuation of thought, positioned at the intersection of the concept and the problem. This transforms what it means for us to orient ourselves in thought. We can list its pathetic traits (the Idiot, the Doubter); its relational traits (the Friend, the Waiter in the café); its dynamic traits (marching, climbing, flying, gliding); or its juridical traits: thought claiming what belongs to it by right, from the Claimant or Plaintiff in a Greek tribunal to the Lawyer (Leibniz), the Empirical Investigator (Hume), or the Judge at the tribunal of revolutionary Reason (Kant). It also includes existential traits, which evoke vital anecdotes from *The Logic of Sense*: Empedocles and his volcano or Spinoza and his spider fights.

Such an inventory – attempted as an experiment in *What is Philosophy?* – does not constitute an exhaustive list of traits that individuate a conceptual persona once and for all, forming a kind of timeless history of figures of Reason. The philosophical consistency of a conceptual persona is neither timeless nor unified; the list of categories is no more closed than the open typologies of signs of cinema, of the Baroque, or of literature. 'Personae proliferate and branch off, jostle one another and replace each other' (WP 71), because they are the object of critical and clinical diagnoses. They are not given but constructed – in a non-arbitrary way, of course, but which is not pre-existent either – and get revived by a philosophy that rolls the dice of the concept anew. This is why the persona is the unknown of a system formed by the relation between concepts and the problematic plane. Unconscious for the philosopher, the persona is only revealed in the critique or revival (*la reprise*) of another philosopher, at the point where the concept is at work and thus, in reality, at the place where the new figure of the conceptual persona disrupts the preceding construction.

POLITICS, PHILOSOPHY AND THE HISTORY OF CAPITALISM

For his part, Guattari produces powerful analyses of the relation between politics and theory, indicating that the formal consistency of doctrines is never univocal, definitive or absolute, and that abstraction is never a first term but rather the result of concrete assemblages of enunciation. Each time we encounter a universal statement of the kind 'cogito ergo sum', it is necessary to determine the particular nature of its enunciating assemblage in order to analyse its formal consistency and the operation of power that enables it to pretend to universality (MU 12).

In sum, the abstract is neither the first term nor the sovereign, hierarchical pole of a proposition that can be extracted from its conditions of enunciation in order to be considered a given in the timeless universe of a sky of Ideas. The relation between theory and practice must be conceived of transversally: the concept is neither a Platonic Idea transcendent to the empirical real, nor a form adjacent to social matter. The concept is not attached to a unique, universal time but rather to a plane of consistency that is always inscribed historically, but which is imperceptible as long as it is not marked by a becoming. In this way, the appearance of the concept in the real does not occur all in one piece (*d'un seul tenant*): the coordinates of existence, the spatiotemporal coordinates, and the subjective coordinates become established in relation to assemblages in constant interaction (MU 11).

In *Anti-Oedipus* and *A Thousand Plateaus*, the critique of the universal is accomplished theoretically and politically: the universal as an abstraction functions as an order word (*mot d'ordre*). This nominalist critique is always accompanied by two logical stakes. First, the universal is not explanatory; instead, it is the universal that must be explained, as Deleuze, as well as Guattari, insist repeatedly, and it must be explained from the point of view of the concrete instance that it explores, of the experience that it configures, as well as of the nexus of social and political forces that it redeploys, contests, or favours. Consequently, the use of the universal as an order word supports a political imperative of domination and is not a logical necessity. The universal as a concept thus gives way to a pragmatics of thought, which opens onto the theory of assemblages, systematically placing theory in a relation of co-constitution with its collective assemblage of enunciation, at the same time as with its endoconsistency. The collective assemblage, similar to the Foucauldian statement, encompasses discursive conditions in the orders of knowledge, but also engages non-discursive conditions: political and pragmatic assemblages and states of facts. Second, it is necessary to analyse the semiotic components (concrete assemblage and abstract machine) that singularise the relation between a given system and a given political assemblage of enunciation. If philosophy no longer concerns the universal, a new interpretation of necessity in thought becomes indispensable, one which concerns neither the universal nor the teleology of history: this is what geophilosophy defines as the constructivism of the concept, in its geopolitical inscription, as becoming. This becoming must be determined as a crisis, not as a linear expression of given material and historical conditions. Without this, thinking would serve no purpose.

The problem is always to be understood on two planes, the political and the conceptual. This is why Deleuze and Guattari immediately refer the question of the emergence of philosophy to that of capitalism. In effect, the question is posited in the same way, since in both cases, given features in given times and places do not necessarily automatically unleash the threshold of emergence of capitalism (Braudel) or of philosophy, between which it is important to avoid establishing a relation of causality. They posit the historical status of the contingent and exigent irruption of such processes for both, revealing the strong link between the history of philosophy and that of capitalism. First, the emergence of capitalism, like that of philosophy, retrospectively unifies all prior history and propels the future forward on a segment of unified history, determining a specific development in a constrained manner. This is why, in the third chapter of *Anti-Oedipus*, Deleuze and Guattari write that there is no universal history except that of capitalism. This does not mean that capitalism is inscribed in an all-encompassing, universal history, but, on the contrary, that it creates the conditions of possibility of such a history: there is no

universal history without capitalism. There is no universal history of civilisations except that of capitalism, just as there is no universal history of
Reason except that of philosophy. It is not that the two determinations are
teleologically programmed in advance, but rather that from the moment
when they occurred (as a contingency), their emergence retrospectively
unifies all prior attempts, through the construction of the universal. From
the moment when capitalism emerged, it unified prior histories because it
configured itself as universal, acting pragmatically as an instance of domination. But this universal is contingent (it is not necessary that it crystallises
at a particular moment).

Nevertheless, from the moment when capitalism crystallised, when it
occurred, it unleashed a necessary and constraining process. This is why
history must be theorised as a mixture of the aleatory and the necessary,
proceeding by contingent leaps, determining a problem (abstract machine,
diagram, or plane) that retroactively produces a prior history without
emerging from it. What is at stake is a transductive crystallisation in the
strict sense that Simondon uses it, even though he did not think of applying
this concept to the history of capitalism: a contingent irruption (chance)
unleashes its own logic, its virtual problem (or abstract machine), from
which the supposed linearity of prior history is retrospectively configured.
This is why 'there is no good reason but contingent reason; there is no
universal history except of contingency' (WP 93). Reason in philosophy
is synthetic and contingent, proceeding through encounters, unpredictable
conjunctions, 'not insufficient by itself but contingent in itself' (WP 93).

How can we deal with this empirical irruption through encounters,
viewing it neither as a teleological universal nor as a causal determination?
Through the concept of the abstract machine, which is installed transversally at the material, cognitive, social and affective levels, as it is set to work
in *Anti-Oedipus*, *A Thousand Plateaus*, and developed by Guattari in *The
Machinic Unconscious* and *Chaosmosis*. Consequently, there is nothing
fortuitous about the link between modern philosophy and capitalism: it
is as strong (and contingent) as that of ancient philosophy with Greece.
In both instances, an aleatory connection produces necessary effects. The
psycho-social conditions of the Greek city-state with ancient Reason, the
psycho-social conditions of capitalist Europe with modern Reason, are
due to the features of deterritorialisation of the Greek city-state, bound
to the Asiatic empires that it deterritorialises. Europe assumes the features
of Greek fractal geography, spreading out into mercantile cities, recoding
them onto the State and onto the generalised convertibility of Capital,
installing a new type of generalised deterritorialisation, which favours
economic domination and conceptual universalism. These determinations
make it possible for Europe to define a properly European transcendental

subject, a privilege that Husserl does not put in question when he defines the crisis of Reason. This privilege is founded on the construction of a subject posited not as one psycho-social type among others, but as Man *par excellence*, in possession of all the 'expansive force' and 'missionary zeal' proper to European capitalism (WP 97).

'Capitalism reactivates the Greek world on these economic, political, and social bases. It is the new Athens. The man of capitalism is not Robinson but Ulysses, the cunning plebeian, some average man or other living in the big towns . . .' (WP 98).

We should not conclude from this that philosophy, now the obligatory ally of capitalism, should be condemned. The link between modern philosophy and capitalism, like that between ancient philosophy and the city-state, is founded on the movement of deterritorialisation of capital, brought to the conditions of immanence of a generalised decoding that distinguishes capitalist assemblages from preceding semiotics. This is why the connection between ancient philosophy and the city-state or that of modern philosophy and capitalism is not ideological (philosophy echoing the exigencies of the city-state or of capitalism). This should not lead to a sociology of modes of thought, a linking of philosophy to the infrastructure of the ancient city-state or to that of modern capitalism, according to the model of a causal determinism (historical materialism). Instead, it should lead to defining a materialism that creates a place for a veritable indetermination in history, for its historicity. It is indeed in the name of real history that it is necessary to reverse the philosophical version that philosophy gives of history: its teleological version. In order to do so, it is necessary to double the concept of history with that of becoming, and to create the concept of geophilosophy.

Philosophy thus appeared in Greece, but through an encounter, 'as a result of contingency rather than necessity, as a result of an ambiance or milieu rather than an origin, of a becoming rather than a history, of a geography rather than a historiography, of a grace rather than a nature' (WP 96–7). The Greek city-state's features of deterritorialisation, linking it to the Asiatic empires, establish the conditions favourable for the emergence of a deterritorialised thought: philosophy is constituted on the basis of contingent chance (or 'grace'), which does not have anything to do with 'nature' but that rather operates rather through the encounter. If Europe assumes the features of the Greek deterritorialisation of the concept on new bases, in doing so it achieves the construction of its Greek moment at the moment it integrates it – this is true for philosophy, as well as for art or science – by claiming a European universality that fabricates a fiction of Greek origins.

This is why it is necessary to explain this conjunction not only as a synthesis, but as a synthesis that is heterogeneous, multifactorial and contingent, to abandon the dream of ethnic purity that specifically links philosophical rationality to the Greek ethos, and to see Greece, as well as Europe, as a non-unified melting pot of very different, heterogeneous influences. And this synthesis is not necessary, but rather contingent, linked to the serendipitous historicity of instances and occurrences, of encounters. Philosophy is thus not linked to its necessary emergence in a given human-ity, but is factual and contingent. This takes nothing away from the strong determination of its rationality, but determines its emergence otherwise, on a geophilosophical plane. Philosophy thus remains historicist as long as it thinks itself in terms of the unity of its history and defines its emergence as necessary, linked to linear history and determined by a form of rationality that, in distinguishing itself from all other forms of rationality, desig-nates itself as the master and conquering form of rationality: European philosophical rationality, manipulating its universality as an instrument of domination.

Quite the opposite: a philosophy that takes into account its real historic-ity is necessarily a philosophy of contingency. This is why it is impossible to respond to the question 'what is philosophy?' without transforming the conception that philosophy has of its own history, that is, without trans-forming the very concept of history and at the same moment proposing a new philosophy.

THE PARADIGM OF CREATION

What is Philosophy? thus does not contain a reevaluation of the question of essence, dispensed with once and for all, but rather an interrogation into the specificity of philosophy as the construction of concepts, which must be understood in a polemical mode as much as in an affirmative one.

Polemicising with discourses of essence that link philosophy to its his-tory, *What is Philosophy?* expresses creation with a sense of humour: if philosophy has a claim to consistency, this has nothing to do with a timeless essence, is not animated by any internal necessity and does not possess any eternal validity. Contingent and variable, philosophy in no way renounces its entire consistency, and is defined instead as construction and diagnosis, in a new conception of historicity. Determining this consistency demands at the same time a critique of philosophy and of the conception that it has of its own history. On the one hand, philosophy thereby shifts from the paradigm of science to that of art, and conceives of itself as creation. On the other, this creation concerns the consistency of the concept as a multiplicity and as a surveying (*survol*) of its own components.

Defining philosophy as creation collapses the epistemological frontiers that guarantee the hermetic distinctions between the discursive formations of science, philosophy and art; indeed, Deleuze and Guattari reduce the objectivity of knowledge and the figure of truth to the creation of the new. Several difficulties follow from this. On the one hand, philosophy and science are indexed on what seems to be the activity of art, that of creation, as new contribution and as sensory production; on the other, creation, considered 'continuous' (WP 8), seems to be defined in a purely negative way, as a difference that subtracts itself from the old, which it rejects, if we understand newness as a rupture with tradition. 'The object of philosophy is to create concepts that are always new' (WP 5).

Here, philosophy assumes two determinations – the creative novelty of concepts and radical singularity – habitually reserved for art. The history of the sciences and of philosophy is thought in terms of the model of a history of works of art that are radically singular, incomparable, and thus unquestionable, and philosophy breaks apart into non-totalisable doctrines, doctrines that are thereby also unquestionable and, in turn, equivalent. The accent put on singular creation seems to open the gate to an atomism and a generalised relativism. There is no element common to doctrines by which we could compare them. What then prevents us from confusing philosophy with science or art in the absence of a universal that is specifically philosophical? Nevertheless, Deleuze and Guattari refuse to allow us to confound them and maintain that art, science and philosophy are established on distinct, heterogeneous planes of thought.

But how is it possible to assign a determinate content to this creation that seems to group philosophy and science with art, and to allow truth to fall back on the criteria of novelty, rupture and anomaly? If the virtue of rupture is derived from what it contests in order to be able to distinguish itself as new, then this definition is as traditionalist as that which proposes that truth is a repetition of the same. It is even completely reactive, and in this sense reactionary, finding its support in the old that it contests. Even worse, it re-establishes a link with linear teleologies of history, being content with reversing them, because it places the old and the new in a relation of succession. It is understood that 'interest' replaces the criteria of truth as measure of adequacy and that this banishes timeless essence, but if interest itself, as that which measures the truth of a proposition, can only boast the criteria of rupture as its guaranty, and if interest may be summarised as saying something 'otherwise', we risk exchanging the eternity of truth as timeless essence and the long history of its development as an oriented evolution for the short, brutal oscillation of rupture, of contestation.

The constructivism of the concept exposes us to this significant difficulty: if a 'concept always has the truth that falls to it as a function of the conditions of its creation' then 'there is no point in wondering whether

Descartes was right or wrong' (WP 27). Even worse, 'when philosophers criticize each other it is on the basis of problems and on a plane that is different from theirs and that melt down the old concepts in the way a cannon can be melted down to make new weapons. It never takes place on the same plane' (WP 28). Constructivism, the new name for transcendental empiricism, implies that the concept assumes sense, not in the antecedent conditions of tradition, but in transforming old concepts into new weapons and responding to problems that did not exist before. Deleuze and Guattari clearly formulate the difficulty: 'In the end, does not every great philosopher lay out a new plane of immanence, introduce a new substance of being and draw up a new image of thought, so that there could not be two great philosophers on the same plane? . . . But how, then, can we proceed in philosophy . . .? . . . Is this not to reconstitute a sort of chaos?' (WP 51). They provide the answer a few lines later: 'the choice is between transcendence and chaos' (WP 51). This in turn presents a difficult methodological circle, which is resolved by the relation between construction and diagnosis.

For this radical singularity aims first to establish for philosophy an endogenous necessity. Different philosophies cannot be measured according to an external standard, one that is artificial and transcendent; they must be evaluated according to the type of systematicity that they institute and according to the systematic consistency that they propose (endoconsistency of the concept as multiplicity), the map of affects that they promote (perspectivism), the multiplicity of pragmatics that they make possible (politics) and for which they are also the diagnosis. The evaluation of a philosophy – as of that of works of art or scientific theories – cannot be the object of a unified, transcendent, pre-existing, exterior measure, because each system, work, doctrine or theory opens a point of view that constitutes its object and because there is no pre-existing unity of discourses, no timeless unity of objects, that would allow them to be aligned according to an external standard. There thus cannot be in philosophy, any more than in the sciences, a logic of truth, deploying its successive figures in the history of Reason. Relying upon the epistemology of sciences of Bachelard, Lautman, Canguilhem, Simondon and Foucault, Deleuze and Guattari thereby define a plural, multiple and discordant philosophy, a philosophy of diagnosis as opposed to a history of truth.

Creation, then, does not simply signify rupture, and novelty does not only signify contestation. To create in a given system signifies constituting, but constituting implies that there is no external, pre-existing object for human thought. This allows Barbara Cassin, for example, to classify Deleuze as a sophist.[2] Art, science and philosophy are not creative because they innovate and refuse the past: this would be a negative and reactionary determinism along the lines of the 'avant-garde', assuming a dialectical conception of the production of the new in contradiction with the old. The value of a concept is not oppositional. 'However, a concept is never valued by reference to what it prevents: it is valued for its incomparable position and its own creation' (WP 31).

But the incomparable opens the way to a radical heterogeneity. What then permits the arrangement of these thoughts into the unity of a philosophy? This is achieved through the determinate and problematic perspective, that is, the partial and reconfigurative perspective that presides over their evaluation, that diagnoses their construction of a concept. Novelty should be less understood as a reaction (negation) than as production, the construction of concepts formulating new problems, presupposing unexpected conceptual personae – the Doubter, the Investigator – none determined by what preceded them, each nevertheless reconfiguring prior doctrines or concepts that they redeploy, but on a new plane. It is thus singularity that explains novelty, just as it determines a 'star friendship', to use Nietzsche's phrase,[3] a monadism of works, a dispersion without communication. This dispersion is not resolved in an atomism but instead promotes, according to Deleuze and Guattari, a politics of thought, one by which the diagnostic impact reverberates by constructing the problematic axis according to which the concepts of prior philosophies can be subjected to examination. This is not relativism but rather a pragmatic perspectivism, the theoretical stakes of which consist in activating the critical re-elaboration of the concept of history, the philosopher having a grip on history as it is being made, this proceeding in tandem with a new, ethical definition of consistency in philosophy: a geophilosophy.

BECOMING AND DIAGNOSIS

The necessity of philosophy is thus endogenous and extrinsic at the same time. It cannot be reduced to an examination of its own history as a totalising university discipline, or to commentary on current scientific and artistic activity, which would be the equivalent of an epistemological retreat. In defining philosophy as the creation of concepts, Deleuze and Guattari seek a constituting exteriority for philosophy that guarantees its singularity as well as giving it a hold on its contingency. Their objection to the history of philosophy is that it remains endogenous without taking into account the necessity, for the concept, of producing a new problem. To metadiscursive or epistemological commentary, they reply that philosophy must maintain its conceptual content or else risk losing everything. The two positions are for them equivalent because both hold philosophy to be a second discourse, and in the end a secondary one, content to reflect upon an exogenous given. But the concept is constructed, it establishes itself as the solution to a problem that it defines: 'A solution has no meaning independently of a problem to be determined in its conditions and unknowns; but these conditions and unknowns have no meaning independently of solutions determinable as concepts' (WP 81).

Geophilosophy thus implies this irruptive, nonlinear history of problems. We can now more precisely define constructivism: the creation of concepts as instances of a solution configuring problems, laying out a plane and a movement on the plane as the condition of a problem, inventing a conceptual persona for the unknown of this problem, as a formula for the individuation of thought. This triadic construction – the concept thought, the virtual philosophical problem and the implied philosophical persona – serves as the maxim for the new 'history of philosophy' proposed by geophilosophy. This triad articulates the real history of philosophy in relation to the series of conceptual necessities produced by a sequence of unpredictable encounters.

In effect, we cannot define the constructivism of a past philosophy without at the same time producing a new construction of the concept, the reason why construction always refers to diagnosis. As opposed to doctrines of truth that position thought in a timeless element, we no longer think in terms of the eternal, but in the present moment that we are already in the process of leaving behind, and which is configured in such a way so as to favour the strategic – that is, the political – becoming of our conceptual practices. In addition, it is not a question of a thought of the present, because the present does not conceal what we are, but rather what we no longer are. We think in the indicative of becoming, in the timely as Foucault said, or the untimely as Nietzsche put it, we who are not concerned with what we are, but instead with the becoming in which we are caught up.

The problem of a philosophy, as a diagram or an abstract machine, is thus indissociable from its actualisation, which can always be assigned a date, even if in itself, as a problem, it does not belong to the retrospective history of the thinker, but to his becoming. The philosophical problem explains the virtue of crisis, the power of rupture, which means that a thought is not given once and for all, but instead knows periods, hours and coefficients of luck and danger. The mutation of thought demands a double analysis on the plane of history and on the plane of becoming: the reason for the succession of periods is not due to history understood as causal succession, but to creation, as rupture, as becoming. Crisis indicates the becoming of a system, and thus its historicity, just as it reveals its uneven, nonlinear, continuity. It is crisis that produces these links in which crisis, as cut or limit, constitutes the ideal cause of continuity. In this sense, cuts are not lacunae or ruptures of continuity because their fractures oblige us to distribute continuity in a new dimension that produces continuity beginning with the contingent irruption of a fracture. The cut thus explains the transversal character of the course of thought and the kinematics of systems of thought. Each philosophy irremediably changes the image of thought, and the construction that each philosophy proposes is no more contained in the preceding dimensions of its work than in the succession of prior doctrines. This is why Deleuze and Guattari specify that philosophy does not stop changing without any of its dimensions being contained in its preceding dimensions. The same is true for the becoming of thought, as for the capacity of thought to transform the world, a world that we are able to act upon precisely because thought has configured it.

NOTES

1. This concept is analysed in Sauvagnargues in *Deleuze: L'empirisme transcendental*, Chapter 9: 'La dramatization de l'Idée', 209–38.
2. Cassin, *L'effet sophistique*, 19–20.
3. Nietzsche, *The Gay Science*, 225–6 (§279).

3. Ecology of Images and Artmachines

In turning his attention to cinema, Deleuze extended the image to the problem of real individuation, freeing it from the restrictive domain of mental representation. This marked a shift from his earlier writings, which restricted the image within the mental sphere of an 'image of thought'. From *Proust and Signs* (1964), where literary invention reinvigorates the morbid image of thought of a pitifully representational philosophy, to *Difference and Repetition* (1968), which calls for a 'thought without images', Deleuze restricts the image to a zone of mental projection, even when he calls for a 'new image of thought'. But, beginning in 1983 with his work on cinema, the image becomes a motor process of sensory differencia-tion: real individuation.

Between these two poles, the image indeed changes its status. The image shifts, according to the logic of the sign in which it is taken up, away from an interpretation deemed mental in 1964 toward the machinic experimen-tation defined by Guattari, which infused their collaborative writing (1970) with a new tension.[1] In *The Logic of Sense* and in the second edition of *Proust and Signs* (1970), Deleuze remains invested in an interpretation of the image founded on signification. Beginning with his collaboration with Guattari, this regime of interpretation definitively gives way to a plural-ism of regimes of signs, semiotic clusters that they define as 'rhizomes' (*Rhizome*, 1976) that do not privilege the mental or linguistic sphere. Like images, signs are no longer devalued as degraded material doubles of a representation or thought, but rather unfold upon maps of affects in an ecological semiotics and an ethology of territory.

Here, the image is no longer consigned to a representative function – an image seen by a consciousness – becoming instead an effect of matter, a movement-image. This movement-image cannot be grasped on a strictly individual or separate plane, or restricted to the effects of human art or cinema. If the image is defined in terms of semiotic individuation, the movement-image is linked to Guattari's work on semiotics and ritornellos presented in *The Machinic Unconscious* (1979) before being developed with Deleuze in *A Thousand Plateaus* (1980). For every movement-image implies a milieu of individuation, a collective assemblage of enunciation and an ecology of images. It is precisely this ecology of images that I would like to define here by linking the problem of the image as individuation to semiotic ritornellos.

From this perspective, art becomes a specific technical, social and political semiotic that is undoubtedly interesting, but which has no special spiritual privilege in relation to other types of movement-images. By linking the assemblage that individuates art in our culture with individuating images – movement-images and time-images defined by Deleuze with reference to cinema – the ecology of individuating images applies to the machine or machines of Western art without presupposing in advance that art is a unity of cultural aesthetics. On the contrary, what is at stake is an interrogation of the 'Art' assemblage – its slow and uneven individuation as a spiritual actor, independent of culture – in accordance with a vital-social perspective, as an image in the Deleuzian sense and as an ecological semiotics in the Guattarian sense: in other words, to see art as an *art machine*.

FROM THE IMAGE OF THOUGHT TO INDIVIDUATION

Once the image is defined as a vital process of differentiation, it is no longer subservient to the problematic of reproduction and sheds its status as copy of an original or imitation of a model. The image, liberated from this representative and reproductive function, reveals its productive potential. Deleuze and Guattari, both singly and together, define any sign as an individuating encounter – what Simondon calls a 'signal' – that gains consistency as a vital perspective, within a regime of signs or an ecological semiotics. In accordance with this conceptualisation, which is both dietetic and political, regimes of signs connect the linguistic, discursive signifier to asignifying material, including vital, technical and social codings. Such semiotics are always plural, characterised by interactions between material and biological codings, between functional qualities and associated milieus. These milieus become defined and diversified through expressive qualities characteristic of social living things, as collective assemblages of habitation.

These semiotics define zones of individuation in the mode of Uexküll's animal worlds, complex clusters of milieus that radiate from living things. These milieus are singular and differentiated but also interconnected, ritornellos of signs that assume an ecological consistency. It seems that a semiotics of this kind invites us to draw a connection between the Guattarian ritornello of *The Machinic Unconscious* and its development in *A Thousand Plateaus*, and the Bergsonian problematic of the image that Deleuze develops in his work on cinema. Henceforth, the problem of the image no longer envelops the status of a thought, capable of reflecting on the effects of its use, as was the case in the image of thought, but concerns rather the production of a subjectivity individuating itself through matter. This is precisely the knot that the cinema books take up in reconfiguring the Bergsonian problematic of the image as sensory-motor individuation, a sensible centre of indetermination tracing its perspective, unfolding its fan of perceptions, actions and subjective and material affections.

It is less a question of a radical shift or even of a theoretical leap than of a spiralling amplification: whole swathes of carefully elaborated arguments – from *Difference and Repetition* to *A Thousand Plateaus*, from *Kafka* to *Spinoza: Practical Philosophy* – concerning individuation defined as differenc/tiation, haecceity, and then the image, are brought to the critique of representation and imitation of the 1960s.

Indeed, image-individuation is present in *Difference and Repetition*, since the philosophy of difference is founded upon a philosophy of individuation in a process of becoming, and is not centred on a substantial individual, a constituted form, an anthropological soul or a logical subject. These impersonal individuations and pre-individual singularities, which owe a great deal to Simondon, imply the double formation of difference as individuation or actualisation on the one hand, and subjectivation or virtual consistency on the other.

These two moments of difference, laid out in the presentation on dramatisation (1967) and in *Difference and Repetition*, are crucial for understanding the solidarity between the critique of representation and the later affirmation of the image as individuation. Differenciation (with a *c*) concerns the movement of actualisation that defines the genesis of individuated forms and stable organisations. These individuals reciprocally assume a virtual differentiation (with a *t*) of intensive singularities that reintroduce chance at every moment into the actual individuated system, and which determine its ideal consistency. Such is the duality of actual individuation and of virtual subjectivation that defines difference. I propose that this duality of difference, presented at the time of *Difference and Repetition* with the erudite formula of differenc/tiation (which along the way does homage to Foucault's analysis of Raymond Roussel and plays with the phonemic substitution b/p), is redeployed with the definition of individuation as haecceity in *A Thousand Plateaus* (1980) and *Spinoza:*

Practical Philosophy (1981), before being unfolded yet again in the study of the cinematic image.

This clarifies the contrasting destiny of the concept of the image: it designates a critique of representative thought from *Nietzsche and Philosophy* (1962) and *Proust and Signs* (1964), to the article 'On Nietzsche and the Image of Thought', published the same year as *Difference and Repetition* (1968).[2] At this point, the representative image of thought appears as a mode of thought captivated by the transcendence of truth, for which Nietzsche and Proust substitute the healthful remedy of a 'new image of thought'.[3] In *Difference and Repetition*, the 'Image of thought', substantialised by its capital letter, congeals into the model of recognition par excellence, becoming the arena for the confrontation with Kant, which makes possible the affirmation of a polemical philosophy of difference as a thought 'without images', that is, a critique of representative Reason, deprived of all transcendent illusion (DR 167). In this case, the image designates the process of representation from which thought must liberate itself.

When Deleuze and Guattari take up the syntagm 'image of thought' once more in *What is Philosophy?* (1991), it is no longer a question of their aversion to representative Reason, but rather a question of the presuppositions of all philosophy. In this context, the image of thought functions as the transcendental condition of thought, no longer as its transcendent, representative illusion. The 'image of thought' is no longer the milieu of deceived thought, but the constitutive dimension that all philosophical thought carries with it, and which every great philosophy transforms. The image becomes the condition for the individuation of thought. The list of such images of thought thereby coincides with that of the great figures of philosophy, for Deleuze as well as for Guattari: Foucault, Spinoza, Nietzsche, Marx and Bergson are said to transform or rather to propose new images of thought because they individuate new theoretical perspectives, creating new concepts. The motor driving this transformation of image-representation into image-individuation therefore functions at the very core of thought, at the point where the image of thought begins to be considered the singular and dated presupposition of thought, in accordance with an ethology of thought that poses the problem of its creative individuation.

It is precisely because the image poses the problem of actualisation that it requires a confrontation with the solutions that metaphysics, throughout its long history, has proposed to the problems of representation, reproduction, imitation and participation. The polemical role that the concept of the image plays in 'The Reversal of Platonism' or in *Difference and Repetition* clearly indicates this: in these terms, Deleuze strives to overturn the trap of representation and the ontological difference between model and copy.

But this polemical project also corresponds to the creative dimension of a new philosophy of individuation, of differenc/tiation, of haecceity, of movement-image.

Haecceity takes up the duality of difference in *Difference and Repetition* and proposes in its turn a non-substantial philosophy of impersonal individuations and of pre-individual singularities. The individual is no longer defined by its form or its function, but by its longitude, a complex relation between speeding up and slowing down, and by its latitude, a variation of power (*puissance*), the power to affect or to be affected. Such an individuation by haecceity, understood as a mode, also diffracts into the two sides of the actual and virtual, henceforth constituting a Spinozist ethology. The actual becomes longitude, speeding up and slowing down; the virtual becomes latitude, variations of power. A body, an organ, or a subject gain consistency through these impersonal and asubjective modes of individuation. In this way, Deleuze and Guattari completely renew the relation between sign and force, obliging us to shift, as they affirm so forcefully in *Kafka*, from a morality of interpretation (signification) to an ethology of power (affect).

The division into latitude and longitude, which replays the distinction between the two aspects of difference – the individuating difference of differenciation (with a *c*), and virtual, subjectivating differentiation (with a *t*) – heralds the duality of the cinematic image. Defined this way, the image takes up Simondonian haecceity and Spinozist ethology: it implies a relation of sensory forces derived from affect – the individuation of which is perfect but not substantial – and diffracts into longitude (the accelerations and decelerations of its actualisation) and latitude (the variation of virtual power). Force is thus not only a composition of relations: it is an image. Such an individuation-image is neither an image-of-the-object nor an image-for-consciousness, neither a psychological given nor a representation of consciousness, neither a view of an object nor a representation of a thing. The image thus abandons the ontology of representation with its ineffable altitudes in order to establish itself on the surface, like sense, within an ethology of sensory individuations: a movement-image that actualises its sensory-motor arc and a time-image that stretches to the point of breaking the sensory-motor arc at the point of its virtual subjectivation.

The ethological map of individuating semiotics, of concrete ritornellos, opens to an ethic of affects and an ethology of bio-social machines. The semiotic of forces (longitude) opens the way to an ethic of power (latitude): in turn, haecceity – which does not define a class of individuals or of preformed beings, but which captures becomings as they are happening – already implies a new philosophy of image-individuation. For its most direct and explosive consequence consists, with regard to the philosophy of art, in the movement from representation, from reproduction, in short, from all of the old ontologies of the image that separate and superimpose model and copy, to a philosophy of becoming, of individuation, and of metamorphosis.

FROM METAPHOR TO THE CIRCUIT OF INTENSITY

From *Anti-Oedipus* to *Kafka*, this new philosophy of individuation through haecceity is deployed in relation to literature and to a critique of interpretation that includes psychoanalysis. Guattari, with the concept of transversality and the distinction between machine and structure,[4] and subsequently with Deleuze, formulates a radical critique of the literary image as a figure or metaphor with respect to literature. Whether it concerns figures of style ('solar anus') or the relationship between the literary character and reality, the old paradigm of imitation is rejected. For imitation, with its procedure of specular reproduction, separates two terms that it takes to be substantial, separate and anterior to their relation, and at the same time assigns to the copy the impossible task of imitating its model. The old ontology of the original and its reproduction is completely destroyed on the plane of logic (in *Rhizome*, we read that it is the imitation that creates its model), of biology (the symbiosis of the wasp and the orchid, animal-vegetable hybridisation replaces the reproduction of the offspring), and of aesthetics (Kafka's work is a machine that opens itself to experimentation, not to interpretation). The image, in this case the literary image, like the work of the unconscious, is understood to be real production, not representation, and is produced through haecceity, the becoming between the orchid and the wasp, between literature and the real, between the image and its model. Between the two terms laid down by the image at the extremities of its constituting passage, a zone of indistinction and indiscernibility is established through a 'capture of force' (see FB), a modulation between forces and materials.

At least two consequences follow from this elegant definition of art as haecceity: first, if, as we have seen, the imitation creates its model instead of being reduced to a secondary production considered to be ontologically distinct, the specular relation of imitation actually conceals a becoming. From *Kafka* to *A Thousand Plateaus*, this becoming is described as a becoming minor that produces a major norm. Mimesis as a process of imitation has therefore always implied a becoming. As soon as we try to produce a second reality (re-production), mimetically imitating a model, we are in reality proceeding by means of an individuation through haecceity, which carries the terms of this relation along to a becoming that redefines them. This exempts art from an analogical theory of resemblance, from reproduction, or from structural homology. Guattari and Deleuze, together and separately, insist repeatedly that it is necessary to shift from interpretation to experimentation, both on the linguistic plane of stylistic variation and on the semantic plane of the individuation of characters or literary journeys. 'Ahab does not imitate the whale, he becomes Moby-Dick, he enters into the zone of proximity (*zone de voisinage*) where he can no longer be distinguished from Moby-Dick', and again: 'it is no longer a question of Mimesis, but of becoming' (CC 78).

The shift from interpretation to experimentation thus exactly reca-pitulates the shift of the image from representation to individuation-image. This is why Guattari refuses all models of psychoanalytic or literary interpretation that reduce the figure (the literary image, the symptom) to an imaginary identification or to a structural correspondence of relations. Nevertheless, this does not imply a critique of the image, since Deleuze and Guattari substitute for the analogical metaphor a becoming-image, a new individuation that creates an original haecceity, a constituting image that carves out a zone of new experience: an ecological image. No metaphor, therefore, if metaphor presupposes a transfer from a zone of literal meaning to a figural one. Nevertheless, the vocabulary of metaphor can be retained, as Guattari does on occasion, on the condition that metaphor is defined as continual variation and the becoming of forces.

The status of the image in art and literature thus turns on the classic problem of art as imitation, on reproduction, and on mimicry in animal ethology, as exemplified by the striking example of the wasp and the orchid. The literary image and becoming-animal engage the same problematic of a shift from imitation (mimesis) to becoming (mimicry).[5] Becoming-animal, the subject par excellence of Kafka's short story 'The Metamorphosis', explores a becoming that affects all literary entities, including characters, in addition to transfiguring literary style. The story concerns neither imaginary identification nor symbolic structure, but a real transformation that affects the style of literature and its modes of syntactic and semantic individuation: the becoming-animal of Gregor and the becoming-minor of language. The image is no longer preoccupied with a specular confronta-tion in the mode of a fantasy (a mental image) or of a symbol (structural homology) when it is conceived of as individuation, the experimentation of a writing machine that explores new vital and social speeds. As soon as the image becomes capture, proximity, intensive composition between two terms that nevertheless remain distinct, it opens a circuit, a sensory-motor arc by means of encounters and the composition of relations between lon-gitude and latitude, and not immediate, instantaneous reflexivity. 'There is no longer a designation of something by means of a proper name, nor an assignation of metaphors by means of a figurative sense. But *like* images, the thing no longer forms anything but a sequence of intensive states, a ladder or a circuit for intensities that one can make race around . . . The image is this very race itself; it has become becoming . . .' (K 21–2).

The individuating model of the becoming-image replaces the representative model of the degraded specular image that separates and hierarchises the model and its copy in the abstract instantaneity of an endless confrontation between two classes of being. No reflexivity is immediate or instantaneous. Every image unfolds across a trajectory. Even between a face and its reflection in a mirror, an uneven circuit is established, rapid though it may be, of kinetic, spatiotemporal dramatisation: step by step, longitude, vibrating with variable speeds, and latitude, varying its power.

THE INDIVIDUATION OF THE MOVEMENT-IMAGE

The image is no longer a representation of consciousness, a mental perception, an internal mini-cinema as Guattari calls it, but is rather given as an apparition of an individuation, longitude and latitude, matter and movement. In order to move from the image as a critique of representation to the image as individuation, it is necessary that it be transferred from the psychic domain of representations in order to undergo material individuation. It is now possible to understand how Deleuze moved from the image of thought as a critique of representation in 1962 to the image as real individuation, as movement in matter and no longer as amputated representation. The circuit by which the image exits the psychic domain of ideations to assume the Bergsonian and Simondonian status of an individuation, is, I hope, clear. This puts the philosophy of cinema at the core of the problem of individuation, which concerns the philosophy of the subject as much as it concerns that of time.

The 'Bergsonian discovery of the movement-image' becomes the point of departure for a philosophy of cinema because it prevents us from setting the psychic image and physical movement in opposition, and not at all because we can supposedly glide from the image as Bergson construes it in *Matter and Memory* to the art of the image allegedly incarnated within cinema. Indeed, the problem is rather an ecological one, that of a sensory-motor perspective becoming individuated as it traverses matter through subtraction.

The image is no longer a mental projection, but is individuated in itself, as matter and movement. This first definition of the image allows it to be posited as the totality of matter in movement, the cinematic material universe: 'This is not mechanism, it is machinism. The material universe, the plane of immanence, is the *machine assemblage of movement-images*'; 'Bergson is startlingly ahead of his time' in allowing us to think of the

'the universe as cinema in itself, a metacinema' (C1 59). In this sense, the image, like Spinozist substance, defines the acentred plane of the totality of movement-images, without yet accounting for their modal individuation. This is what Deleuze calls the plane of immanence, indistinctly matter = image = movement: 'We may therefore say that the plane of immanence or the plane of matter is: a set of movement-images' (C1 61). On this plane, it is not possible to distinguish any individuated image because everything reacts on everything else. If Deleuze now establishes a correspondence between Bergson's philosophy and his own study of cinema, it is because the modal individuation of sensory images allows matter and perception to be rigorously dealt with on the same plane. In this system, in effect, the thing and the perception of the thing make up one and only one image, one and only one reality, but which is referred to one or the other of two systems of reference: the universe as a metacinema, the set of image-movement-matter, or the individuated image as a sensorial interstice that traces its myopic perspective across matter.

The problem of perception – and this is where the encounter with cinema is decisive – can only be broached from the starting point of the acentred plane of the set of movement-images, and not from the perceiving subject for whom images appear following the paradigm model/copy of imitation, which phenomenology takes up again for its part with intentionality. The technical invention of cinema was necessary in order for perception to appear (in the photographic sense) as the ecological individuation of a movement-image.

The movement-image signifies nothing other than this *sensory* (image) *motor* (movement) arc. Thus the image, in the ordinary sense of an individuated movement-image, is a plural individuation of differential movements, which form fluctuating composites of varying power. Such a mode of individuation, as we have seen with haecceity, presupposes neither unity nor stable identity, but rather composes a material and transitory relation of forces. Individuation is defined neither by its unity, nor by its identity, but by a cutting operation that detaches, in the mobile universe of forces, a provisional relation of variable speeds and affects. Such images become individuated and detached from the acentred universe of matter through selection, neglecting everything in other images that is not of interest. In other words, perception is produced through subtractive framing, which attracts incomplete images to a privileged image in the mobile universe of material forces. This is why the moving image is, strictly speaking, of the same order as matter and provides neither a secondary copy nor a psychic translation of it. Perception is individuation.

The individuated-image emerges through a cinematographic mode, through editing and framing, folding and interiorisation. The finite perceptive image, whether it is technical-social or vital, emerges from infinite acentred movement through the subtractive operation of vital framing. Perceiving, for a specific image – an organic body or a cinematographic machine, with no privilege accorded to the living or to the human – involves tracing a myopic diagonal across the other images. The production of the cinematographic image, as of that of any vital image –human, animal, technical or vegetal – determines this cut among the acentred movement-images. The image subjectivates in unfolding its arc, shifting from perception-image to action-image by way of the affection-image. These three states of matter correspond at the same time to a genetics of the subject and to a semiotics of cinema. We might even say that a kinetics or a cinematography of the subject is invented alongside a physics of cinema.

In two respects, cinema is revealed to be not only decisive, but the necessary condition for this recognition of the differential individuation of images. This is due to the way in which it exhibits its technical moment, offering human perception a fascinating access to the visible that is no longer referred to the human mediation of the presumably artistic hand or eye. The camera controls this non-centred access to the individuation-image and impels us to traverse the circuit that strains the human perception of the spectator and binds it and extends it to a movement-image, which to us seems acentred because it is not produced by the reflex of human perception or held hostage by the consciousness of an artist.

We shift from the acentred universe of movement-images (the cinema-chinic universe) to the subjectivated body of second images without ever leaving the immanent plane of forces. This is the lesson cinema can teach us better than the other arts of its time. First and foremost, because it offers a captivating glimpse into states of matter that are not dependent upon a human centre – a gaseous and liquid perception – and in that it cuts or illuminates its objects in ways that are not recognisably human. Better than the other arts, cinema allows the extra-individual, social and technical aspects of all other art images, visual or aural, to be shattered, and demonstrates that they also do not merely add another spiritual layer to ordinary human perception, but rather cut a zone of subjectivation across matter in a different way, captured in a material form.

The example of cinema is thus necessary to define the status of such images, indifferently individuated-images and art images, because these photo- and cinematographic images individuate their technical perspective without needing to manifest themselves to a (human) consciousness in order to appear. Relatively acentred, we have no need to refer them datively to a human subject who would have started by experiencing them, and, consequently, no need to define them as duplications of an object that they would strive to reproduce. This is how photography inserts perception into matter, as Bergson said.

This encounter between cinema and individuation does not, however, grant any privilege to cinema, as if cinema could flatter itself for incarnating the art of the movement-image more intimately than the other arts. But it is necessary to insert this encounter between cinema, perception and the arts into the short history of Western art in order to convey the scope of the technical and industrial crisis that cinema, on the heels of photography, imposed on the landscape of the arts at the end of the nineteenth century. The fine arts, uptight and aloof in their distaste for mass and industrial production, justifying their arrogance based upon their emphatic self-definition as *beaux arts*, undergo a savage and mechanical profanation with the emergence of photography and cinema. This transformation does not, however, grant cinema any technical privilege and is noteworthy only for its impact on the Western consciousness of the arts, which places the spiritual privilege of an artistic consciousness, with its exquisite surplus value of sensibility and of archi-perception, at the apogee, as the cultivated and mystical apotheosis of natural perception. The camera, more visibly than language, the paintbrush, the body or the musical instrument, superimposes its industrial mask on the discredited body of the artist and grafts the mechanical features of the camera onto the eye of the cameraman. This has earned for cinema and photography their equivocal status as mechanical reproducers, lacking in art because incapable of spiritual representation and bound to the vulgar duplication of the real. In *Man with a Movie Camera*, Vertov already refuted this aestheticising fracture, making the cine-eye visible, effecting the individuation of the mechanical image at the level of the social material of cities, creating an entirely new sensory-motor blister (*cloque*) vibrating with new ways of affecting and being affected.

This is true retrospectively of all the other arts once they are understood as a capture of forces and not as inspired exceptions that spiritualise ordinary perception. In the same way, the most modest finger painting or music created through tapping one's foot imply an ecological zone of visibility of this kind, one that is indiscernibly technical, living and social, as well as individuations of movement-images. Now that individuation is not that of a subject and is not defined by a universal logic of a species or by the anthropological substance of perception, any more than by the aesthetic work (*mise en forme*) of an artistic genius, we can understand all images – from the organic to the social, from the living to the technical – as Guattari says so forcefully, to be on the environmental, social and mental plane of ecology.[6] All of the arts thus implicate these modes of individuated, differential and specific images, introducing their material and social semiotics into the core of matter. The definition of the image as a haecceity – the longitude of movement-images, the latitude of time-images – was made possible because of the emergence of cinema. Nevertheless, these concepts do not apply exclusively to cinema as a type of art, nor to art as a specific type of individuation in human cultures, but rather apply to all individuation. This should encourage us not only to apply these concepts to art history, like Thomas Kisser, who writes of the time-image in relation to Titian and Watteau, or Gregory Flaxman who interrogates the longitude of the history of perspective.[7] It also makes it possible for us to connect the problematics of the image to the ecological semiotics of the ritornello, freeing ourselves from many of the idealist assumptions of aesthetic theories, which define art as archi-perception, a universal anthropology.

NOTES

1. Deleuze and Guattari, 'La synthèse disjunctive', in *L'Arc* 43 (1970): 54–62, special issue on Klossowski. The first text co-written by the two authors and which, as its title indicates, concerns the disjunctive writing machine that they are in the process of creating.
2. For a more complete analysis of these movements, see Sauvagnargues, *Deleuze: L'empirisme transcendental*, Chapter 3, as well as Sauvagnargues, *Deleuze and Art*, also Chapter 3.
3. Deleuze, *Nietzsche and Philosophy*, 103; *Proust and Signs*, 94–102; *Two Regimes of Madness*, 308.
4. Guattari, *Psychanalyse et tranversalité*. This book is absolutely decisive.
5. Zourabichvili, *La littéralité et autres écrits sur l'art*.
6. See Guattari's *The Three Ecologies* and *Chaosmosis*.
7. Kisser, 'Visualität, Virtualität, Temporalität', and also 'Carnation et incarnation: Logique picturale et logique religieuse dans l'oeuvre tardive du Titien'; Flaxman, *Gilles Deleuze and the Fabulation of Philosophy: Powers of the False*, vol. 1.

PART II: DELEUZE, AESTHETICS AND THE IMAGE

4. The Concept of Modulation in Deleuze, and the Importance of Simondon to the Deleuzian Aesthetic

In Deleuze, art occupies a determinant position: a philosophy of immanence and becoming that strives to constitute a metaphysics of the event necessarily encounters the question of art on a triple plane. First, the sensible effects of works historically raises the problem of creation and of the mutation of cultures. Second, the disparity between the sensible effect of art and philosophy demands a critique of representation, which is relevant as much to art understood as imitation as to the status of a philosophy of works. Third, art is at the centre of a 'semiotics', in the sense that Deleuze defines it in his studies on cinema, as a theory of signs irreducible to linguistic determinations (C2 29).

Deleuze affirms that art participates, just as much as philosophy and science, in the becoming of thought, but that their domains, as well as their methods and their effects, remain irreducible, independent and estranged. Their difference must be thought in terms of heterogeneity and not abstractly reduced to the identical under the authority of the concept. Nevertheless, Deleuze does not in any way intend to deprive philosophy of the excellence proper to it. The fact that art and science are equally creative justifies us in positing that 'philosophy creates concepts in the strict sense' (WP 5) and in affirming its irreducible specificity. But it is precisely the fact that philosophy concerns the creation of concepts[1] that at the same time suggests the urgency of thinking art in philosophy, without reducing the sense of art to the philosophical concept, or renouncing thinking about art philosophically.

It is the concept of modulation that makes it possible to extract from art the concepts that a theory of art requires, and that makes it possible for philosophy to learn from the experience of art in order to theorise the relations between thought and the sensible. If the semiotics that Deleuze proposes for cinema combines the systematic force of philosophy with a theory of the sign that eludes linguistic domination, if Deleuze chooses to use the term 'semiotics' over 'semiology',[2] this is because it is no longer a question of thinking about art as if it is a language, or of ordering sense according to discursive significations, but of elaborating the relations between matter and form, which brings with it new requirements. In art, matter that is not linguistically formed, that is irreducible to a statement, is nevertheless not amorphous: it is 'formed semiotically, aesthetically and pragmatically' (C2 29). Deleuze deploys the Simondonian concept of modulation to think through these new relations between matter and form.

Simondon's contribution is decisive, and this is the occasion to establish the importance of a thinker whose theoretical fecundity, little recognised during his lifetime, did not escape Deleuze's attention. As early as 1966, Deleuze reviewed the abridged version of Simondon's thesis, which had appeared two years previously. Simondon defended his doctoral dissertation in 1958 under the direction of Merleau-Ponty.[3] In his review, Deleuze hailed Simondon as a creator of new concepts: 'The new concepts established by Simondon seem to me extremely important; their wealth and originality are striking, when they're not outright inspiring' (DI 89). Simondon in effect proposes a critique of the substantial subject that coordinates a constellation of original concepts: the problematic, disparation, signal, resonance, crystallisation, membrane and modulation. Beginning in *Difference and Repetition*, Deleuze assimilates these concepts and organises them into an original theory, the Deleuzian 'disparate' (*dispars*) doing homage to Simondonian disparation, while Simondonian semiology, derived from the philosophy of nature and Wiener's information theory,[4] provided Deleuze with the physical frame he needed to move from a 'logic of sense', centred in a Husserlian mode on the production of idealities in thought, to a 'logic of sensation',[5] in which thought, produced by the brutal encounter with a heterogeneous, sensible sign (WP 199; see also PS), can henceforth be grasped as 'heterogenesis'.[6]

For his part, Deleuze elaborates a philosophy of the constitution of the sensible from the perspective of a critique of the substantial subject,[7] which allows him to appreciate the power of the Simondonian critique of individuation. This marked a confluence between two thinkers that did not prevent either divergences or critiques. The technical (*technicienne*) and positivist inspiration of Simondon, as well as his interest in the sciences, encountered in the young Deleuze a thought permeated by Anglo-Saxon empiricism, and their confluence operates at the level of a fundamental thesis concerning the constitution of subjectivity. Simondon demonstrates, in effect, that the individual, whether it concerns a subject or a being of any kind, is never given substantially, but is produced through a process of individuation. He understands this process in terms of problematic 'disparation', that is, as an act, a relation. The subject is not given; it is constituted through its process of individuation. Deleuze completely assimilates this conclusion, his studies of Hume and Nietzsche having prepared him to integrate it into his own doctrine. He does not take up the concept of 'disparation' in name – in contrast to 'modulation', which he employs frequently without mentioning Simondon – but he does integrate the Simondonian analysis of disparation and of the problematic, both of which are necessary for understanding modulation.

The term 'disparation', which Simondon borrows from the psychophysiology of perception,[8] designates the production of depth in binocular vision and addresses the asymmetry of retinal images, an irreducible disparity that problematically produces, through the resolution of their difference, binocular vision. Each retina is covered by a bi-dimensional image, but the two images do not coincide due to the difference in parallaxes, as anyone can see by closing one eye and then the other.[9] There is thus no optically available bi-dimensional image that can resolve what Simondon calls 'the axiomatic of bi-dimensionality' (two images that between them lack coherency), 'axiomatic' designating in Simondon the objective structuration of a field, in this case that of vision. To resolve bi-dimensional disparation, the human brain integrates it as the condition of coherence of a *new* axiom: tri-dimensionality. Volume, or depth perception, resolves the bi-dimensional conflict by positively creating a new dimension, tri-dimensionality, in the absence of a retinal image. As Simondon described it, 'the perceptual discovery is not a reductive abstraction, but an integration, an amplifying operation',[10] indicating that in depth perception, visual volume is achieved not through the reduction of disparity – the elimination of the difference of parallaxes – but rather through an operation, an inventive construction that adds a new dimension that the isolated retinal image does not contain. It is the pair of disparate retinas that require this amplifying operation, which is what constitutes 'disparation'. Disparation is thus simultaneously 'problematic' and creative. 'Problematic' refers to the disparity, the difference, between the retinal images in so far as this difference is not reduced, but, on the contrary, provides the opportunity for the constitution of a new dimension.

Far from reducing disparation to the psychophysiological phenomenon of vision from which he derives it – even if, as we shall see, perception does not constitute a random example of it – Simondon extends it to all individuation, to any production of existence on whatever scale one

is situated (physical signal, living being, collective body, idea): any singularity is produced through problematic disparation. Following Kant,
Simondon thus elevates the problematic to the dignity of the condition of
emergence of a difference, of a sense. What is at stake, Deleuze observes,
is an 'objective category of knowledge' and 'a perfectly objective kind
of being', and not a 'fleeting uncertainty' (LS 54). 'This category of [the
problematic] acquires in Simondon's thought tremendous importance
insofar as this category is endowed with an objective sense: it no longer
designates a provisional state of our knowledge, . . . but a moment of
being' (DI 88, with modification).

Deleuze appropriates this analysis as a fecund method that facilitates the
thinking of productive difference by avoiding what he judges to be unaccep-
table in the Hegelian dialectic: the motor role of the negative, the primacy
of opposition, and the resolution of difference by means of a dialectic that
produces the identity of difference and of identity, at the very place where
Deleuze is seeking to affirm difference. The conflict (the incompatibility
of two retinal images, for example) thought as disparation, is difference
and not opposition, and it is resolved through construction (the creation of
a new dimension), through affirmation and not negation. Thus, 'the idea
of "disparation" is more profound than the idea of opposition . . . And,
in Simondon's dialectic, the problematic replaces the negative' (DI 87–8).
What interests Deleuze is 'the primacy of "disparateness" in relation to
opposition' (DR 330 n. 12),[11] which allows him – while avoiding the dialectical suppression of difference – to think, in alignment with Simondon,
that all events are produced problematically through disparation and thus
that 'the individual is not just a result, but a *milieu* of individuation' (DI
86, with modification). For the individual is neither prior to nor contemporaneous with its individuation, because what defines the conditions of an
individuation is 'the existence of a "disparation," the existence of at least
two different dimensions, two disparate levels of reality', which implies
a 'fundamental *difference*, like a state of dissymmetry' (DI 87). We can
thus appreciate the degree to which Deleuze was interested in Simondon, a
thinker of difference who defined the mode of the event as the problematic
(LS 54), and who judged that a philosophy of becoming required a new
logic, a thought 'in terms of milieu'.[12]

For his part, in his critique of the substantialised subject, Simondon
insists on the fact that any individuation occurs through disparation in a
milieu that does not pre-exist the individual, but on the contrary is constituted by a *transduction*,[13] for which the crystal furnishes the simplest
image, and which proposes the correlative appearance of the individuation and its milieu in problematic tension: 'the transductive operation is
an individuation in progress',[14] through a resonance between different

realities (for the crystal, the crystalline seed and the supersaturated solution) that the process of individuation puts into communication. It is indeed Simondonian disparation, a *metastable* relation between two orders of different realities that enter into resonance, that allows Deleuze to think 'a mode of individuation that is precisely not confused with that of a thing or a subject'. Deleuze reserves for it the term 'haecceity', a nuanced tribute to Simondonian theory.[15] Haecceity concerns thought as much as the production of signs or signals since it thematises the event, the emergence of a singularity on whatever scale: a human idea, a molecular encounter, a distinct atmosphere, *five o'clock in the afternoon*.[16] This is also Simondonian. We thus understand that the mode of being of thought, like that of the work of art, can be defined as 'problematic',[17] as a heterogeneous tension that produces the conditions of its resolution. Like Simondon – and even if on this point he invokes Kant – Deleuze turns the problematic into a 'discordant harmony': 'Ideas are essentially problematic' (DR 168; 189–90),[18] the Idea functioning as the problematic field that determines thought. But if Deleuze owes this objectivity of the problematic as much to Kant as to French epistemology, it is with Simondon that he relates the problem to the creation of thought and signs.[19] Ideas and problems are no longer reduced to an anthropological field, for the sign no longer refers to a philosophy of spirit, but rather to a philosophy of nature.[20] As soon as there is the production of a material effect, the emergence of a signal as a haecceity resolves a problematic tension. For Deleuze as for Simondon, the theory of the sign is substituted for a theory of physical causality. We can thus appreciate the extent to which the Deleuzian definition of the signal and the sign is indebted to Simondon: 'By "signal" we mean a system with orders of disparate size, endowed with elements of dissymmetry; by "sign" we mean what happens within such a system, what flashes across the intervals when a communication takes place between disparates' (DR 20).

In effect, Simondon locates information 'between the two halves of a system in a relation of disparation';[21] even if this information is not signaletic in the crystallisation that proceeds step by step, it is at the level of the living being, and presupposes the tension of the system in the midst of individuation. Deleuze substitutes the theory of the simulacrum for the vocabulary of information, which 'seizes upon a constituent *disparity*' (DR 67) and allows us to explain repetition as differentiation rather than as resemblance (of effect to cause, of thing to essence). It is the 'disparate' (*dispars*), 'difference in itself . . . which relates heterogeneous series and even completely disparate things' (DR 120), which causes sensibility and thought to emerge as a 'resolution of a difference of potential', that is, as an intensive difference.[22] Simondon's influence on the Deleuzian theory of intensive difference is thus not negligible, even if Deleuze reinterprets the physical theory of the communication of information within the frame of his own work on the heterogeneity of the sign (DR 22–3).

The theory of problematic disparation determines the status of modulation, which assumes in the Deleuzian aesthetic an increasingly determinant position, to the point of functioning in *Francis Bacon: The Logic of Sensation* and in *Cinema 2: The Time-Image* as the decisive concept in a philosophy of art. How can philosophy account for the effect of art, on the double plane of the effect produced by the material (which assumes form in the work) and the effect produced on the recipient, the beholder? How, on the canvas, does Francis Bacon's brush stroke produce an effect that transmutes the sensory material (pigments and binders adhering to the surface) into expressive qualities, which extract from the sensible what Deleuze calls 'expressive features' (WP 183)? How does art – all of the arts – inscribe the production of its sense into the working of material? Alternatively, how are these expressive features received? How do they produce their effect on humans? By problematic disparation, which functions as much at the level of the relation between form and matter in the sensible body of the work as on the plane of the effect produced by art. We can thus think of aesthetics simultaneously as a theory of the sensible and as a theory of art. Just as Simondonian disparation makes it possible to think sense perception, but is raised by Simondon to the rank of a cosmological concept accounting for phases of being, aesthetics in Deleuze makes it possible to simultaneously think the being of the sensible and the production of sense in culture. More precisely, positioning the problem in this way, in terms of disparation, allows us to overcome what Deleuze, in 1966, called the 'wrenching duality' of aesthetics, split between a theory of sensibility as the 'form of possible experience' and 'the theory of art as the reflection of real experience' (LS 260).[23] We recognise in this formulation the Kantian duality between aesthetics as a theory of sensibility, the transcendental aesthetics dealt with in the *Critique of Pure Reason*, and aesthetics in the modern sense, coming from Baumgarten, who defines the effect produced by the beauty of a representation, analysed by Kant in the *Critique of Judgment*. It is quite remarkable that Deleuze, in *Difference and Repetition*, theorises the problem of art from the Kantian position, which serves as both frame of reference and as the critical stake. Down to his last published text, 'Immanence . . . A life',[24] Deleuze maintains this founding inspiration: that thought, in its vital and corporeal conditions, must be seized in terms of its transcendental conditions of exercise. Nevertheless, he critiques the Kantian position by substituting for transcendental idealism the claim, constant in his work, to a 'transcendental empiricism', which radicalises the Kantian project by conducting a critique of the substantial subject (hence the expression transcendental *empiricism*, which is a substitute for the *idealism* of the Kantian critique). It is within a Kantian frame that Deleuze interprets the extremely powerful theory of Simondonian modulation.

Let us return, then, to the 'wrenching duality' (LS 260) that plagues Kantian aesthetics, for which Deleuze precisely establishes the conditions of resolution: the methodological critique of representation. Kant 'splits' aesthetics (at the same time that he constitutes it) into 'two irreducible domains' (DR 68), the theory of the sensible and the theory of art, because he positions the relation between thought and the sensible in terms of representation. On the one hand, he assumes sensations to be already made as the matter of intuition, relating them only abstractly to the *a priori* form of the representation, reducing sensation to a simple receptivity that he opposes to categorical spontaneity. On the other hand, the *a priori* form of experience, categories of understanding and *a priori* forms of sensibility, abstracted from the matter of sensation, can now only define *possible* conditions of experience. From this fact, he 'splits' the two parts of the Aesthetic, separating the objective element of sensation from the subjective element of pleasure and pain (DR 97–8). Because Kant opposes the matter of sensation, received passively, to the spontaneity of the categorical form, he can only retain from the real 'its conformity to possible experience', while the theory of the beautiful, itself caught up in a struggle with 'the reality of the real', now only retains it in the form of the subjective element of representation. In this way, the Kantian theory of the transcendental remains subjected to representation: separating the transcendental form from sensible matter, it can now only determine the conditions of an experience that is only possible, and not those of a real experience. Deleuze, following Bergson, demonstrates that the possible is only ever a general idea, one that is abstract and representative, because it misrecognises the relations between thought and the real, is revealed to be incapable of explaining its own genesis, and patterns itself implicitly on the empirical. In effect, it is necessary that such a set of conditions be first empirically given in order for abstract thought to retrospectively subtract a few conditions from it and declare after the fact: such and such other configuration *would have been* possible. Kant, the 'prodigious' inventor of the transcendental, the discoverer of critical philosophy (DR 135), in the end submits to representative dogma, replaying the opposition between passive matter and active form. He divides Aesthetics in two because he bases it on what can be represented in the sensible (DR 56), and conceives the relations between thought and the sensible in terms of the opposition between form and matter, instead of positing thought as an encounter with the sensible.

It is precisely from art that Deleuze expected to find a solution to 'transcendental empiricism' for philosophy: 'The work of art leaves the domain of representation in order to become "experience," transcendental empiricism or science of the sensible' (DR 56). This indicates that it is the work of art, as experience, as actualised performance, that realises in its own mode what philosophy cannot produce without calling upon it for help: a critique of representation. The role of art turns out to be crucial and paradoxical. It is from art, in so far as it is real experience, that philosophy awaits theoretical renewal, but this renewal is not produced conceptually: it is elaborated on the plane of artistic work (creation and reception being confounded). It is indeed, however, a question of a theoretical reform, because the work becomes the occasion for a new philosophy: 'Everything changes once we determine the conditions of real experience . . . the two senses of the aesthetic become one, to the point where the being of the sensible reveals itself in the work of art, while at the same time the work of art appears as experimentation' (DR 68). The work of art is an experimentation with the sensible, on the sensible, because it brings about a creation of sense on the plane of the sensible, and because it compels thought. For Deleuze – and this applies to art as well as to philosophy – what compels thought is the object of a disruptive, violent and empirical encounter, one that is vital and not a matter of recognition: thought is produced in the heterogeneous encounter with the sensible, and not in the element of thought (recognition). The object of the encounter 'gives rise to sensibility with regard to a given sense', and that which is given is not a sensible being, or the separation between amorphous matter and an empty form, but 'a sign', 'the being *of* the sensible', 'that by which the given is given'. It is the object of the encounter, the sign, that is the 'bearer of the problem – as though it were a problem' (DR 139–40); it is the sign that is produced through problematic disparation. Sense is not pre-existent, but, as Simondon makes perfectly clear, is 'the signification that will emerge when an operation of individuation discovers the dimension according to which two disparate reals can become a system'.[25]

The theory of the sign as the relation between thought and the sensible, that is, as aesthetics, demands that we return to the conditions of opposition between matter and form. It is here that the theory of modulation intervenes as an explicit critique of any *hylomorphic* doctrine that, according to Simondon, refers to the Aristotelian distinction between form and matter (notably in terms of sensation, which Aristotle thinks of as an imprint that communicates the form of the mould but not its matter), and also to the Kantian separation between sensation, amorphous matter, intensive size and the form of sensibility.[26] Simondon refuses the quest to 'grasp the structure of being without the operation, and the operation without the structure'[27] – exactly as Deleuze demands that we think categorical structure and the genesis of thought together in the sensible encounter. Thought is representative when it divides structure and operation, and prohibits itself from thinking the process that it itself sets into motion in becoming actualised, just as much as it misrecognises real individuations. Everywhere, thought divides the active, conditioning form from unformed matter. In order to grasp the process of knowledge, as well as material, living, or technological formations, it is necessary, according to Simondon, to situate oneself in the middle (*au milieu*)[28] of what hylomorphic thought has broken apart, in the interstices between the merely abstract form and that matter that it splits in two, and whose opposition cannot withstand even the weakest, concrete examination of an operation of natural or technical individuation.

Take the example of moulding, prototype of human technics, but more importantly, the example of reference for hylomorphic thought, for which it appears to present a convincing validation. Doesn't it consist of the imposition of an external form (a mould) upon a passive matter (clay)? First, Simondon replies, clay is not just any random, inert material, but a determinate material, not only endowed with its own forms (properties of clay, variable plasticity), but also given preliminary form by the artisan (prepared). Next, the mould is not an abstract form, but a material frame, realising in a material form its geometric shape through the work of selecting and the assembling of material. If we wish to hold onto notions of matter and form, we have to admit that both the clay and the mould present the same complex as matter and form. In fact, the abstract application of the notions of 'matter' and 'form' impede reflection, because it is the operation of assuming form (*mise en forme*) that counts.[29] The theory of the imprint assumes that the active form of the mould impresses its form on passive matter. That's not it at all. Of course, clay compressed in a mould comes out of it after a determinate length of time in the form of a brick, but what has actually happened? According to Simondon, not the imposition of a form, but a *reciprocal* 'assumption of form' (*prise de forme*) between the mould and the material, which Simondon proposes to call *modulation* (continuous and temporal moulding).[30] Of course, the mould endures after the operation, while the clay is turned into a brick. But what counts is that the frame of the mould and the material *modulate*, enter into a common system, an associated milieu, and together realise an operation of individuation (the brick) through a continuous exchange of information. This causes a 'zone of an average and intermediary dimension' to appear between form and matter, that of the singularities that are the start of individuals in the operation of individuation.[31] Thus, neither form nor matter suffices to explain individuation. 'The true principle of individuation is the genesis itself in the process of operating, that is, the system in the process of becoming, as energy gets actualized. . . . The principle of individuation is the unique manner in which the internal resonance of *this* matter in the process of assuming *this* form becomes established.'[32]

Each molecule of the clay enters into communication with the pressure exercised by the surface of the mould, in constant communication with the geometric form concretised in the mould; the mould is as informed by the clay as the clay is by the mould, having to resist, to a certain point, the deformations of the material (the constraints that it exercises on the mould).[33] What this very simple, canonical example shows (the mastery of clay having marked the emergence of the Neolithic threshold) is that at the level of technics itself, where the hylomorphic scheme appears to be triumphant, the individuation (of the brick) puts into play 'a common operation and at the same level of existence between matter and form', a differentiation that operates in such a way that the mould and the clay 'modulate' together, concretely interacting, 'and this common milieu of existence is that of force',[34] that is, the quantity of energy that is actualised in the modulation clay-mould during the production of the brick.

This distinction between moulding (an abstract conception that opposes matter to form) and modulation (as a continuous 'assumption of form' between properties of material and the concrete action of form) has much to offer to the theory of art. Modulation makes it possible to deal with, on the same plane, the shift from material to expressive features in the work, and the encounter between thought and the work, because in both cases what occurs is the production of a sign, which is no longer referred to the ideality of a meaning, but which 'modulates' through problematic disparation. This explains why Simondon is presented by Deleuze in *The Logic of Sense* as the author who proposes 'a new conception of the transcendental', 'of great importance', because he liberates individuation from the substantial subject, and makes it possible thereby to position the transcendental, no longer as the act of a substantial and constituting subject, but as an actualisation, which generates subjects and objects at the same time. Modulation makes it possible to theorise this reciprocal assumption of form (*prise de forme réciproque*), rather than thinking of the object as constituted by the subjective form. It makes possible, according to Deleuze, a new definition of the transcendental field, liberated from subjectification by the subject-form, detached from a consciousness, posited instead as 'impersonal and pre-individual' (LS 102) because it is produced by the encounter, in the interstices of the heterogeneous elements that are thought and the sensible, in their very difference, as the problematic resolution of their disparation that produces a new dimension: sense actualised as an event. This event is the haecceity that emerges through the modulation of disparate elements: a singularity. This is why 'this world of sense has a *problematic* status: singularities are distributed in a properly problematic field and crop up in this field as topological events' (LS 104). Simondon is a decisive philosopher for Deleuze: he makes possible 'the first thought-out theory of impersonal and pre-individual singularities' (LS 104 n. 3).

It is thus possible for Deleuze to interpret Simondonian modulation as a logic of sensation that heals the rift in aesthetics between the theory of sensibility and the theory of art. It is the same disparation that modulates in sensation the relation between the sensible and the felt (*du sensible au senti*), and in thought, the relation between sense and the sensible in the encounter with the work (*du sens au sensible à la rencontre de l'oeuvre*). Thus 'perception will no longer reside in the relation between a subject and an object, but rather in the movement serving as the limit of that relation . . . Perception will confront its own limit; it will be in the midst of things . . . as the presence of one haecceity in another' (TP 282). Modulation makes it possible to be inserted at the level of matter itself in order to think it as the bearer of singularities and expressive features. We thus shift from the static opposition between form and matter to a zone of average dimension, one that is energetic and molecular, which makes it possible to think an 'energetic materiality in movement, carrying *singularities or haecceities* that are already like implicit forms . . . that combine with processes of deformation' (TP 408). In other words, art does not consist in imposing a form upon matter, nor in producing a subjective effect upon a sensibility, but in '*following* a flow of matter' (TP 373), that is, in exploiting material expressive features in a 'synthesis of heterogeneities' (TP 330), a 'synthesis of disparate elements' (TP 343) that conjoins the expressive forces of the material and those of affect in the consistency of the work.

'It is no longer a question of imposing a form upon a matter but of elaborating an increasingly rich and consistent material, the better to tap increasingly intense forces' (TP 329).[35] This is why Deleuze turns art into an experimentation that has a bearing upon 'the being of the sensible', instead of only finding in art an effect of representation, as Kant proposed. Art, like modulation, can be defined as a capture of forces: the 'community of arts', 'their common problem', is to be found here: 'In art, and in painting as in music, it is not a matter of reproducing or inventing forms, but of capturing forces. For this reason no art is figurative' (FB 48). On the one hand, we move away from the opposition between form and matter to the constitution of an expressive material at the level of the work itself, an advantage for the analysis that aims for a veritable epistemology of material. On the other hand, the relation between the work and the spectator, the theory of affect, can also be comprehended in terms of modulation.

Thus, in *Francis Bacon: The Logic of Sensation*, colour is defined as 'a temporal, variable, and continuous mould, to which alone the name of *modulation* belongs, strictly speaking' (FB 108).[36] Deleuze cites

Simondonian modulation as a technological model, and sets it in relation
with Buffon's interior mould. Modulation allows us to avoid resemblance
and to instead think a heterogeneous relation that is temporalised between
the material of art and the sensation that it forms. Just as it allows pictorial colour to be thought, modulation defines the difference between
the photographic image (mould) and the cinematographic image, which
substitutes the mobile cut for the static equilibrium of the immobile cut, in
which modulation 'constantly modifies the mould, constitutes a variable,
continuous, temporal mould' (C1 24).

It is the relation of art to expression that is at play in colour, as in the
cinematographic image, and Deleuze tries to think this relation without
relying upon imaginary resemblance or structural analogy, which turn art
into a copy of a sensible model or a capture of an intelligible structure.
The theory of the simulacrum made it possible, as we have seen, to think
repetition without resemblance, and instead as differentiation (at the level
of the living being, of the concept and of art). Beginning with his work with
Guattari, Deleuze substitutes for this theory a theory of becoming – becoming-animal, becoming-minor – which makes it possible to think expression
in art without abandoning its mimetic responsibility, but in moving from
an imitation based on resemblance to a symbiosis of a vital kind, a coevolution, an aparallel becoming.[37] The theory of art, alongside theories in the
human sciences, must be purged of the theory of the imaginary likeness
(*semblable*), as well as of the theory of structural homology: '[imaginary]
resemblance and [structural, symbolic] code at least have in common the
fact that they are *moulds*, the one by perceptible form, the other by intelligible structure' (C2 27). At the same time, Deleuze banishes the imaginary
(and with that, any psychoanalytic theory that absorbs the work into the
interpretation of its author or recipient) and the structural (and with that,
any formalist theory reducing the effect of art to its internal structure). The
concept of modulation opens a new path for the philosophy of art. Against
hermeneutics, which attaches the work to the subject, and against structuralist or sociological interpretation, which locates in the work the effectivity
of objective structures, modulation is 'an entirely different thing'. It retains
from moulding the heterogeneity of opposing forces, but it extracts from
them 'a new force'. Putting in contact heterogeneous forces that produce
through disparation an irreducible singularity, the work produces its effect
in the problematic field that links creator and recipient in a real becoming,
which at the same time takes into account the mutation of cultures.

This is why, according to Deleuze, modulation 'is the operation of the
Real' (C2 28). For a theory of sensation, it is not 'the common action of the
feeling and the felt', as Aristotle proposed, or the 'power that co-emerges
in a certain milieu of existence or synchronizes with it', as Merleau-Ponty

proposed;[38] it is neither coexistence nor communion, but difference and indiscernibility, disparation on the plane of forces. Modulation explains how we can define art through the operation of 'render[ing] visible forces that are not themselves visible' (FB 48; DR 139 ff.):[39] the theory of art is in solidarity with a theory of sensation, understood materially as a force that is exerted on a body, but through modulation, offering the senses 'something completely different' starting with the forces that constitute it (FB 48). The disparate (*dispars*) sets heterogeneous series in relation; modulation as a process of differentiation explains that force, a condition of sensation, is not felt, but produces through disparation a new effect, one that is creative and problematic: sensation, carried to its supreme exercise, aesthetic affect and percept. This allows Deleuze to propose a transcendental Aesthetic 'more profound to us than that of Kant' (DR 98) that joins together feeling and artistic experience.[40]

If modulation is 'the operation of the Real', this is because we feel by means of 'a mobile covering-up of sets which are incompatible, almost alike and yet disparate' (C2 129).[41] Modulation makes possible the conjugation of the indiscernibility of opposing forces in their heterogeneity. In effect, it is no longer a question of figurative resemblance or of structural identity, but of a modulation by disparation that at the same time constitutes the work and its public, the artist and his or her milieu. Deleuze's application of Simondonian modulation to aesthetics makes possible the insertion of oppositions 'into the milieu' that tear aesthetics apart, without overcoming them in a Hegelian way but rather in positioning them in their constituting difference as the 'indiscernible' point of the objective and the subjective, of the imaginary and the real (C2 8–20). The sign unites the two branches of aesthetics split apart by Kant, on the condition of liberating the sign from its dependence on linguistics and no longer reducing it by analogy to a statement. The following definition of the movement-image characterising classical cinema is applicable to all kinds of signs: 'it is the modulation of the object itself' (C2 27), that is, the differentiation by which a 'signaletic material' – a material that is nonlinguistic but which is capable of exerting effects on perception, and is variable according to the art in question – 'includes all kinds of modulation features' (C2 29). We can thus understand why a theory of the arts requires a semiotics, a theory of signs that is not reducible to verbal utterances, but which is concerned with their pragmatic and aesthetic effects.

Two decisive consequences for the theory of the arts follow from this. First, it becomes completely futile to distinguish the fine arts from technics because the same modulation process operates in the two cases, and in *A Thousand Plateaus* makes it possible to simultaneously think technology (metallurgy, for example) and art (music, for example) (TP 406–15).[42] In both cases, a given social body enters into modulation with given haecceities of matter, and extracts from this a singular assemblage that defines, at the same time, the state of technics and the position of art, quite variable depending upon the case. Architecture, for example, is in solidarity with a technical knowledge of materials (the wood and stone of sedentary architecture, but also the skin of the tent or the ice of the igloo of the nomad), as well as with a form of power determining human installation on a site, which implies a given mode of dwelling and valorises a given form of expression. A theory of the arts thus requires a global theory of culture, which does not separate the technical threshold and aesthetic taste from the political type of power, which together define the mode of individuation of a given society and the status that it designates for the arts as well as for technics.[43] As with technics, art is grasped in its social dimension, and both converge to cause the emergence and distribution of social subjects (F 57–8) in a process of individuation that does not apply an external form (a social form) to inert matter (the individual), but which modulates human, material and social forces in producing a singular, social form.

Second, art is nevertheless not reducible to technics such that it does not require a specific kind of analysis. Deleuze devotes a number of his works to literature, painting and cinema, but not a single title can be found that refers to a technical use, even if the analysis of technics is determinant for the constitution of the concepts of 'apparatus' and of the 'machine' linked to it.[44] Deleuze distinguishes 'technical composition' from 'aesthetic composition'. Technical composition concerns the working of material in which a certain knowledge, a certain capacity, a practical competence, and an assemblage of social modes of production and of fabrication are all in play. 'Aesthetic composition', for its part, concerns the work of sensation, the way in which a technical composition turns out to be capable of producing the sensible consistency that causes the shift from feeling to an aesthetic 'bloc of sensations' (WP 164). This distinction between art and technics recalls, in a sense, the Kantian distinction between *art* (in the classical sense of technical competence or *poesis*) and aesthetics (in the sense of the subjective quality of the representation);[45] nevertheless, it modifies the frame. For Kant, heir to a conception that goes back to Greek Antiquity and which Simondon criticised, the ideal dignity of the beautiful ravishing the spirit is compared, term for term, to the servile and utilitarian dignity of technical work, indispensable to the survival of the body. For Deleuze, art 'begins with the house' (WP 186), which is immediately technical and aesthetic at the same time. For a vitalist philosophy, art belongs to life, not to spirit, and it is constituted on the plane of animality as dwelling, coadaptation of the living being and its terrestrial milieu, what Deleuze calls a 'territory'. Thus, art begins with an animal that 'constructs a home', that territorialises, that modulates with the forces of the earth to produce a new and singular expressive space. This relation between art and territoriality is crucial for articulating art, as matter of expression, to the relation between the animal and its world: art is 'in a milieu' (*au milieu*), art modulates functions of life in expressive features, and this is why it requires an ethology of life as well as one of culture. Thus, art as technics concerns the way in which materials (*matières*) are captured and assembled into matter (*matière*) of expression. From this perspective, it is the technical assemblage that demands its own aesthetic analysis. 'Still from the standpoint of the assemblage, there is an essential relation between tools and signs' (TP 400). Hence Deleuze's subtle position: the work of art is not reducible to its technical apparatus since it must provoke a specific effect on sensibility. But, in this sense, there is also art in technics, for every tool also functions as a sign and reveals an expressive nature. However, the work of value is not reducible to its mode of fabrication, in the sense in which it can be imitated (Kant). Finally, true artistic invention resides in the treatment of material. Thus, Deleuze can simultaneously hold that a work of art 'is never produced by or for the sake of technique' (WP 192), because it is a composite of sensations, but also that artistic imagination exclusively operates on the technical plane: 'For there is no imagination outside of technique' (TP 345).

Hence the important relation between music and metallurgy (TP 411), or between Baroque art and its 'material traits' (FLB 4) such as travertine and coloured backgrounds.[46] Technics determines the problematic field in which invention takes place. As we have seen, 'events bear exclusively upon problems and define their conditions [solutions]' (LS 54, with modification), and the aesthetic event always intervenes as the material solution to a problem of expression for which the resolution is technical, in the sense that it takes place through the invention of a material in the process of becoming expressive. This is the principle of an epistemology of art.

Having demonstrated the importance of the concept of modulation to the philosophy of art, I shall conclude by addressing the relations between Deleuze and Simondon. Deleuze outlined his thought on difference beginning with his first article on Bergson in 1956.[47] Between the thinker of individuation and the thinker of difference, the determinate points of being as becoming, non-organic vitalism and the critique of substantialism sufficiently indicate a kinship of inspiration, without reciprocal influence, stemming from a shared Nietzschean and Bergsonian heritage. Deleuze borrowed the theory of disparation and the problematic directly from Simondon, and thus, as we have shown, the concept of modulation as well as the concepts of 'crystallisation' and 'membrane' that will realise an analogous future in the analysis of art. Deleuze does not systematically credit Simondon regarding the articulation of the problematic and of difference.

When he praises Proust, for example, for having 'shown us once and for all' that 'individuation, [whether] collective or singular, proceeds not by subjectivity but by haecceity, pure haecceity' (TP 271), we are obliged to correct this statement: it's really about Simondon. In the same way, we would have liked Simondon to be credited when we find in the middle of an argument devoted to individual difference in Leibniz the following conclusion: '*In this sense, the individual is the actualization of preindividual singularities*, and implies no previous determination. The contrary must be noted by observing that determination itself supposes individuation' (FLB 64).

As Muriel Combes indicates in a work devoted to Simondon, he is treated more as 'a subterranean source of inspiration' than as a 'work of reference', and Deleuze is inspired by him 'much more than he cites him'.[48] But, starting in 1966, Deleuze hails the ontological audacity of Simondonian philosophy. A major, underestimated reference in his first works ('encounters between independent thinkers always occur in a blind zone' [F 42]), Simondon's philosophy allows him to move from a philosophy centred on its internal history to a philosophy of life that borrows from the contemporary sciences and their methodological instruments. Thus, we can say that the reference to Simondon is at its maximum and most ignorant of itself in *Difference and Repetition*, and that in this work, Deleuze does not do justice to him because he is preoccupied with pinpointing the differences that separate them. All references to Simondon thus operate through a work of critical distancing, because Deleuze is above all concerned to establish his own doctrine and because he refuses the Simondonian conception of the individual as phased between the pre-individual and the trans-individual, caught between an inferior, pre-individual dimension and a superior dimension, between the Great and the Small. All references in *Difference and Repetition* systematically explore the critique of this dyad of the Great and the Small, which traps Simondon, according to Deleuze, in a Platonic dyad.

On the other hand, the technical-social aspect in Simondon, the aspect that receives the most attention from contemporary commentators,[49] is insufficient for Deleuze, because the analysis does not move in the two directions that preoccupied him in the 1970s: the critique of the Ego, inspired initially by psychoanalysis, and then radicalised as a critique of psychoanalysis itself, and political and social critique, inspired by Marx, which while critical of Marxism was always careful to recognise the theoretical fecundity of Marx. Already in his 1966 review, Deleuze concluded that Simondon weakened his analysis by restoring to psychic and to collective human individuation 'the form of the Self' (DI 89) that he had done away with in an ethics that is in the end conservative. Simondon's indifference to

Freud and to Marx explains why his originality passed unnoticed during an era dominated by reference to these two authors. Beginning with *The Logic of Sense*, Simondon becomes the object of ever more intense praise, and he is a constant interlocutor in Deleuzian thought. In this sense, Deleuze inaugurates Simondonian studies.

To bring this study of art and modulation to a conclusion, we would still need to envisage the importance of Canguilhem and Foucault for the determination of the concepts of the 'minor' and the 'major', and the importance of ethology (Uexküll) for the theory of becoming. This triple field of investigation marks at the same time the importance of art to Deleuze's philosophy, and its originality. Borrowing major concepts for a theory of art from a metaphysics renewed by the epistemology of science indicates that it is necessary to think art in the perspective of a cosmology. Having recourse to support from biology (Ruyer) mediated by Spinoza makes possible an ethology of culture. Finally, thinking knowledge as power and visibility (Foucault) turns art into an essential component of cultural mutations. It is Deleuze's force and originality to have known how to conjugate these sectors, disparate in appearance, in order to extract from them a theory of the sensible effect of works that at the same time proposes a logic of creation.

> The conditions of a true critique and a true creation are the same: the destruction of an image of thought which presupposes itself and the genesis of the act of thinking within thought itself. (DR 139)

NOTES

1. Deleuze affirms this principle as early as 1956. See the first lines of the article, 'Bergson, 1859–1941', in *Les philosophes célèbres*, 292–9. This has been published in English in *Desert Islands*, 22–31.

2. This is what distinguishes semiotics from semiology, which reduces signs to linguistic signs; semiotics was invented by Peirce. See Deleuze and Guattari, *A Thousand Plateaus*, 142 n. 41; Deleuze, *Cinema 2*, Chapter 2.

3. Simondon, *L'individuation à la lumière des notions de forme et d'information*. Doctoral thesis submitted to the Faculty of Letters and of Human Sciences at the University of Paris in 1958 and published by Presses Universitaires de France in 1964. *L'individu et sa genèse physico-biologique: L'individuation à la lumière des notions de forme et d'information* was published as well, thanks to the efforts of Jean Hyppolite. This is the work that Deleuze read and reviewed positively in 1966. See Deleuze, 'Gilbert Simondon: L'individuation et sa genèse physico-biologique'. This review has been published in English in *Desert Islands*, 86–9. Once Simondon's work had been exhausted, a new organisation of his thesis was published

in 1989. This edition retained the second part, unedited to that point. See Simondon, *Individuation psychique et collective: à la lumière des notions de forme, information, potential et métatstatique* (Paris: Aubier, 'L'invention philosophique' collection, 1989). François Laruelle, its editor, wrote in the Preface that finally 'one of the most inventive works of French philosophy of the twentieth century had been reconstituted and published'. It was nevertheless necessary to wait until 1995 for those works first published by Presses Universitaires de France to be reedited: Simondon, *L'individuation et sa genèse physico-biologique*, Preface by Jacques Garelli (Grenoble: Millon, collection 'Krisis' collection, 1995). This is the work that will be referred to in the current essay, substituting where necessary its pagination for Deleuze's citations.

4. See Simondon, 'L'amplification dans les processus d'information', presented at the fifth philosophical colloquium at Royaumont, including the discussion with Wiener, MacKay, and Poirier, summarised in *Cahiers de Royaumont* 5 (Paris: Minuit, 1962).

5. See Deleuze, *The Logic of Sense*, Ninth Series, 'Of the Problematic'; *Francis Bacon: The Logic of Sensation*.

6. On 'heterogenesis', see Alliez, *La signature du monde, ou, Qu'est-ce que la philosophie de Deleuze et Guattari*, translated into English by Eliot Ross Albert and Alberto Toscano as *The Signature of the World, or, What is Deleuze and Guattari's Philosophy?*

7. This is the theoretical backbone of Deleuze's first published work, *Empiricism and Subjectivity: An Essay on Hume's Theory of Human Nature*.

8. Simondon, *L'individu et sa genèse physico-biologique*, 203 n. 15.

9. See Deleuze, *Difference and Repetition*, 51: 'Stereoscopic images form no more than an even and flat opposition, but they depend upon something quite different: an arrangement of coexistent, tiered, mobile planes, a "disparateness" within an original depth. Everywhere, the depth of difference is primary.'

10. Simondon, *L'individu et sa genèse physico-biologique*, 206. Throughout this analysis, we can discern Merleau-Ponty's influence. 'Behaviours create significations that are transcendent with regard to the anatomical apparatus, but which are nevertheless immanent to behaviour in itself', Merleau-Ponty wrote. Simondon grants that the synthesis between two images is not the act of the epistemological subject and is effectuated at the level of the phenomenal body, but he refuses intentionality and substitutes objective disparation for it. See Merleau-Ponty, *Phénomenologie de la perception*, 266–70. My translation.

11. Deleuze specifies this in the second note that he devotes to Simondon (*Difference and Repetition*, 236 n. 12). In the first note (120 n. 25), he does refer to Simondon, but in the midst of a development critiquing the great and the small: 'On the importance of disparate series and their internal resonance in the constitution of systems, see Gilbert Simondon.' But, he

adds: 'However, Simondon maintains as a condition the requirement of resemblance between series, or the smallness of differences in play.' Here, it is a question of a site of theoretical divergence between Deleuze and Simondon that, as we have seen, does not exclude their points of convergence.

Simondon's influence is much more important than explicit commentaries on *Difference and Repetition* allow, and in according disparation the status of a theoretical alternative to opposition, Deleuze implicitly recognises it. For the dialectic (in the sense of the Hegelian dialectic, defined as a contradiction that is resolved through the work of the negative) is, for Deleuze, the overt theoretical adversary. Deleuze refuses to allow that the relation is changed through opposition; he refuses the logical and real process of the overcoming of the negative. As he understands very well, 'pluralism sometimes has a dialectical appearance', but he adds that it is 'the profound enemy'. Here, Deleuze's fundamental inspiration is Spinozist: the negative does not exist; only affirmation has ontological reality. He adds, with Nietzsche, that affirmation is the affirmation of its difference. If Deleuze plays Nietzsche off Hegel, it is because, 'in Nietzsche, the essential relation of one force to another is never conceived of as a negative element in the essence. In its relation with the other the force which makes itself obeyed does not deny the other or that which it is not, it affirms its own difference' (*Nietzsche and Philosophy*, 8–9). Deleuze situates his thought in a 'generalized anti-Hegelianism: difference and repetition have taken the place of the identical and the negative, of identity and contradiction. For difference implies the negative and allows itself to lead to contradiction, only to the extent that its subordination to the identical is maintained' (*Difference and Repetition*, xix). For Deleuze, Hegelian logic remains a 'false movement', that is, it remains at the level of mediation posited as the movement of the concept. Deleuze will never stop opposing this mediation in the concept, this thinking of movement first and foremost through the process of the concept, also indicating by this opposition the proximity of his own theoretical engagement to that of Hegel.

12. Deleuze and Guattari, *Rhizome: Introduction*.
13. Simondon, *L'individu et sa genèse physico-biologique*, 30. Transduction refers at the same time to process in being, and to the logic of this process (32 and 34), through a reversibility of 'ontological and methodological problems', which is not unrelated to Hegelian effectivity, but which Deleuze, for his part, sets to work as early as 'La conception de la différence chez Bergson', in *Études bergsoniennes*, 79–112: 'A philosophy of difference . . . always works on two planes, the methodological and the ontological' (112).
14. Simondon, *L'individu et sa genèse physico-biologique*, 31 and 75ff.
15. Deleuze and Guattari, *A Thousand Plateaus*, 261 n. 33. This tribute is nuanced for, as the note specifies, it is an error to write 'ecceity', deriving the term from *ecce*, 'here is', while Duns Scotus created the concept

beginning with '*Haec*', or 'this thing'. But this is a fruitful error because it allows Simondon to define individuation as a process, an emergence, the occurrence of an event, putting emphasis on temporal emergence and not on the constituted individual. Nevertheless, it is a tribute because Simondon thematises 'ecceity' as a power of matter (*L'individu et sa genèse physico-biologique*, 47ff.).

16. Federico García Lorca, 'Lament for Ignacio Sanchez Mejias'. Translator's note.

17. Deleuze, *The Logic of Sense*, 'Ninth Series, 'Of the Problematic'.

18. It is worth noting (and this is an influence both Deleuze and Simondon share) that this distinction between the problem and the solution, this attention brought to bear on the problem in itself as constitutive of its solution, of course comes from Bergson, but also from French epistemology, which requires, according to Deleuze, 'the use of the word "problematic" as a substantive'. Deleuze does homage to Bachelard (*Difference and Repetition*, 140 n. 9), to Bouligand and Canguilhem (163 n. 22), and especially to Lautman, who defined the problem as a transcendental instance, one which does not exist outside its solutions but that determines them as a veritable Idea (163–4).

19. This more concerns an encounter than an influence since Deleuze developed the theory of thought produced by the involuntary irruption of the sign in his earliest works, notably in his analysis of Proust and the first version of *Proust and Signs*, published in 1964.

20. On this point, we can see an evolution in Deleuze's thought, from *The Logic of Sense*, which articulates the event in relation to the production of sense (1969), to *Rhizome* (1976), in which regimes of signs no longer refer exclusively to language or even to human thought.

21. Simondon, *L'individu et sa genèse physico-biologique*, 221 n. 30.

22. 'The privilege of sensibility as origin appears in the fact that, in an encounter, what forces sensation and that which can only be sensed are one and the same thing, whereas in other cases the two instances are distinct. In effect, the intensive or difference in intensity is at once both the object of the encounter and the object to which the encounter raises sensibility' (*Difference and Repetition*, 144–5).

23. This citation also appeared in 'Renverser le Platonisme' in *Revue de Métaphysique et de Morale* (October–November 1966): 434. It was then taken up in the appendix to *The Logic of Sense*. At the same time, it was subject to an important development in *Difference and Repetition*, 68ff.

24. Deleuze, 'L'immanence: Une vie . . .', 3–7.

25. Simondon, *L'individu et sa genèse physico-biologique*, 29.

26. Simondon, *L'individu et sa genèse physico-biologique*, 28.

27. This expression is found in Simondon, *L'individuation psychique et collective*, 148.

28. On this point also, the kinship between Simondon and Deleuze is remarkable.

29. It is only with *A Thousand Plateaus* that Deleuze recognises the degree to which the Simondonian analysis of matter and form is remarkable, first because it makes possible a critique of hylomorphism from Aristotle to Kant (which is important to Deleuze), and second because the Simondonian critique treats the concept as an assemblage. In effect, Simondon accuses theoretical thought of being incapable of theorising an act as simple as moulding due to a lack of scientific concepts (the Ancients were only familiar with stable equilibrium, lacking the notion of *metastability*, the achievement of modern physics), and especially due to the fact that it maintains or (implicitly) applies a socialised representation of labour to technological analysis, confusing the technical operation with the abstract order that the master transmits to the slave, who executes it. The hylomorphic scheme is thus embedded in the ancient representation of labour, and refers to a sociology of the division of labour. But Simondon does not pursue this incisive critique in the direction of a contestation of the social typical of his era, and he remains indifferent to Marx. This is one of the reasons for his obscurity on the French intellectual landscape in the 1960s and 1970s, and the reason that encouraged Deleuze to chastise him for being lukewarm.

30. Simondon, *L'individu et sa genèse physico-biologique*, 45.

31. Simondon, *L'individu et sa genèse physico-biologique*, 58.

32. Simondon, *L'individu et sa genèse physico-biologique*, 46.

33. The mould must 'limit the expansion of the plastic earth and statically guide this expansion by developing a force of reaction equal to the pressure of the earth'. The reaction of the sides must be slightly more than the pressure of the earth for the mould to be filled correctly (without air pockets). 'The reaction of the sides is thus the static force that guides the clay during the process of filling by prohibiting expansion in certain directions' (Simondon, *L'individu et sa genèse physico-biologique*, 42). This also requires that the sides display a slight elastic flexibility, which can be reduced (thin wood becomes deformed but returns in place while an iron mould deforms just a bit). The mould opposes its elasticity to the plasticity of the clay. It is this negative action (by which the mould 'stops' the deformation of the clay, limiting its expansion) that has been interpreted as an active setting into form (*mise en forme active*). 'The mould limits and stabilises more than it imposes a form: it provides an end to deformation, terminating it by interrupting it along a defined contour: it modulates (*module*) the set of strands [of clay and] plays the role of a fixed set of modulating hands, acting as kneading, immobile hands' (*L'individu et sa genèse physico-biologique*, 40).

34. Simondon, *L'individu et sa genèse physico-biologique*, 41.

35. This definition of art as a capture of forces obviously finds its point of departure in Nietzsche. In this respect, it is a question of comparing the way that Deleuze determines force in the studies devoted to Nietzsche and Foucault.

36. Remember that this is the definition that we find in Simondon: 'a modu-
    lator is a continuous temporal mould . . . to modulate is to mould in a
    way that is continuous and perpetually variable' (*L'individu et sa genèse
    physico-biologique*, 45).

37. These notions, thematised beginning in *Rhizome*, are determinant for
    comprehending the substitution of becoming-animal or becoming-minor
    for the theory of imitation. They involve a detailed analysis of Deleuze's
    relation to biology and notably to Uexküll's ethology, and provide a
    well-determined sense to the perpetual example of the aparallel relation
    between the orchid and the wasp, which Deleuze borrows from Proust.
    To go into detail here would take us far afield. It is sufficient to point out
    that it involves the same conceptual problem: articulating art to life and to
    sensation in the frame of a philosophy of nature. The theories of becom-
    ing-animal and of ethology are articulated precisely with Simondonian
    modulation: like the latter, together they function to define a theory of
    feeling and of the expressivity of art.

38. Merleau-Ponty, *Phénoménologie de la perception*, 245. The relation
    between Merleau-Ponty's thesis and that of Aristotle is indicated by
    Renaud Barbaras, 'La puissance du visible: Le sentir chez Merleau-Ponty
    et Aristote'.

39. 'The task of painting is defined as the attempt to render visible forces that
    are not themselves visible. Likewise, music attempts to render sonorous
    forces that are not themselves sonorous' (*Francis Bacon: The Logic of
    Sensation*, 48).

40. In effect, *Difference and Repetition* proposes a transcendental Aesthetics
    and logic that constitutes the Deleuzian analytic, while Chapter 3, 'The
    Image of Thought', presents a dialectic of representative Reason. What
    Deleuze says of Nietzsche's *Genealogy of Morals* – that it is a critical
    replaying of *The Critique of Pure Reason* – is eminently true of *Difference
    and Repetition* as well.

41. Simondon, *L'individu et sa genèse physico-biologique*, 209.

42. Here, the authors simultaneously refer to Simondon, Leroi-Gourhan (a
    thinker of technics), and Worringer (a theorist of art). See Leroi-Gourhan,
    Le Geste et la parole, translated into English by Anna Bostock Berger as
    Gesture and Speech; and Wilhelm Worringer, *Formprobleme der Gotik*
    (Munich: Piper & Co., 1912), translated into French as *L'Art gothique* by
    D. Decourdemanche (Paris: Gallimard, 1941), and into English by Herbert
    Read as *Form in Gothic*.

43. On this point, it would be necessary to examine the influence of Foucault,
    and to compare the Foucauldian apparatus to the Deleuzian assemblage,
    a question that goes beyond the bounds of this article. (On this precise
    question, see Chapters 11 and 12 in the present book. Translator's note).

44. In particular, in a series of notes indirectly addressed to Foucault, written
    in 1977 on *The History of Sexuality: The Will to Knowledge*, and pub-
    lished in the *Magazine littéraire* 325 (1994): 59–65 under the title 'Désir et

plaisir'. These remarks have been translated into English by Ames Hodges and Mike Taorima as 'Desire and Pleasure' and included in *Two Regimes of Madness*, 122–34. Here, the assemblage is thought as a technical assemblage: 'For example, feudalism is an assemblage that inaugurates new relationships with animals (the horse), with land, with deterritorialization (the knight riding away, the Crusades), with women (courtly love and chivalry) . . . etc. These are totally crazy assemblages but they can always be pinpointed historically. I would say for myself that desire circulates in this heterogeneous assemblage, in this kind of symbiosis: desire is one with a determined assemblage, a co-function' (124–5). Similarly, in *A Thousand Plateaus*, where the analysis of the technical phylum allows us to think the co-functioning of man and nature in terms of symbiosis (in conformity with the analyses of *Anti-Oedipus*, which explicitly take up this theme from Marx and Engels' *The German Ideology*). For the assemblage is first and foremost territorial: the assemblage extracts a territory from the milieu; it is the assemblage that allows us to think the coevolution of the human and nature in terms of milieu, the back-and-forth of modulation. Thus, it is in conformity not only with Deleuze's work on ethology, but also with the Simondonian thesis of individuation: 'The territory is more than the organism and the milieu, and the relation between the two . . .' (*A Thousand Plateaus*, 504). But the assemblage sets in relation technical, social and natural forces and produces a mode of culture that is at the same time aesthetic, social, political and natural. 'Every assemblage is basically territorial . . . The territory makes the assemblage' (503–4). Captured in the modulation of the assemblage, the expression of life becomes a semiotic system (a regime of signs) while the content becomes a pragmatic system. The distinction between the form of expression and the form of content, from Hjelmslev, typical of the logic deployed in *Kafka*, *Rhizome* and *A Thousand Plateaus*, allows us to connect the expressive (semiotic) to social transformation: the assemblage is always a machinic assemblage and an assemblage of enunciation. We do not have space here to correctly analyse those concepts that are relevant to the definition of art as a becoming-minor. '[E]xpression in it [the assemblage] becomes a *semiotic system*, a regime of signs, and content becomes a *pragmatic system*, actions and passions . . . This is the first division of every assemblage: it is simultaneously and inseparably a machinic assemblage and an assemblage of enunciation' (*A Thousand Plateaus*, 504).

45. Kant, *Critique of Judgment*, §43.

46. 'Wölfflin noted that the Baroque is marked by a certain number of material traits: horizontal widening of the lower floor, flattening of the pediment, low and curved stairs that push into space; matter handled in masses or aggregates, with the rounding of angles and avoidance of perpendiculars; the circular acanthus replacing the jagged acanthus, use of limestone to produce spongy, cavernous shapes . . .' (*The Fold: Leibniz and the Baroque*, 4): here we can observe the characteristic mixing, the assemblage

of tools (limestone) that makes possible and co-produces morphological inventions.

47. Deleuze, 'Bergson, 1849–1941', *Desert Islands*, 22–31.
48. Combes, *Simondon, Individu et Collectivité: Pour une philosophie du transindividuel*, 5–6. This has been translated into English by Thomas LaMarre as *Gilbert Simondon and the Philosophy of the Transindividual* (Cambridge, MA: MIT Press, 2013).
49. It was necessary to wait until 1993 for a comprehensive work to appear that does justice to Simondon: G. Hottois, *Simondon et la philosophie de la 'culture technique'*. It was followed by Actes du colloque organisé par la Collège International de philosophie: *Gilbert Simondon, Une pensée de l'individuation et de la technique* (Paris: Albin Michel, 1994), and by Combes, *Simondon, Individu et Collectivité* (see n. 48).

5. Deleuze: Cinema, Image, Individuation[1]

PART I:
THE IMAGE: BERGSON, DELEUZE AND CINEMA

> The Bergsonian discovery of a movement-image, and more profoundly, of a time-image, still retains such richness today that it is not certain that all its consequences have been drawn. (C1 xiv)

In his early work, Deleuze utilises the expression 'the image of thought' to describe the way thought represents its own power and, occasionally, mutilates the definition of its use in an abstract way (PS 94). Twenty years later, he no longer restricts the image to the mental domain of ideations. The image departs from the psychic domain of representations and assumes the Bergsonian sense of an appearance, of the very givenness of matter (*d'une donnée en soi de la matière*). The 'Bergsonian discovery of a movement-image' henceforth prevents us from setting the psychic image in opposition to physical movement. This, then, is the point of departure, of 'such richness today that it is not certain that all its consequences have been drawn', that enables Deleuze to develop an entirely new semiology of cinema, starting with a philosophy of the image that does not reduce it to the mental domain. Deleuze's very curious attempt to create a taxonomy and classification of images relies upon an inventive reading of Bergson: 'nothing can prevent an encounter between the movement-image, as [Bergson] considers it, and the cinematographic image' (C1 xiv).

Deleuze's philosophy of cinema is not satisfied with simply adding a chapter to the philosophy of art, which is so decisive for him. Rather, this philosophy simultaneously elucidates the conjunction between matter, movement, image and time. The fact that these discoveries are made in relation to cinema, a recent industrial art, indicates once again the methodological importance of a concrete analysis of the arts for philosophy and indicates that the semiotics of the image relies upon a kinetics of movement.

THE IMAGE: MATTER IN MOVEMENT

Matter and Images

Deleuze's definition of the image, elaborated following Bergson, is of such a disconcerting simplicity and novelty that it is difficult to grasp. The image is not a representation of consciousness or a psychological given internal to the brain. Nor is the image a representative of a thing, a perception of an object (*une visée d'objet*), or a double. It is an appearance (*une apparition*), one to be rigorously understood as situated on the plane of forces: 'Let us call the set of what appears "Image"' (C1 58).[2] The image is produced as an appearance, a composition of relations of forces, a system of actions and reactions at the level of matter itself, such that it does not need to be perceived, but rather exists in itself as disturbance, vibration and movement. If the image is a reality and not a mental picture (*une visée mentale*), neither is it a representation of consciousness (a psychological given) or a representative of a thing (a perception of the object, *une visée d'objet*).

In these terms, the image is not a phenomenon. Bergson posits an image in itself that undoes any intentionality. The image does not need to manifest itself to a consciousness in order to appear. This makes possible a definition of an image that is completely acentred and that does not need to be referred datively to a subject who experiences it or to be posited as the duplicata of an object that it targets. Such an image is strictly immanent and prohibits any dualism of consciousness and things. In this way, the image inserts perception within matter, as Bergson intended.

Thus understood, the image is identically image and movement: it is no longer a support, but a relation of forces, a system of forces and reactions. Perceptions and brains are images like any other, consisting of actions and reactions, forces and movements. Deleuze expresses this with the concept of movement-image, through which he pays homage to Bergson, but into which he also injects his reading of force and power according to Nietzsche, and of individuation as a composition of movement according to Spinoza.

Thus, the image is a plural individuation of differential movements that compose fluctuating groupings whose power varies. Such a mode of individuation assumes no unity, no stable identity, but rather composes a relation of transitory, material forces. Deleuze takes from his reading of Spinoza the definition of a modal, non-substantial individuation, which he terms a 'haecceity'. Any body whatever individuates by means of the grouping of parts that belong to it under specific relations of variable speed (*de vitesses et de lenteurs*), or longitude, and as a function of the affects of which it is capable under a specific degree of power, or latitude. An individuation is defined neither by its unity nor by its identity, but detaches itself, in the mobile universe of forces, as a provisional relation of speeds and affects. Deleuze combines this definition of the individual with the complementarity between relations of force and evaluation in Nietzsche. Such a sign, or complex of relations of forces, does not refer in any way to a signifier, but only to a state of power, or, more precisely, to a state of forces (a semiotics of images) that corresponds to a specific affect (an evaluation of their power). This allows Deleuze to develop a semiotics of cinema as a typology of images and signs.

The image refers to a relation of forces, a composition of actions and reactions and variable speeds for which we are able evaluate the state, the differential relation of forces that are present. A variation of power corresponds to such a relation of forces. Defined in this way, the image is a composition of relations of forces and duration, affection and variation in power. A first result follows from this, which breaks with classical theories of the image as representation: the movement-image is strictly of the same order as matter; it proposes neither a second copy nor a psychic translation. On the contrary, in the world where 'image = movement', matter, the image and movement are equivalent.

The Movement-Image and its Three Varieties

Rigorously speaking, images are the only things that exist. Such a realism of the image must be taken literally: the image does not represent a reality of another order, but is rather itself all of its reality. With this new and decisive definition, the image is thus not a mental snapshot, a double or a fiction, but a real composition of relations of differential forces, consisting of varying speeds and of fluctuating actions and reactions, and which also experience variations of power of affects. These images interact instantaneously with each other so that in reality we cannot separate them or differentiate one from the other.

In this universe of universal variation, we must then conceptualise *special* images, which introduce the pulsation of a temporal interval between material actions and reactions. Here, we shift from matter – physical, acentred movement – to special images that are vital perceptions, cinematographic images, individuated images, or images that are relatively centred for the time that their relation endures. Such images become individuated and detached from the acentred universe of matter through selection, ignoring in other images anything that is not of interest. In other words, perception is produced through subtractive framing, a framing that attracts incomplete images that refer to a special image from the mobile universe of material forces. Perception is nothing more than an individuation of an image. The finite perceptual image emerges from infinite, acentred movement by means of this subtractive operation of vital framing. Perceiving, for a specific image – an organic body or a cinematographic machine, with no privilege accorded to the living or to the human – thus consists in tracing a myopic diagonal across other images. We move from the acentred universe of movement-images to the subjectivated bodies of second images without ever leaving the immanent plane of forces.

The image is thus a reality. But in certain, specific conditions, a delay or temporal interval slows down the instantaneous succession of action and reaction. This delay marks the point of insertion of the subjectivation of an image on the plane of matter itself. Owing to this gap (*écart*), the image becomes individuated by acquiring a sensory zone that separates the movement received from the movement executed. The individuated image turns its perceptive surface toward the movement received and, after a delay that promotes its individuation, effects a singular motor response. Perceptive framing provokes a motor response, causing a sensory zone of the sensory-motor circuit to emerge in the tissue of images. In this way, we shift from perception to action through affection.

Cinematographic images are subjective images of this kind. All at once, Deleuze invents a classification of cinema and a taxonomy of the image that answers to the material and immanent constitution of the subject, of the individuated image, whether it be organic, human or artificial. It is necessary to insist on the radical novelty of such a genetic account of the subject, one that finds its point of departure in a material semiotics of the image. Deleuze systematically returns to the first chapter of *Matter and Memory*, which makes possible a shift from movement to perception and offers a stunningly economic definition of subjectivity, one that does not propose an already completely formed substantial subject, but which proceeds genetically toward its constitution. Perception-images, affection-images and action-images are subjectivated images not because they refer to a subject as a support for these affections or because they are referred to a subject who experiences them. They are subjectivated images because they are dilated images that integrate the sensorality (*la sensoralité*), the affect and the motricity of a provisional centre between the action and reaction of forces. Physical matter folds, curves in on itself (*s'incurve*), individualises itself, and endows the image with a sensory zone of affection that separates perception and action. Owing to this delay, the sensorial interval of a provisional centre of indetermination unfolds in perception-images, affection-images and action-images.

It is no longer appropriate to distinguish living images from technical images, any more than it is appropriate to refer the cinematographic image to the eye of the cameraman or to any human support. More precisely, the interest of cinema derives from what it offers to human perception in terms of acentred images; gaseous, liquid or solid perception-images; affects of machines; and non-human perceptual intervals and cuts. The subjective movement-image of cinema also makes the gap between the perceived image and the effective movement perceptible, but it does so in an accomplished, independent and stimulating artistic mode, offering images that the human body alone would never have been able to provoke.

The Cinematographic Image

The movement-image thus serves as the frame for a free and mobile classification of cinema according to types of montage and modes of actualisation of movement-images. The perception-image of cinema, like the living image, doubles the action that it experiences with a sensitive membrane: instead of dissipating itself immediately in action, it develops a zone of affect between its sensitive surface (perception-image) and its motor surface (action-image), by which it exposes and carves out its subjective receptivity in experiencing itself, in vaporising the circuit between perception and action and in referring movement to a quality as an experienced state (affection-image), instead of to acts (action-image) or to bodies (perception-image). As soon as movement-images are referred to a centre of indetermination, they divide into perception-images, affection-images and action-images: these are the major categories that dominate the classification of *Cinema 1: The Movement-Image*. If all films mix the three varieties of movement-images, it is possible to distinguish styles and works by referring them either to the perception-image, which valorises long shots and panoramas (Mann's Westerns), or to the action-image, which privileges medium shots and rapid, segmented montage (Hawks's film noirs), or to the affection-image, with its close-ups (Dreyer, Ozu).

The cinema is thus not an 'art of the image' in the ordinary sense of a reproduction and projection of photograms, but rather the art that responds best to the contemporary problem of the movement-image. While this makes cinema particularly interesting, as industrial production and as art, it does not confer upon it the privileged possession of the image. The image is in no way limited to the visual, but rather concerns all sensory appearances (*apparitions sensibles*), including sound and tactile images. Any complex of relations of forces is an image, and this is why Deleuze defines art as a capture of forces, not as a representation or imitation of nature. 'From one art to another, the nature of images varies and is inseparable from the techniques used: colors and lines for painting, sound for music, verbal descriptions for novels, movement-images for cinema, etc.' (TRM 210).

Thus, in the two volumes entitled *The Movement-Image* and *The Time-Image*, the concept of the image does not designate an operation that is specific to cinema, but describes matter itself, as movement-image. The image has a physical range before producing its aesthetic effects, and the titles 'Movement-Image' and 'Time-Image' designate a real exposition of relations of forces before serving as categories that allow us to classify and think about cinematic productions. The semiotics of the image is embedded in the physical frame of the movement-image, to which Deleuze adds a time-image in order to answer to a gambit that concerns science, art and philosophy equally: thinking movement according to a metaphysics of becoming and causing time to emerge directly within the image. The kinetics of movement and the philosophy of becoming are allied in offering a supple frame for a new classification of cinema. Art and science enter into resonance with each other.

BECOMING, IMAGE AND MOVEMENT

In no longer opposing matter to representation and in calling for a philosophy of becoming that privileges change over static or spatialising theories of movement, Bergson made it possible to define a world of universal variation, in which everything is image and matter, where images become mixed and confused with one another, sliding into each other in an acentred mode. Images – vibrations of matter and blocks of space-time – only become individuated through a relative framing, forming unstable and provisional zones that we must be careful not to see as centres of determination. If, in effect, it is a question of centres, their effect of perspectival framing results rather from indetermination, a hiatus, or a temporal dilation.

This transformation of the concept of the image corresponds to the transformation of the concept of movement and sheds light on the surprising suture that Deleuze operates between the appearance of cinema and Bergson's philosophy. With the theory of the movement-image, even though it is introduced by means of a literal commentary on the opening pages of *Matter and Memory*, Deleuze actually exposes a complex apparatus (*dispositif*) that is hardly Bergsonian, in which the status of time and of movement, the state of the sciences and that of Bergsonian philosophy, converge to explore problematics that are very different from and foreign to Bergson: the technical invention of cinema as an industrial art enables a judgement about relations of time and movement and the elaboration of a semiotics that refers to a physics of forces, not to a signifying interpretation that causes the image to fall back on discourse. It is necessary to think the new social world of speed and images as a function of the theories of space-time that they demand, and to set the role of the image in the industrial age – the age of the acceleration of motor displacements and the diffusion of sensory images – in relation to its new place of strategic operation for the theory of knowledge and the philosophy of nature. The cinema emerges, not as a passive effect, but as an implied actor, as a creative response, as much as an economic or commercial one, to this new problematic.

In order to elucidate this inventive logic of the image, it is important to think the correlation between philosophy and science, and between industry and art. Science, art and philosophy all confront the same problem: how do we move away from a static and transcendent conception of movement to a veritable kinetics of becoming? The image gains access to reality – 'You may say that my body is matter, or that it is an image: the word is of no importance' – in a single moment of philosophy, the first chapter of *Matter and Memory* (1896).[3] Bergson derives these conclusions from the transformations affecting contemporary science, which substitute a kinetic cosmology for the static universe of classical mechanics, a cosmology in which space and time turn out to be as indissociable as matter, light and energy. As the philosopher who explicitly devoted himself to furnishing the science of his time with the metaphysics that it required, Bergson embraced this conjunction. From Bergson, Deleuze retained the analysis of the image and of movement, the conjunction between philosophy and science, and, of course, the task of thinking becoming, but he extracts from these theses a consequence that is not Bergsonian. The new kinetics of movement requires that we think the image as a mobile cut of duration (*durée*). However, thinking the image and movement together requires that we proceed by means of a semiotics of the image that specifies and precisely analyses the movement-image and its three varieties, and that shows how movement and time are composed in the image. Deleuze opens the cinematographic movement-image, with its three varieties of perception, action and affection, to a new type of image, one that does not extend itself into a sensory-motor response, but that rather opens to the affect of time. Time emerges within the hiatus of movement and the affect of force is liberated in the sensory-motor interval, just as the subjective image detaches itself in the caesura between actions and reactions. This is the time-image, which corresponds to the shift from actual movement to the temporal virtual.

The New Conception of Movement and of the Image

The inevitable conjunction between this new conception of matter in movement and the invention of the cinematograph was initially a response to a historical crisis in psychology, which Bergson attempted to resolve in *Matter and Memory*. It had become impossible to remain satisfied with the duality of consciousness and the thing, of the image and movement, in short, with the old dichotomies between subject and object, the psychic and corporeal. The old separation of the corporeal and the psychic turned out to be untenable in a world always putting 'more and more movement into conscious life, and more and more images into the material world' (C1 56). Bergson thus established a continuity between matter and perception, complete matter being nothing other than the set of images, while perception refers these images to the limited action of a singular image.[4] This conception of acentred image-matter and of perception as a subtractive zone of indetermination demanded a new conception of movement and of change.

The cosmological crisis of movement corresponded to the crisis in psychology. Spatial displacement became change by subordinating the conception of movement to that of becoming. Movement, including the most simple displacement, never implies a simple change of position affecting an invariable moving object in inert space. Every passage through a trajectory is an act during which the moving object itself is transformed, in addition to everything else in which it moves. In this way, we shift from a static conception to a kinetics of movement, which restores the temporal aspect to motor displacement and opens displacement to becoming. From being conceived of as spatial displacement, movement now vibrates in time. This is why Deleuze establishes such a strong relation between Bergson's philosophy, the status of the movement-image, and the invention of the cinematograph.

Deleuze thus treats the cinematographic image as the sensory laboratory in which the relations between movement and time are worked out. This approach is paradoxical if we recall that Bergson himself dismissed cinema as the final avatar of a long tradition hostile to becoming, incapable of thinking movement as anything other than a succession of immobile poses. According to Bergson, cinema falls under the auspices of a spontaneous metaphysics of intelligence and models itself on natural perception. A film consists of a static band of inert photograms disposed spatially, one after the other, on a perforated piece of film, abstractly animated in a mechanical stream. There is no transformation in this succession, no unpredictable novelty, no becoming in these images that have been falsely animated. This new technique became for Bergson the model of a *cinematographic illusion*, proceeding through a reconstitution of movement starting with immobile poses. Deleuze strove to overturn the judgement by which Bergson discredited cinema by applying the analyses of the image and of movement that Bergson developed elsewhere to the seventh art. To achieve this, Deleuze pedagogically divided his critique into three moments.

First, movement cannot be reduced to the displacement of a moving object in space. Rather, displacement must not be conceived as a static relation between elements in space, but rather as a veritable change that affects the moving object as much as the whole in which it moves. Movement is reality itself, not an accident occurring to an invariable substrate traversing inert space.[5] Thus movement must not be confused with the space traversed, but refers to a veritable duration (*durée*), in what effectively constitutes a Bergsonian thesis.

However, in Deleuze's estimation, we must not identify the cinematographic procedure with spatial juxtaposition. For, in a second thesis, there exist at least two ways of reducing movement to a succession of static poses, one that corresponds to ancient science and the other to modern physics. Cinema belongs to the second series, and falls completely under the modern conception of movement. We could identify cinema with a metaphysics of the eternal that corresponds to ancient science: this is what Bergson does in concluding that cinema amounts to the same thing as composing movement with eternal poses, as in Antiquity, or with immobile cuts, as in the classical age. In both cases, one fails to deal with becoming. But at the same time we can, as Deleuze proposes, see that cinema in reality presents an absolutely new problem to thought, one that responds to the modern paradigm of movement and that cannot be thought under the ancient paradigm.

While ancient science proposed to think the eternal, modern science presented a new task to thought: to think becoming and the production of the new. Bergson wrongly believed that cinema imitated the reduction of movement to the identical, even while he called for, through making a correlation to modern cosmology, a 'total conversion of philosophy' in conformity elsewhere with his project of giving 'to modern science the metaphysics that corresponds to it'.[6] Bergson underestimated the degree to which the invention of cinema corresponded to this necessity. The arts, and cinema in particular, responded to this new conception of movement. This is the third thesis, which directly formulates the principle already implied by the two preceding ones: that movement is becoming.

In these terms, cinema 'fully belongs to the modern conception of movement' (C1 7) and emerges as 'the organ for perfecting the new reality' (C1 8). In its technical operation, cinema corresponds to the age of modern physics. It refers movement to any instant whatsoever, no longer to privileged instants, and inserts a regular interval between immobile photograms that it aligns on the film and inscribes into the technological line of time as an independent variable. In Antiquity, the conception of movement was subordinated to intelligible Forms, which reconstituted movement on the basis of transcendent elements. In the modern age, Kepler, Galileo and

Descartes no longer decompose movement starting with intelligible poses but proceed to its sensory analysis (calculating an orbit, a falling body) on the basis of immanent, material elements, static cuts extracted from the moving matter of the universe. The dialectical order of poses in Antiquity gives way to a succession of random instants. Cinema also involves a succession of equidistant photograms on a surface animated by a system that moves the images along. This is why Bergson rejects the cinematographic apparatus as a new victory for the abstract conception of movement, the juxtaposition of immobile cuts in accordance with an external unspooling. By contrast, Deleuze holds that cinema actually involves a kinetics of movement. At the core of its apparatus, in the framing that animates each shot, as well as in montage, cinema deploys mobile cuts and makes acentred images possible.

Cinematographic images frame and stabilise a perception through the linking of actions and reactions, a perception that is both mechanical and living, endowed with a non-organic vitality and a subjectivity, not because the image refers back to the eye of a cameraman or because it presents a projection that resembles natural forms, but because it explodes the perceptions of the camera onscreen, its affects of light, colour and sound. In framing other images, the cinematographic image functions as a living image endowed with a singular vitality that decentres, transforms and shatters human perception. With cinema, framing and montage become semiotic operations that allow us to perceive a new relation between movement and time.

Framing temporalises movement, playing on the mobility of the camera and especially on the cuts and connecting shots of the montage. The mobile camera extracts its points of view as a new mode of transportation, introducing perception into the limits that mechanical prostheses allow, creating and linking together new continuous visibilities as soon as we shift from the fixed plane to the animated plane. With the resources of the travelling camera, which allows for a variation in angles and points of view, the camera becomes a mode of transportation that combines visual angles, as in the famous example of Murnau's *The Last Laugh*, in which the camera, mounted on a bicycle, descends an escalator and crosses the hall, thereby creating a cinematographic plane that is projective, perspectival and temporal (C1 22). Such a shot projects a perspective and motor axis into things that at the same time makes possible a creative perception of its object. Cinema does not only consist in points of view; rather, through montage, it enters into the very composition of the image. Vertov, a cinematic genius, defined the 'cine-eye', capable of 'coupl[ing] together any point whatsoever of the universe in any temporal order whatsoever' (C1 80–1), and proliferated, in *Man with a Movie Camera*, procedures of slowing down, acceleration, fragmentation, superimposition and high-speed editing (C1 84). In these instances, cinema does not consist in enhancing human perception but rather in decentring it, causing it to lose its stable points of reference and its familiarity to attain to a non-human perception, no longer 'hewn out in solids' (C1 80, modified) following the pattern of our possible action. Cinema slides between the chinks in matter and makes it possible for perception to attain a liquid or gaseous state through a diversity of procedures that procure visibilities at different speeds and affects (*à des vitesses, des lenteurs ou des affects*) that human perception, on its own scale, is incapable of distinguishing.

Cinema thus does not reconstitute movement with fixed cuts (*coupes fixes*), but rather renders change perceptible through the mobility of its framings and by the cuts and continuities of montage. In these terms, as a contemporary art, cinema of course does not have privileged access to the image, but it does have privileged access to the movement-image. With cinema, we definitively leave behind the static metaphysics of Antiquity or the Classical era and enter the era of becoming, of the movement-image and the time-image.

The new status of the movement-image promotes the emancipation of non-discursive arts: we are now able to think in images without translating the image into discourse. The image is a sign in itself, which attests to the independence of semiotics from signifying interpretation and meaning. With the cinematographic image, the philosophy of art proposes an inventive typology of signs that is founded on a logic of forces. To think art is to think the image that causes the affect of time to surge forth in the actualisation of movement.

MOVEMENT AND TIME

Movement no longer consists of translation across space, but rather of radiation (*rayonnement*), vibration, qualitative change, and affection of the whole (*le tout*). The material equivalence between movement and image depends upon this demonstration. Any spatial displacement implies a temporal transformation, one that affects the moving object as much as the whole in which it moves. This is why movement does not only imply a relation of displacement or of transformation between the objects or parts that move; movement also expresses duration (*la durée*). Movement pertains not only to a change of a moving object, but to the affection of a whole. Following Bergson, Deleuze explodes supposedly stable elements between which movement 'occurs': that which moves changes and vibrates temporally as much as the whole in which it moves. 'Our error lies in believing that it [what moves] is the any-element-whatevers, external to qualities which move. But the qualities themselves are pure vibrations which change at the same time as the alleged elements move' (C1 8–9).[7] Deleuze defines a hyletics of fluent matter (*hylétique de la matière fluente*). Matter is energy, and the equivalence between matter and light, the condition of possibility of the invention of cinema, bestows a luminous, shining capacity upon matter-movement, which explains why the image is given not as a static body, but as a vibrating block of space-time.

This conception of movement, which Deleuze elaborates in effect through his reading of Bergson, has important consequences for the philosophy of becoming and for the semiotics of cinema. First, the status of totality changes. Just as movement can no longer be reduced to the displacement or transfer of a unitary moving object in static space, consisting rather of incessant transformation and change, the image becomes equivalent to matter in movement, in its energetic and temporal becoming. Once we restore to movement its double aspect of transfer in space and change in duration, the cinematographic shot can no longer be identified, as Bergson did, with a static cut. Every element must be thought according to this new scheme of totality that conjoins variation or duration to the actual existence of parts (*parties*) in space (C1 19). This conclusion was already implied in the initial definition of the image as haecceity, as a relation of forces specified in the instant as a composition of variable speeds (longitude) and of a variation of power in duration (latitude).

What is at stake is less a duality of movement than an oscillation of forces between spatial actuality and temporal virtuality. The actualisation of force in an instant is inseparable from its virtual becoming. Any actual individualisation implies the double movement by which the virtual is actualised even while the constituted individual is singularised by being dispersed in intensive becomings. This conception of becoming radically changes the conception of the whole (*le tout*), which we must no longer conceptualise as an actual multiplicity, a set given according to a unitary or identitarian scheme, but as a whole that endures and experiences transformation. This is why Deleuze, following Bergson, defines the whole as the incessant capacity to allow the new to emerge, even more so in terms of the relation. In effect, according to Deleuze, the relation remains always exterior to its terms; it is not a property of objects, but rather a transformation of the whole. The whole, thought as multiplicity in becoming rather than as a closed totality, loses its unity and stability to be instead conceived as becoming. The whole changes, being created in accordance with a system of relations that are always exterior to their terms: this is what Deleuze calls the 'Open' (*l'Ouvert*).

The conceptualisation of a whole that is open, as multiplicity in becoming, is a decisive methodological principle. This is not only because it permits us to define a mode of individuation in becoming for each level of totality – whether it be universe, image or atom matters little – but also because it changes the logical conception of the relations between part and whole. Movement refers the elements it transforms to open duration (*la durée ouverte*). It thus has two sides, circulating between the actual parts that it modifies and the virtual whole that it transforms. Like any other material reality, the cinematographic shot also presents these two sides: the transfer and modification of parts and the change in the whole in duration. The 'extraordinary advance' that Bergson instigates in the conception of the universe can thus be explained more precisely: the universe is 'a cinema in itself, a metacinema', an assemblage of movement-images, a 'machinic' assemblage and not a mechanical one, mechanism implying a closed system and actions involving contact that no longer correspond to this open totality. If Deleuze describes the universe as a cinema in itself, it is because he defines it as the material set of images, as the plane of matter or 'plane of immanence': an acentred universe where everything reacts upon everything else, one that knows only forces – longitudes and latitudes – and in which subjects form without any transcendent detachment (*décrochement*). On the immanent plane of matter, a subjective image separates out, creating a provisional zone of individuated perception. The subjective image, a mobile cut in a universe in a state of becoming, is defined by framing, cutting and connecting with other images. Subjectivity emerges as a temporal and sensory interval between images that are also in motion.

Thinking movement as becoming entails that we reverse the relations between movement and time. Here too we shift from a statics of space to a kinetics of becoming. It is no longer a question of subordinating time to cosmic movement in accordance with the ancient hypothesis of time numbered on movement, but instead of making time a condition of movement. In the ancient formula, time was subordinated to extensive movement, which measured it. The ancient cosmological hypothesis linked time to the circular movement of the world, making time literally turn around cardinal points as around celestial joints. Deleuze applies Shakespeare's splendid expression, the time 'is out of joint', to modern cosmology. Movement no longer links time to the cardinal points of the rotation of the stars; it is rather movement that depends upon time. Released from its cosmic hinges, time becomes the condition for the transformation of the whole and becomes emancipated from movement, for which it now becomes the principle. 'Time is no longer related to the movement it measures, but rather movement to time that conditions it' (CC 27–8).[8]

The image and movement thus open to the question of time. This is why Deleuze condenses some of his boldest presentations on metaphysics in the books on cinema, in which cinema is revealed to be a field of experimentation for thought. Movement opens to time just as the time-image emerges from the movement-image. We recall that the movement-image unfolds, fan-like (*en éventail*), the varieties of perception-image, affection-image and action-image. With the time-image, a new regime of the image carves out, at the core of the movement-image, a mode of becoming that is no longer suspended in the actualisation of movement. With the emergence of the time-image, cinematographic art becomes inscribed in a Bergsonian universe, cinema no longer treating movement as the displacement of a stable object across surrounding space, but as the intensive variation and real vibration of qualities in time.

From Movement-Image to Time-Image

In shifting from *The Movement-Image* to *The Time-Image*, we do not only move from one epoch of cinema to another, but also from a mode of individuating narration to an intensive description, from a regime of qualified space and ordered time to the direct experience of becoming. For its part, cinematographic art explores Bergson's philosophical innovation: spatial movement and actual displacement in reality presuppose the intensive vibration of the virtual. Time pulsates behind movement. At all points, the intensive becoming of time accompanies the actual movement of history. The time-image surges forth in the interstices of the movement-image.

Drawing upon Bergson, Deleuze already conceptualised the movement-image as a subjective suturing of action and reaction. In the acentred universe of material actions and reactions, the subjectivated image extends itself and carves out a vital centre of indetermination around itself, tracing a sensory arc of perception, affection and action between the movement experienced and the executed movement. Any individuated image opens a perspectival spectre (*un spectre perspectif*) that shifts from perception to motor reaction through sensory affection. This relaxation, characteristic of the subjective movement-image, is raised to a superior power in the time-image. In the sensory-motor circuit, the affection image is already thickened by an intensive layer, one that the time-image makes even more dense. The affect of the time-image corresponds to this experience of thought, characteristic of modern cinema but also present in any image, which marks the failure of the sensory-motor circuit in favour of a vision or an affect. This experience of thought stretches the interval of the movement-image to the breaking point. Within the sensory-motor circuit, the affection-image already developed this sensitive, vibrating disturbance, detached from the actual. The time-image makes affect vibrate even more intensely, shattering the sensory-motor connection.

The shift from movement-image to time-image allows us to describe the shift from classic cinema to post-war cinema. With neorealism, the personified narrative of classic cinema gives way to a vision, wherein history, plot and action are undone. The movement-image of classic cinema defined individuated characters in an ordered narration that permitted us to follow their actions. Whether in a Hawks-style film noir, in which the epic posture contracts to the side of action and dilates in being dispersed in the milieu in which it is actualised, or a Ford-style Western, wherein action is tailored to fit a landscape framed and animated by a sky pulsating with colour, in the case of the movement-image, a defined subject perceives, experiences and acts on the world. With Italian neorealism, as, for example, in De Sica's *Bicycle Thieves* or Rossellini's *Stromboli*, a new type of character, one now in the guise of spectator, endures a share of the intolerable and the possible exuded by an event. Stereotyped characters are replaced by floating subjectivities who, in the weakness or relaxation of their motor capacities, experience the visionary intensity of a situation.

The political and historical condition for sensory-motor failure is the rupture of the connection between human and world that characterised the post-war period. Situations no longer extend into actions, instead redoubling their perceptual situation: we become prey to a vision, affect prevailing over action in the image. Detached from actual sensory-motor engagement, the time-image directly pits sensibility in a struggle with virtual forces of dissolution and of transformation of the real. Deleuze precisely establishes the conditions of this rupture: perceptions and actions 'ceased to be linked together' (C2 40). They no longer constitute a unified and individualising sensory-motor link that leads from perception to action. We depart from the organic to approach what Deleuze calls the 'crystalline', the coexistence of the actual and virtual in an image that causes time to emerge directly in the shot, as in, for example, films by Welles or Ozu.

The result is a profound mutation of cinematographic style, which shifts from organic narration to intensive description. Space ceases being a place to coordinate or to fill, and characters become visionaries. Sensory-motor conditions are eroded, transforming the possibilities of spatiality and the modes of subjectivation in these spaces. Transformation systematically affects perceptions and actions, the fields and modes of subjectivations of characters. We shift from a motor image, which becomes dissipated in inchoate movements, to what Deleuze calls pure, sensory affects or 'visions': pure optical or sound situations. The character is no longer a sovereign agent, a subject of his or her action, becoming instead the passive and enchanted vector of a perception. It is at the same moment that perception is put into contact with thought rather than being extended into an action, and that the image ceases to adhere to movement to instead encounter time. What is at stake is less an abandonment of the sensory-motor schema or its overcoming, than an adventure that affects the movement-image itself, at its very core. Deleuze specifies that the sensory-motor connection is neither displaced nor replaced, but rather 'shattered from the inside' (C2 40), strained to such an extreme limit that it can no longer make motor output correspond to sensory input. If Deleuze, following Bergson, conceived of the sensory-motor as a living image that doubles the material actions and reactions with a sensory surface on the reverse side, the failure of the sensory-motor schema opens the living circuit of the image to the experience of time.

In these terms, the modern cinema of the time-image does not imply that progress is being made in terms of the image or of the cinematographic art, but rather indicates the troubling intrusion of the virtual, of the effect of time, into an image that is no longer destined to give a living response. The interval of affect, which separates the subjective perception-image and the action-image, causes the time-image to emerge within the movement-image. The time-image is thus not the interior of the movement-image, but is rather exterior to it as its intensive lining; the time-image is neither hidden nor more profound than the movement-image, but is rather different and direct, and, in truth, dependent on the rupture of the sensory-motor connection. It is only in this way that the time-image presupposes the movement-image.

In cinema, as well as in art in general, it is never a matter of imagining that there is an overcoming, a historical succession or a causal progression between two types of image; at most, we should think of a rupture, interstice or interval. Thus, it is necessary to avoid the aesthetic trap that consists in translating the privilege of the time-image in terms of a reality that is 'more profound', 'more beautiful', or 'more true' (C2 40, 270). Rather, the time-image erupts in the fracture of the movement-image and refers to a new political relation between the human and the world; in preventing perception from immediately being extended into action and resulting in movement, the time-image puts thought directly into contact with time. The sensory-motor schema is ruptured because the political conditions of action are no longer present in the contemporary assemblage: 'The modern fact is that we no longer believe in this world' (C2 171). But this political pessimism is doubled by the necessity for art and specifically for cinema – the art of the masses and of power structures (*puissances*) – to oppose a pedagogy of the image to ambient mediocrity (*à la médiocrité ambiante*), a pedagogy that calls for a people who are missing and which, through its visions, frees perception from the ordinary habits of opinion, thereby 'tearing a real image from clichés' (C2 21).

PART II:
THE CINEMATOGRAPHIC SUBJECT — FROM THE
SENSORY-MOTOR ARC TO THE VISIONARY

In Deleuze, the semiotics of the image relies upon a physics, or rather upon a kinetics, of movement, which renews philosophy at the same time that it renews the theory of cinema. First, perception and matter are now only distinguished by degrees. Matter includes the set of images, while perception opens a myopic perspective onto images, taking a particular subjectivated image, *a* body for its centre or frame. Next, matter and image are identified with one another, matter being nothing other than a vibrating block of space-time. Finally, in this acentred universe, subjectivity emerges in an immanent mode, producing its own framing, making cuts, creating interstices between images.

It is this definition of subjectivity as framing and cutting that we will explore here. Deleuze accords to cinema – a recent art and one that had previously received little attention from philosophers – a decisive explanatory capacity: only an analysis of cinema allows us to elucidate the question of the subject by means of analysis of the image and of the determinate cinematographic procedures of framing and editing. For Deleuze, it amounts to the same thing to ask how a perception forms and how an image becomes individuated: it is at this juncture that, for Deleuze, Bergson's philosophy and cinema converge.

THE INDIVIDUATION OF THE IMAGE

Only images exist, since the image is defined as an assemblage of relations of plural and differential forces that compose floating and provisional zones of individuations in the acentred universe of matter. Thus, everything is image, movement, or force. In this universe of forces and movement, of acentred actions and reactions, it is not possible, rigorously speaking, to distinguish partial images. Everything interacts with everything else. This point of departure, which identifies matter with the image in movement, that is, with force, designates it as 'a flowing-matter [*une matière-écoulement*] in which no point of anchorage nor centre of reference would be assignable' (C1 57). This is what defines the 'plane of immanence' as an infinite set of images in movement, the in-itself of the image or flowing-matter. This plane of immanence presents matter in becoming in an acentred mode by suppressing the anchorage of the subject as the horizon of the world, that is, by eliminating the least transcendent opening (C1 57–9). Defining the plane of immanence as acentred or as immanent amounts to the same thing because it is the absence of transcendent anchoring on the side of the subject (perception) or on the side of the object (the world perceived) that assures the immanence of the plane. The plane of immanence is thus, by definition, acentred. In addition, defining the plane as immanent and acentred follows from two convergent theoretical requirements. First, it was indispensable to begin with movement and not with perception in order to genetically demonstrate how perceptions and subjects become centred. Acentred matter is the condition of the individuation of images. In short, the perceptive image forms as an individuation, which produces a relative centre in a floating and provisional mode, a zone of subjectivation.

Second, this is why it was necessary to deduce perception and not to begin with it, as phenomenology does too quickly, according to Deleuze, at the cost of presupposing what it was supposed to demonstrate. Hence the importance of the point of departure: the state of things in perpetual change, the plane of forces of matter, from which perception emerges as interval, cut and temporal lapse.

How, then, do image-subjects form? How do we move from the acentred movement-image of matter to this new species of movement-image, the centred, perceiving and subjective image? This genesis of perception from matter permits Deleuze to propose a truly immanent definition of subjectivity, following the path laid out by Spinoza: to think the subject as a mode, not as a substance. The image depends upon a definition of individuation as modal haecceity that Deleuze elaborates at length, from *Difference and Repetition* (1968) to *Spinoza: Practical Philosophy* (1981), by connecting Simondon to Spinoza's theory of finite modes. Like all compositions of relations of force, images become individuated by means of a function of distinctive parts that belong to them under specific relations of variable speeds (*rapports de vitesses et de lenteurs*), or longitude, and of affects or variations of power (*puissance*) that these relations are capable of producing (latitude). There is an individual as soon as a modal individuation provisionally stabilises a determinate relation according to which certain forces become singularised. But the theory of cinema formulates this individuation in terms of a genesis of perception. The image becomes individuated in detaching itself from the plane of other images, and it detaches itself from the plane in intervals by producing a perceptual hiatus that prevents the linkage of the other images. In this way, we shift from acentred matter to subjective perception.

CINEMATOGRAPHIC FRAMING

The subject effect is produced when the gap between the action and reaction of the movement-images is sufficient to generate perception, that is, an illumination (*un éclairage*) exerting a subtractive effect on the other images.

The subject-image is produced in this gap, such that the subjectivity of images actually occurs in the interval, at the moment when the relaxation takes place that distances and separates action and reaction, one from the other. Where actions and reactions are instantaneously linked together, we are on the plane of immanence of complete matter where everything reacts on everything else and where the individuated image is not to be found. By contrast, the interval opens up where action does not dissipate in reaction, but is rather propagated and unfolds in a movement-image, according to the three varieties of perception-image, affection-image and action-image.

Deleuze thereby draws our attention to the convergence between Leibniz and Bergson in saying that subjectivity traces out a finite perspective, but he goes further by demonstrating that it amounts to the same thing to say that perception is subtractive, subjective and extracts a specific point of view from reality. Subjectivity proceeds through framing. From this, Deleuze derives a new and strange theory: perceptive images are cinematographic and they propagate a sensory zone of sensory-motor subjectivity within the interval of forces. In this way, a second image forms that is excluded from other images, and which becomes individuated by presenting a sensory surface to them and by opposing its singular motor power (*sa puissance motrice singulière*) to them. This power is endowed, in addition, with a power of affection that allows it to experience its nascent interiority. In this way, subjectivity reveals its cinematographic status, for it is distinguished from other images by its perceptual framing and active editing that favours the cutting and the relinking of other images.

How can we assimilate the cinematographic image to the formation of a subject? By starting from acentred matter, Deleuze neutralises the distinction between the organic and the machinic, the living and the technical. The temporal interval between action and reaction favours the emergence of subjective images whether they be human, living or cinematographic, without granting any privilege to the anthropomorphic or the natural. One of the most powerful aspects of this theory of individuation is that it allows us to treat technical images and biological images, the cinema and the living, on the same plane, not by 'humanising' cinematographic images, but simply because in this universe of forces, the human origin of such images is of small importance in terms of their material composition. Here, Deleuze follows Spinoza: the difference between artificial and natural images is perfectly secondary, and cinematographic images are defined exactly like other material images, that is, by cutting and editing. This is reinforced by the fact that cinematographic images allow us to experience movement and perceive 'a bit of time in a pure state', as Proust desired, better than our natural perception could, because they are not, like human perception, subject to human action and its impoverished attempts to stabilise becoming by submitting it to the spatialising categories of our possible action. Cinema is thus better positioned than a psychological or phenomenological analysis of the human to allow us to respond to the question, what is a perception? But, since we should not to reduce this question overly quickly to this anthropological mode, we should deal with it in this other form: how do images become individuated? Only the analysis of cinema could guarantee this mutation. This is the decisive importance of the concept of the image, and the reason why cinema is so important to Deleuze.

THREE TYPES OF MOVEMENT IMAGES

The image becomes individuated through unfolding its fan-like range (*dépliant son éventail*) of perceptions, actions and affections, a process that applies to the human subject as much as to the cinematographic image. The three moments of the constitution of the subject thus correspond to the three types of movement-images. The semiotics of the image allows the taxonomy of the cinema to correspond to the genesis of the constitution of the subject, a *kinetics* of the subject.

The genesis of the subject thus corresponds to the formation of the movement-image and to its three types. The image becomes individuated in cutting the automatic linking of material actions and reactions and in unfolding, between the movement received and the movement executed, its range of perceptions, actions and affections. These types, which constitute the operations of subjectivity, consist in subtraction for the perception-image, a creative incurvation for the action-image, and a reflecting intensity for the affection-image.

The subtractive perception-image forms the first operation, or the first 'material moment' of subjectivity. The perception-image transforms action experienced into perception and, in its interactions with other images, neglects anything that does not directly interest its action. Perception acts thereby through limitation, by taking away or 'subtracting' from other images anything not directly of interest to it. Its framing is subtractive. Here, Deleuze takes up a Bergsonian motif that he deploys and transforms throughout his work: subjectivity is disjunctive, subtractive and creative. The subject is distinguished as a singularity in that it neglects anything that does not enter the path of its possible action in the tissue of the real.

We move continually between the perception-image and the action-image, between subtraction and incurvation. For perception, in ignoring anything in reality not of interest to its action, curves the universe around its operative possibilities as around a centre that consists of nothing more than a positive indetermination, an interval. The action is a 'delayed reaction of the centre of indetermination' (C1 64). Indetermination favours this delay, which provokes a (temporal) waiting period at the same time that it provokes a (spatial) rupture. At stake is a topological and chronogenetic definition of subjectivity that supplements Bergson's definition of perception with the contributions of Simondon and Spinoza. Bergson indicates that perception cuts the acentred set of images by creating its singular and limited framing. Simondon pursues the analysis on the plane of organic matter. Biological differentiation occurs when matter folds, becomes incurved, and forms a membrane, that is, a polarised surface that is selectively porous and chemically capable of selecting what it incorporates and what it excludes, thereby differentiating an interiority and an exteriority, such that 'at the level of the polarised membrane the interior past and the exterior future confront one another'.[9] Deleuze shifts from the living membrane to the cinematographic image by substituting the operations of framing and montage for this chemical polarity, and by explaining perceptual selectivity by its action of subtraction in relation to the requirements of its actions. In this way, subjective disjunction is revealed to be subtractive and creative at the same time.

This second material operation of subjectivity thereby creates the action-image, which curves or bends the universe around its motor possibilities. The centre of indetermination thereby produces its two effects of centring and of indetermination. It *centres* the universe around its zone of creative *indetermination*, that is to say, it frames it in relation to a possible action: in so doing, it differentiates itself from the object that it separates from itself and which it holds at a distance, in the spatial depth of its point of view but also in accordance with the temporal interval of its possible action. The perceived object and the active subject become individuated in concert with one another, for they form two surfaces of the same temporal and topological interval. Perceptual, sensory-motor space, in incurving and in folding, differentiates things that present their surface of virtual interaction to the subject, while action holds them at a distance, in the sightlines of its possible intervention.

Subjectivity thus necessarily appears as a sensory-motor schema by injecting indetermination into the dense tissue of matter. Action is not satisfied with unfurling a sensory-motor response; in a creative mode, it brings forth something new. Something happens, something unpredictable is produced. The action-image, the second material operation of subjectivity, thereby responds to perception by a motor discharge.

This sensory-motor discharge implies the intermediary of the affection-image. While this third operation of subjectivity does not guarantee the shift from the *sensory* (perception-image) to the *motor* (action-image), it does create the possibility of surpassing the subjective movement-image. The affection-image not only unifies the sensory-motor arc by linking perception and action, it also marks the point of coincidence between the object perceived and the acting subject. It is in the affection-image that the cut is produced as a disjunctive synthesis, creative of a subjectivity of indetermination and of the temporal interval. This cut marks a subjective interiorisation, a power of existence by which the image becomes individuated in affecting itself. We can thus interpret the affection-image as a form of *cogito* on the condition that we remain well aware it is not a question of a reflexivity of thought that would affect itself through an act of consciousness, as in Descartes, but of an auto-affection of force (*force*) that experiences its own variation of power (*puissance*). Thus, the third material aspect of subjectivity indicates exactly the point where force is folded, experiencing its variation in power and revealing itself as reflecting and intensive.

The affection-image indicates the point of subjectivation, a pocket of indetermination (*la poche d'indétermination*) from which the bundle of subtractive perception and creative action emanate. Affection marks the shift between acentred matter and subjective differenciation. As power of subjectivation, it actualises an individuation and cuts the undifferentiated plane of immanence. But, in a movement typical of Deleuze's philosophy, and which demonstrates clearly how important the philosophy of cinema is for the elaboration of the entirety of the system, the affection-image not only indicates the cut by which a force individuates itself within the undifferentiated tissue of forces in becoming. It indicates at the same time and with the same intensity the moment of differentiation by which force, instead of actualising itself, becomes virtual and experiences its power, no longer as a point of actualisation or as a defined individuation, but as a vector of the dissolution of individuation, as, precisely, intensity. Affection thus divides itself between the moment of subjective actualisation, thanks to which forces take a determinate form, and that of virtual differentiation, by which force experiences the power of the whole and is exposed to the event of becoming. In this way, we shift from the movement-image to the time-image.

FROM THE MOVEMENT-IMAGE TO THE TIME-IMAGE

The definition of affection becomes redoubled in the shift from the movement-image to the time-image, from organic narration, actualised around the epic schema of a sensory-motor action individuated in the form of a determinate person, to the crystalline description, neutral and 'unqualified'. In the movement-image, time appears only indirectly, in the guise of montage. The time-image, raising the affection-image to a superior power, ruptures the sensory-motor schema. The acting and perceiving individual is submitted to the pure force of affection, to a vision. The situation no longer prolongs itself into a motor response (*en motricité*). Thus, the heroine of *Stromboli* (Rossellini 1950) can only sob as she gazes upon the eruption of the volcano, which literally overwhelms her capacity to respond. Exposed to the power of nature, she experiences sensory-motor failure, and in the unravelling of her capacities of response, she experiences the affect of the pure event.

Enduring the liquidation of the sensory-motor response, the character exchanges the possibilities of action for new visionary qualities, which cause the new to appear as an event, instead of reducing it to the linkage of parts of a story. The organic, narrative story is organised according to the linear tissue of a linking together of causes and effects. The event proves to be 'the possibility for something else' (TRM 234), a possibility that did not exist before but which is created by the event in accordance with the modes – impotency, passivity and the experience of violence – Deleuze established in his earliest studies of Proust, in 1964, as the conditions of creation. This is precisely why Deleuze makes of the Proustian formula cited above – 'a bit of time in a pure state' – the very indication of success in art. Creation consists in this being overwhelmed, a situation in which time emerges in a sublime and violent mode: the character is no longer a sovereign actor, the subject of his or her action, but the passive and enchanted vector of a perception.

Here, Deleuze evokes a definition of the sublime, which allows him to link neorealist cinema to a new form of romanticism. This is because the sublime, according to Kant, is defined precisely by the excess and dispro-portion by which the subject finds herself submerged and at the same time undone by the enormity (the mathematical sublime) or power (the dynamic sublime) of a natural phenomenon. Deleuze connects the Kantian sublime to Bergsonian intuition and valorises, in contrast to Kant, the moment of impotence and passivity: the subject, unable to respond, is no longer capable of neutralising the event by means of motor escape, but instead finds him or herself riveted, without defence, to the power of affection. The sublime causes the sensory-motor cliché to fail, for action, like intelligence for Bergson, is 'anthropological', impoverished and reductive because it spatialises duration, reducing the real to human proportions so that it becomes inoffensive and convenient. This is why Deleuze considers the sensory-motor response to be a cliché of common sense.

In opening this cliché to vision and to the affect of time, the character experiences a change. He or she ceases valorising movement in order to per-ceive the virtual affect of time in that moment, in an intensive way. In order for the shift from the sensory-motor spectator to the visionary of the time-image to occur, it is necessary that response or reaction become radically impossible, such that the character can no longer escape the impact of the affect by executing a reaction. In short, the causal and psychological path of movement must be blocked in order to set off the explosive violence of the event as vision. The reason for the violent outbreak of the time-image is thus opposed to that behind the sensory-motor hiatus, which dissipates the quality in motor energy instead of converting it into thought. 'Subjectivity, then, takes on a new sense, which is no longer motor or material, but temporal and spiritual . . .' (C2 47). Thus, in a sense, subjectivity pursues its own undoing: the dilation of the time-image redoubles the interstice of the movement-image by bringing it to its point of rupture, while at the same time, within the indiscernibility of the actual and virtual, it is not only the affect in time that we experience, but 'time itself' (C2 83).

Not only do the three modes of the movement-image – perceptive, active and affective – constitute a genetics of the subject and a semiotics of cinema, but the irruption of virtual time in the dilation of the affection-image marks the point at which we shift from an indirect, empirical and actual relation to time to its direct and transcendental vision. The philosophy of the individuation of the image proposes a semiotics of cinema, and the theory of cinema renews the philosophy of the subject and of time. It was indeed necessary for genetics to become semiotics in order for the subject to be defined in an immanent mode. Reciprocally, it was also necessary for the theory of signs to rely upon the kinetics of the image in order for it to be possible to elaborate a philosophy of cinema that could address the matter of images, rather than assuming the theory of discursive acts as an epistemological model, subordinating cinema to literature and to linguistic schemes of interpretation. These different stakes – an immanent definition of the subject and the independence of the philosophy of art, and especially of cinema as a logic of forces, and the determination of relations between movement and time, and between actual and virtual – converge upon this properly Deleuzian invention: the subject is always defined by an act of subtraction. Individuation always entails cutting the flows of other images. Deleuze already affirmed this in the disjunctive theory of subjectivity and pursued its analysis with the machine as the cutting of a flow during the years when he was co-writing with Guattari. But here, individuation is neither presented in an energetic sense, as the legislation of a difference of potential, as during the era of *Difference and Repetition*, nor as a tendency toward organisation and molar stratification, as in *A Thousand Plateaus*. Here, it is defined as a sensory-motor arc capable, when it becomes blocked, of opening by way of a vision to the affect of time.

Deleuze had to encounter cinema, the technics of framing and editing images, in order to explore the simultaneity of movement and time, the indiscernibility of the actual and virtual in the image. The typology of cinematographic signs aims to propose a new theory of cinema, and at the same time the semiotics of the image renews the ethics of individuation. *The Movement-Image* and *The Time-Image* make it possible to follow the transformation of this theory of individuation, in its continuity and coherence, but also in its inventiveness and capacity for rupture. This allows us to observe, in addition, how Deleuze composes his own philosophy by means of cuts, folds and linkages, connecting segments of disparate doctrines into an enduring, active and original montage.

NOTES

1. This chapter integrates two previously published articles by Sauvagnargues, eliminating major repetition between the two. Part I contains the entirety of 'L'image: Deleuze, Bergson et le cinéma', in *L'image*, ed. Alexander Schnell (Paris: Vrin, 2007), 157–76. Part II contains an edited version of 'Le sujet cinématographique: de l'arc sensorimoteur à la voyance', in *CINéMAS, Revue d'études cinématographiques/Journal of Film Studies* 16.2–3 (2006): 96–114, special issue on Deleuze and cinema. Translator's note.

2. Bergson, *Matière et mémoire* (1896), in *Oeuvres*.

3. Bergson, *Matter and Memory*, 20; Bergson, *Matière et mémoire*, in *Oeuvres*, 171.

4. Bergson, *Matière et mémoire*, in *Oeuvres*, 173.

5. Bergson, *La Pensée et le Mouvant* (1934), in *Oeuvres*, 1381.

6. Bergson, *L'Évolution créatrice* (1907), in *Oeuvres*, 786. My translation.

7. See also Bergson, *Matière et Mémoire*, in *Oeuvres*, 337.

8. Deleuze cites this line from Shakespeare's *Hamlet*, Act I, Scene 5, in 'On Four Poetic Formulas That Might Summarize the Kantian Philosophy', in *Essays Critical and Clinical*, 27–35.

9. Simondon, *L'individuation à la lumière des notions de forme et d'information*, 228.

6. The Table of Categories as a Table of Montage

In proposing to think of the table of categories as a table of montage, Deleuze demonstrates the degree to which the invention of cinema, as an industrial technology and as a new form of art, transforms the problem of thought for philosophy. The table of montage makes a completely new image of the table of categories possible, and this surprising alignment transforms our view of both thought and cinema.

It may seem risky to compare the technique of cinematic montage to the activity of thought itself. But in proposing this equivalence between the two tables, Deleuze is not simply indulging in a poetic distraction, engendering a hybrid monster or chimera, imitating the surrealist grafting of the sewing machine of the mind to the dissection table of the editing room. In reality, this operation transforms the status of the image, including the verbal and poetic image, because it overturns the habitual boundaries between thought and creation. This explains the role that cinema assumes as a technique for Deleuze: the points of view of the camera, and especially the montage of shots – their sometimes homogeneous, sometimes heterogeneous connections, as in false continuity editing – indicate the decisive role of framing, cutting and montage in achieving the linking of shots that compose the film.

In proposing to think of the table of categories as a table of montage, Deleuze is not trying to weaken thought by reducing it to a technological scheme, any more than he is trying to conjure away the effective, technical constraints of montage by linking them, by analogy, to the virtual cut of thought. The proposition here is much more radical: thought proceeds by means of cutting and collage, and cinema makes possible a new logical figure of thought, which corresponds to a new philosophy of the image.

THE IMAGE OF THOUGHT

In philosophy, the table of categories classically answers to the question of how thought functions, what operations it requires, and what logical structure it brings into play. Deleuze names this problem – how to think thought, how to describe its inventiveness? – 'the image of thought' in the first phase of his work. From the first appearance of this expression in *Nietzsche and Philosophy* (1962) and in *Difference and Repetition* (1968), the term 'image' is used in a relatively pejorative sense. Because it establishes a suspect reflexivity or reflection, the image, in providing a representation to thought, deforms thought and indicates the faulty and distorting manner in which thought reflects upon its own activity. The 'image of thought', in the works that lead to the definition of transcendental empiricism at the time of *Difference and Repetition*, always signals the way thought implicitly represents its own activity. The image and representative thought are thereby in solidarity.

This is why Deleuze concluded the first version of *Proust and Signs* (1964) with a chapter entitled 'The Image of Thought', revealing the degree to which philosophy needs art and literature. Proust introduced an image of thought that rivals that presented by philosophy, proposing that thought erupts involuntarily in response to the violent appearance of the sign. 'Thought is nothing without something that forces and does violence to it' (PS 95).

Proust transforms the very way we represent thought to ourselves: thought is no longer docile, humble and submissive, and is not deployed in the diligent or complacent mode of the student endowed with good will, careful when necessary to make use of a method to arrive at the truth. Thought is rather contrary and turbulent and responds abruptly to the impulse of the sign, harnessing all of its resources, despite its urgency and lack of preparation, in an attempt to respond to an intrusive event that takes us by surprise. The act of thinking seems neither natural nor serene, but rather proceeds in relation to a shock, a secret torsion, or a violent experience: we think due to the harrowing contingency of an experience that resists our capacity to know. It is in this sense that thinking may be considered creation.

Proust makes it possible for us to understand the genesis of thought because he is a novelist, and so brings precise, microscopic attention to the sensorial modes of creation. Logical thought is preoccupied more with the validity of its judgement than with the contingent circumstances of its conception. Emphasising the *a priori* less, the novelist describes the adventures of thought and opposes the image of thought proposed by rationalist philosophy. 'The act of thinking does not proceed from a simple natural possibility; on the contrary, it is the only true creation' (PS 97).

This new image of thought, transmitted by art, transforms the givens of the problem. Deleuze no longer proposes to obtain a thought without images, or to purge thought of its tendency to imagine thought: thought makes an image of itself, in a mode that is much more troubling and decisive.

THE TABLE OF CATEGORIES

Of what does a table of categories consist? Since Kant, the logical grid of categories structures our possible judgements and distributes our concepts according to closed, completed and static determinations. These unified, objective connections allow us to classify our concepts and organise our experiences by referring them to the constituting activity of the subject. The form of thought is patterned on the nature of the thinking subject, defined in advance. This is why Deleuze turns out to be hesitant toward categories and proposes, in *Difference and Repetition*, that it would be better to replace them with empirical and nomad notions. However, once the status of thought has been transformed, a new conception of categories becomes possible. It is in this second sense that the table of categories becomes a table of montage.

In effect, a table must not be understood as something static, a surface upon which the operations of thought are distributed, an inert support for logical interventions, the erection of a plane for the attribution of judgements and distributing different, possible mental activities among the faculties in relation to their proper use. It must be understood in terms of its dynamic operativity, not as an outline of a frozen architecture, but rather as a plane of action, a plane of montage, a list of pragmatic instructions, or as an ephemeral and transitory succession of mental acts staging a guerrilla operation within thought.

The table of categories thus operates in the two modes that characterise a table of cinematographic montage: cutting and connecting. In cutting between shots, it introduces a supplementary movement between points of view, and reintroduces continuity in proposing an inventive assembling of shots. These two activities of cutting and connecting are strictly complementary. It is impossible to cut without connecting, and even more impossible to connect without cutting: cutting is the decisive act of montage. Cutting selects and identifies the unities that it reclassifies according to the specific ordering of the montage. In combining shots in a series, it aligns them in a succession that is truly creative, which in turn transforms each shot that has been thereby combined.

In his first article on Bergson, in 1956, Deleuze defined thought in the following way: 'A great philosopher creates new concepts: these concepts simultaneously surpass the dualities of ordinary thought and give things a new truth, a new distribution, [an extraordinary] way of dividing up the world' (DI 22, with modification).

Thinking proceeds through cutting or division (*découpage*), and when it is creative, the lines of articulation of these 'extraordinary' divisions no longer pass through the ordinary coordinates of everyday thought. A creator invents new categories, new ways of laying out lines of thought, and in so doing, changes the world. It is the categories themselves that assure the creativity of thought, plotting new pathways of circulation for concepts. Thinking thus consists in opening new pathways for thought, which in turn transform both the tissue of the world and our neural pathways. In making new cuts in the tissue of reality, new properties of reality are set down that, in turn, affect us.

With this new definition of philosophical thought as creation, we obtain an equally new definition of the image. Now, in order to transform our image of thought, Deleuze needs cinema just as he previously relied upon Proust. But, at the same time, the definition of the image has changed: it is no longer the passive and appropriate (*convenu*) reflection of a representation that thought creates of its own power, but the acts of cutting, framing and montage by which thought insinuates itself in matter. The image is no longer a representation of consciousness, but, in a manner that is much more decisive and dangerous, is the movement of matter. It is in this third sense that the table of categories becomes a table of montage. Thought is produced by a framing of shots and by montage, that is, by the reassembling of framings (*ré-enchaînement de cadrages*).

MOVEMENT-IMAGE

By defining thought as an inventive means of carving out (*découper*) our relation to reality, Deleuze is in actuality proposing a new philosophy of the image. This constitutes the programme of the two volumes on cinema, *The Movement-Image* (1983) and *The Time-Image* (1985): the transformation of our conception of thought and of our conventional notion of cinema, and the operation of these two transformations in relation to each other.

The image is no longer an exclusively mental experience, a psychic phenomenon, or a point of view (*visée*) of consciousness, instead becoming a relation of forces, an image in itself, a movement-image, as Bergson sought in *Matter and Memory*. The table of categories no longer appears as a table of montage only because the categories divide and cut (*sectionnent and découpent*) reality differently; more profoundly, it is necessary to recognise that the categories, in their operative mode, are the conditions of framing and cutting that allow thought to be creative. When we think, we actually cut and reframe relations in reality that are effectively new, except when we use the clichés of conventional cuts. Thought thus functions as a table of montage, but only when we think in new terms. If not, thought is content to use the framing provided by tradition. Deleuze develops this new conception thanks to the movement-image: with the movement-image, we obtain a much more intense definition of the subject as an image, and of thought as framing and cinematographic montage. The cinema as an experience of thought radically transforms philosophy.

This is why Deleuze determined that it was necessary to set Bergson's *Matter and Memory* in relation to the invention of cinema, the industrial creation that has transformed our modern experience of art. Cinema implies a definition of the image in movement, each framing effectuating a mobile cut such that we no longer oppose the movement of bodies to the image in consciousness. The image effectively appears as a change, a transformation of constituent parts and the affection of the whole. For his part, Bergson proposes a definition of the subjective image as a cut, an interval between other images or a framing. Thus, we can understand the very creation of subjective thought as an act of subtractive cutting, as an act that emerges in the interval between other images by proposing its singular framing of reality.

In these terms, the consideration of the table of categories as a table of montage assumes a new and fourth sense. When we think, we operate a cut that causes us to emerge as a subject, in the operations of cutting and framing that characterises the image. Our subjective perception inserts itself into the flow of other images. This is why Deleuze relies upon Bergson, and why he had to encounter cinema as a philosophical problem.

In *Matter and Memory*, Bergson starts from the infinite variation of matter in the sense of the actions and reactions of material images in movement. We must first situate the image on this plane of forces of matter, wherein no centre yet puts forth a preferential point of view. This acentred definition of images in movement explains the complex notion of the 'plane of immanence' in Deleuze's thought: the set of all images is determined on this plane, which he calls the plane of immanence because it is composed of the flux and reflux of material forces, without being traversed by any transcendent point (*pic*). On this plane, the actions and reactions of material images link up in a state that is too animated to allow us to distinguish bodies, unities or sets. The image is absolute movement, a field of forces, and strictly speaking, nothing exists other than this immanent field of forces. Matter is not hidden behind the image and the image does not reflect matter for a consciousness: the image is directly temporal fabric, energetic matter and blocks of space-time.

Movement-images must initially be defined this way, on the plane of immanence, in terms of the universal reactivity of images, matter in movement, and actions and reactions that link up and react to each other instantaneously, without any privileged point of view allowing for the definition of new unities or subjective framings.

FROM THE MOVEMENT-IMAGE TO SUBJECTIVE OPENING

In order for a subject to emerge on the acentred plane of images, a framing is sufficient, one that introduces a new system and permits other images to vary mainly as a function of one image, which has contact with them on one of its surfaces and reacts to them on another of its surfaces. This is how subjective images are created – as provisional centres and especially as zones of indetermination that introduce into the world of movement-images a gap or an interval between a movement received (perception) and a movement executed (action). These subject-images are thus 'separated' (*écartelées*) images that reflect the actions that interest them in the form of perception, and respond in the form of action. Between the sensory surface of perception and the motor reaction, the sensitive surface of affection is carved out. All of these secondary images, whether they are perceptive, mechanical or living, are defined by this simple gap, this elongation, the insertion of a temporal slackening or interval that separates the actions and reactions of matter. The subject is nothing other than this gap, and this gap consists in a cinematographic framing. In this case, all images are referred to one image; in other words, they are framed. When we think, when we produce ourselves as subjectivity, we act like cinematographic images: we frame other images.

We needed cinema to be in a position to understand what anthropological analysis or even the phenomenology of human perception were incapable of explaining to us, because their starting point is not the acentred plane of matter. Perception does not consist of an image in which matter is reflected for an attentive consciousness; an image is not a representation of matter, but is rather matter itself, minus all that does not interest us. Photography is already in things. Deleuze borrows this startling definition from Bergson: perception is equal to matter itself, but neglects in matter all that does not interest our action, all that we come across but which we do not pay attention to. The living thing and the perceiving subjective image are nothing more than the slackening between action and reaction, owing to which certain movements are reflected as perceptions experienced, while the movement received is refracted by this sensitive prism to become a motor response. To perceive is to act or trace a fluctuating, murky zone of possible action within the totality of matter. The objects that our perception cuts out, the surfaces that we select, thereby reflect our capacity to take hold (*notre capacité de prise*) of the world.

For Deleuze, as for Bergson, perception draws its myopic diagonal, its zone of possible action, across matter. In these conditions, we see that Deleuze gives perception a cinematographic twist: to perceive is to frame and to cut between images. Perception consists of this mobile and living cut, 'an operation which consists exactly of a *framing*' (C1 62, with modification). On the one hand, perception extends its sensory, subtractive and myopic diagonal across matter, while on the other, its selection corresponds exactly to the gap that its sensory-motor arc introduces within matter. This is how subjects are produced, through framing and cutting.

We must draw the consequences of this extraordinary vision very carefully. The perceiving image corresponds to a centre of indetermination. Subjects are thus constituted on the immanent plane of matter by means of a simple distension (*étirement*) that expands the interval between images and allows the sensitive range (*éventail*) of a sensory-motor arc to be inserted between action and reaction. In these terms, all perception is characterised by a vital framing and cutting, and the cinematographic framing through which we enact our categorical cutting also corresponds to this sensory-motor power, whose vital affect fluctuates as a function of encounters, states and hours. Our thought responds to the sensory-motor mode by which we insert ourselves among the other images.

Here, Deleuze rejoins Spinoza: our thought corresponds to the cutting our body performs among images. In this way, our table of categories responds to the framing and mobile insertion of our body. The philosophical subject and the cinematographic image unfold their sensory range of perception and action, of perception-image and action-image. The sensory interval of affection, by which the subject experiences the movement traversing it, is carved out between perception and action. With the affection-image, the movement experienced, intercepted and extended between perception-image and action-image shifts from the motor to the perceptual: movement stops performing a translation to instead express a transformation, becoming a quality. During this shift from the perception-image to action-image, movement becomes absorbed in affection. All of the categories Deleuze uses to elaborate the relation between Bergson and cinema, all of the sensory categories that constitute the semiotics of cinema, are contained in this formulation.

With the three determinations of perception-image, action-image and affection-image, Deleuze explains how *one* cinematographic image, an immanent singularity, '*a* life' – which is nothing other than this minute subjective interval – is carved out, expands (*gonflent*) and unfolds in the acentred plane of immanence. With this, we bear witness to the cinematographic genesis of the subject. This subject, a fold between images, befits a human or living image as much as an artificial one, a percept of a camera. The operations that select and frame at the level of living matter perform an active and subtractive collecting (*recueil*), not always in the same way, but with the same capacity for framing. The artificial perceptions of our instruments of capture frame, like the biological eye situated at the level of matter itself (*monté à même la matière*). Deleuze also follows the lessons of Bergson and Spinoza in this instance. Consciousness is modal. There is no reason to privilege the human eye as if it were a spiritual seed piercing matter with its psychic ray: the eye is composed of the same substance as the rest of the universe, and the human, a material mode among others, is distinguished neither by its strangeness, its extra-material essence, nor by its divine purity.

In this universe, there is no predominance of spirit over matter, of man over animal, or of the living over the inert. Subjective images are technological, biological or human, and do not include any differences of essence, only differences of modes, bodies or organisations of parts. But whether we are dealing with a technological image or a living image, the eye of the camera or that of the living human operating the cut unfolds, in a sensorial manner, a sensitive arc among the images that constitute the rest of the world. In all of these cases, the difference between subjective images and the non-sensory images has to do with framing: in the case of the subjective image, all of the *other* images are referred to this centre of reference; in the case of inert matter, this framing does not take place because no centre is proposed as an instance of cutting and selection. The only real difference between images hinges upon the operation of framing by which certain images are selected amidst other images by subtractive perception. The subject is indeed a centre of reference, but this centre is a centre of indetermination, one that is provisional and fluctuating and in no way a transcendent nucleus.

Thus the table of categories turns out to be a table of montage, because thought enacts its corporeal situation. This allows us to define subjectivity in a perfectly immanent way. Philosophy derived this definition, one that radically transforms thought, from cinema.

CINEMATOGRAPHIC MONTAGE

Only cinema could give this vision to philosophy. The experience of cinema was necessary to open access to the acentred production of subjectivity because, when we consider the problem of the image on the scale of the human, we begin with perception rather than deducing it. Our thought, embedded in our bodies, gives us the immediate security of the human experience, and we thereby assume an already-constituted subjectivity as our point of departure. Cinema, the last born of the arts, in its machinic actuality – with its technological prowess but also its lowly status as an industrial curiosity or side-show attraction – was not directly in commerce with the great Ideas of culture. Cinema offered its animated shadows, its slapstick, and its naïve plots with a perceptual signaletics still unequalled in the art world. It allowed us to feel a technical convulsive jolt and a perceptive shimmering (*une lueur perceptive*) vibrating in foreign matter. Cinema presents a theatre of shadows on the material plane of the screen, a shimmering that cannot be absorbed in the consciousness of the cameraman or of the spectator because it is spread out indiscriminately on the screen, bathing faces in its watery light.

Given its status as a minor art and its burlesque productions, cinema introduced the following fact into the consciousness of the twentieth century: between the perception of consciousness and the reality of matter, many intermediary stages become illuminated, many stages of perception develop and become sensible. The perception of the camera gives us access to such stages, as do the percepts of videos, digital pulses, acoustic echoes, telescopic waves, or any other aspirator of visibilities that sweeps through our universe and produces images that are completely perceptual, deprived of bodies. Cinema, as an artistic technique, furnishes thought with a mode of perception that is non-human but nevertheless perfectly operative, and which is also capable of provoking our deepest emotional response. Cinema projects us onto the plane of matter and allows us to deduce the existence of images that are, if not acentred, at least weakly centred or clearly extra-human: water dripping from our hands, clouds racing across the sky, a beauty mark. In sum, cinema allows us to experiment in the acentred plane of immanence, no longer restricting perception to human intelligence or to animal life separated from matter. Thanks to the experience of machinic framing and of technological perception, cinema put its own capacity for conceptual invention, through framing and montage, at the disposition of philosophical thought. Just as in 1964 Deleuze needed Proust to elucidate the affects of thought, in 1983 he called upon cinema to transform philosophy. The sensorial power of the novelist made possible a more accurate grasp of the affects associated with thought and of the nature of its operation. The perception of cinema makes thought capable of discovering its own responsibility to invent and its framing of the forces of matter. Cinematographic montage consists of nothing else.

What is cinematographic montage if not the composition of a plurality of framings? Of what do all of our perceptions consist? With framing, a *shot* (*plan*) – cinematographic, in this case – is constituted and is restricted by cutting, and the montage consists of the inventive linking of a succession of shots, causing the sequences and shots to vary.

Thus, the shot causes movement to intervene in two aspects: as movement in the ordinary sense, that is, as sensory-motor translation and displacement in space, the action of characters and the movement of the camera. But movement is also introduced much more decisively in another way, one that concerns montage and no longer framing. Each shot affects the totality of the film; each framing makes the whole vary in a state of becoming. Movement does not concern only the relation between parts in space; it also affects the change of a whole that is transformed in duration: it is not only displacement, but becoming. Thus, the displacement of forces gives way to the affect of the image, effecting the transition from the movement-image to the time-image.

This duality of movement – motor displacement, sensory affection – allows us to comprehend the duality between movement-image and time-image, a duality that in reality concerns all movement since movement involves not only the translation of an object in inert space, but also temporal affection, that is, the vibration of qualities in a state of becoming in a whole that is transformed. In reality, any perception already combines these two aspects. A perception – all perceptions – for example, that of your eyes in the process of reading this sentence, consists of a sensorial movement, the displacement of the retina that follows the line on the paper. Any perception includes its individual movement, but something else as well: every perception consists in an individuation of movement.

Perception does not necessarily engage the individual movement of a body, taken between the sensorial and the motor, an individuated unity of matter that bears the sensitive plate (*la plaque sensible*) of a perceptive face. It is necessary to go further and say that all movement already individuates a perception, whether or not there is a body designated to serve as the vector of it. Cinema has shown us that this body can be reduced to a minimum, to the apparatus of an eye, and even, at the limit, to movement itself, which we should describe less as 'individual' (the movement of a defined body) than as 'individuated', or the beginning of an individuation. The frame in itself is such a movement, always implying the affective assumption of a relation with duration, with the transformation or affect of the whole.

The double power of movement is expressed with framing and montage: the displacement of parts in a set and the affect of the whole. Movements – the beginnings of individuations of framings – imply this vibration, this initiation of individuation that we should understand as much on the scale of the cinematographic shot as on the scale of perceptual affect by which we humans explore reality. The stylistic power of cinema, the technological affect of a surveillance camera, or the vision of an animal's eye:

all raise the same problem. The affective expression of framing is not an anthropomorphic theory that is exclusive and applicable only to humans or to living beings to the exclusion of the technological and the material. In reality, it becomes applicable as soon as a framing is initiated, as soon as an image is enlarged on a screen. A sensory-motor arc draws a curve, one that individuates and thus reflects its sensitive surface between the perceived movement and the executed movement: the temporal affect of its force as an image.

THE ACTUALITY OF MOVEMENT,
THE POWER OF TIME

This is how we should understand the shift from *The Movement-Image* to *The Time-Image*. Everything is given with *one* framed image, which unfolds starting with the plane of acentred images. Such subjective images – cinematographic or living – require only a gap, a fan tapering to a point (*cet éventail en pointe*) that separates actions and reactions, and which prevents them from vanishing instantly, one inside the other. Instead of actions immediately becoming dissipated in reactions, an action that has been slowed down by the vibrating interval of a sensibility is reflected in a movement experienced, and reverberates in perception. Between the sensitive surface of a movement transmitted perceptively and the motor reaction of a corporeal response, the sensory surface of affection develops. This is the critical apparatus of signs, the typology of categories that Deleuze proposes to apply to cinema.

The physics of movement serves as the frame for the inventive cutting of these categories of cinema, which Deleuze considers to be neither closed nor finished, but which he offers as a toolbox to accompany cinematic pleasure and to enhance our perception. This typology of images, whose elaboration begins with an inventive reading of Bergson, enchants the cinephile: the movement-image, unfolding its range of perception-image, action-image and affection-image, the time-image hollowing out and fracturing the movement-image at its core. This material typology of the image simultaneously provides a theory of the constitution of the subject and a material semiotics of cinema, as well as making its critical resources accessible for filmic analysis.

The divisions of filmic analysis thus correspond to a philosophy of invention and of the creation of thought, concerning the encounter between thought, movement and time. The relation between movement and time is the following: as long as you are preoccupied with the sensory-motor, or as long as cinema is preoccupied with action, individual perception, the affection of characters, and characters and heroes, then the movement-image has individuation as its aim and is interested in narration and in a plot that deploys characters and actualises them in reality. By contrast, when the affection-image makes its power felt and when relations of forces no longer concern a body as a sensory-motor individual, instead actualising their own power – or, to adopt the categories that Deleuze used in 1980, in collaboration with Guattari in *A Thousand Plateaus*, at the point where a haecceity (a body seized as a relation of forces) experiences its latitude (that is, when a force, instead of consisting simply in the actualisation of a movement, experiences its own variation of power) – we shift from the movement-image to the time-image. The screenplay no longer consists of the individuation of a story, placing the hero in a defined situation that he transforms, rather, as in the films of Nicholas Ray, a power dissolves the characters and the action, and the character, enchanted or surprised, becomes the vector of a sensation and no longer serves as the instrument of the transformation of reality. In this way, the movement-image cedes to the time-image.

This shift is of concern not only to the becoming of cinema, defining the succession from the movement-image of pre-war cinema to the neorealist time-image usually associated with post-war cinema. It concerns the vibration between movement and time, which does not orchestrate the succession of two epochs or provide a reason for a stylistic mutation. In reality, the time-image exists from the first indication of movement because it emerges at the point where the sensory-motor arc ruptures. It affects the cinematographic image from the beginnings of cinema. But it only begins to prevail with the desolate framings and the wanderings of characters in the any-space-whatevers of post-war Italian cinema, just as it glimmers, in Ozu's films, in the interval between a bowl and a bottle in equilibrium on a table, or in the pure framing of a window isolating a factory chimney. There is nothing historical about the tension between these two kinds of images: rather, they concern gestures (*amorces*) and directions orienting the stylistic description. The contemporaneity of these two images demonstrates how, in Deleuze's thought, actual movement and virtual becoming – the constituted, solid, individuated individual and the gaseous, dreaming, vaporous subject – are implicated with each other.

In effect, for Deleuze, individuation and subjectivity are not the same. The sensory-motor arc individuates in an organised body assuming form, becoming defined, structuring its provisional identity, becoming actualised. But any actuality is surrounded by a virtual cloud of intensity, which involves the becoming of forces, the dissolution of forms, transformations that agitate structures and trouble constituted organisations. The virtual troubles the actual and revives it. The time-image is created with the rupture of the sensory-motor arc, in the layer of affection (*flaque d'affection*) that signals the sensitive zone of the individuated arc. The movement of displacement is transformed into expression and action is transformed into quality. The rupturing of the sensory-motor arc permits the time-image to appear. At this point, we exit the regime of the individual and of individuation, that of the actual and of the movement-image. We enter the informal and intense zone of a subjectivity that surpasses any personal individuation and that undoes any constituted form. For Deleuze, the virtual vibrates within the actual. From his early encounter with Proust, Deleuze has always thought of art as that which allows us to experience a bit of time in a pure state. The virtual pulsates beneath the actual, and philosophy – creative thought – seeks to theorise becoming. Thought is effectively defined as an encounter, an intense collision with an image upon which we cannot act, but that asserts itself as affection. Thought becomes creative through the penetrative violence of the sign. This is how thought creates the new and how it transforms the table of categories into a table of montage.

PART III: SCHIZOANALYSIS: TERRITORY, ECOLOGY AND THE RITORNELLO

7. Ritornellos of Time

Ritornello: the four syllables of this naïve, infantile word evoke the repetitive games, songs, dances and nursery rhymes of our childhoods. Even though the ritornello finds its origin in sophisticated music, it always threatens to devolve into tedious and sclerotic song. Guattari uses this term to approach the problem of time from a truly singular perspective, that of repetition, but repetition considered in the striking terms of the individuation of living beings, beings that territorialise in temporalising. The ritornello unleashes spatiotemporal rhythm and measure in an aesthetic and sensory mode, as habit, habitation and habituation.

We approach the question of time through this singular and vital vector of temporalisation, of an individuation that assumes consistency and subjectivates in configuring its milieu. It is a time that is ecological, referring to sensory beings: it is not a time of existence or an encompassing, cosmological time. From the start, the ritornello is pluralised and foliated, neither homogeneous nor unitary. It puts us in the most concrete of situations, that of rhythmic time (*temps battu*), pluralised by the discordant set of diverse rhythms by which we configure ourselves. The church bell, the factory siren, the clock of the town hall or station: all 'beat' diverse kinds of time, just as much as our circadian rhythms, the rhythm of our days and nights. Is it necessary to unify these diverse kinds of time according to a homogeneous unit of measure? In choosing the term 'ritornello', Guattari vigorously resists this obligation.

The ritornello does not concern the status of abstract time, but rather the diverse, rhythmic modes of temporalisation. It does not concern the goal of isolating the transhistorical dimension of time in general, but rather of capturing it in the place where it is modalised by one or several ritornellos. Referring to the 'basic rhythms of temporalization – what I call ritornellos' (MU 108), Guattari warns us that 'time is not sustained by humans as something that is imposed from the outside. There is no interaction between time "in general" and man "in general"' (MU 107, with modification).

There is nothing one-dimensional about time. Time is neither bound to the trajectory of the earth, the ecological rhythm of the planet in its orbit around the sun, nor to the time of uni-linear consciousness, the vector of an interiority that it unifies and extends. Just as what is at stake is not time 'in general' (that is, the concept of time), comforted by the twin fiction of 'man in general', this time is not lived, isolated in the bound state of a subjectivity given in advance. This is not the time of memory, of a consciousness strained by the intrusion of the future and the persistence of the past. Nor is it situated within a cosmological frame that refers the rhythm of days, months, seasons and years to the movements and regular periodicity of the stars: a mobile image of eternity. Since Guattari is not pursuing time in general, cosmological time does not provide a unifying frame for all of our moments, an objective cycle of eternal return of the same that would measure our durations (*durées*). Cosmological time itself represents the local ritornello of the planet Earth in terms of its spatial trajectory, an ecological vessel of the individuation of terrestrials, one that is otherwise extremely local in the context of the universe. Neither objective, cosmological time, nor a time of consciousness 'in general', ritornellos express time less as it is lived (*vécu*) than as it is inhabited (*habité*), as bundles of sensory signs by which we extract a territory from surrounding milieus through consolidation and habit. For habit very much concerns the temporal milieu in the form of repetition, but valorises the attainment of consistency as well as the crisis by which we attain consistency when we interiorise time as a power of transformation, by stabilising it as a milieu and as a habitation.

TRA LA LA

The ritornello gets its start in the simplest of ways, with the little song a child sings in the dark. In this instance, time is approached not only from the psychic point of view of its actualisation, but also from that of its habituation, by a small, mutating zone (*foyer*) of subjectivation seeking to affirm its consistency in duration by modulating its entrance into a 'time . . . "beaten" by concrete assemblages of semiotization': 'A child singing in the night because it is afraid of the dark seeks to regain control of events that deterritorialised too quickly for her liking and started to proliferate on the side of the cosmos and the Imaginary' (MU 107). The fact that this example concerns a child brings with it a whole set of problems: rhythms of reassurance to conjure away fear and the precarious consolidation of an identity; genetic rhythms of psychic development, play and learning, wherein repetition is affirmed as a mode of constitution of the self; and socialised and sensory-motor scansion of a musical rhythm, set into variation against a social background. The child who sings in order to gain equilibrium and reassure herself does so in conjunction with a whole assemblage of subjectivation, one that sets the songs she has been taught in operation, even if she whistles a variation. This operation permits her to create a sense of being at 'home' (*chez soi*) that has its beginning in a vocalisation, a socialising motricity. This is not an isolated individual warding off her fear of the dark, although it does concern a child conjugated with the solitariness of the singular (*conjugé au solitaire du singulier*). A young singularity makes an attempt to inhabit her world, and this applies to every first time, every beginning, every new departure. The axis from which Guattari considers repetition is that of crisis, rupture and reaction (of milieus to chaos). He views habit from the striking perspective of becoming.

Repetition is crystallised in crisis and is consolidated by mutation. Building on *Difference and Repetition*, Guattari activates the two aspects of habit: a formative repetition that risks petrifying into a mechanism of reproduction, and the precarious, vacillating grasp (*prise*) that attempts to arrange a favourable dwelling place. The play of difference and repetition reveals that repetition itself is, first and foremost, differentiating. A habit is not given once and for all; it is given one time, inscribed as a temporal rupture, before becoming consolidated. In the fashion of the first temporal synthesis, as described by Deleuze, the ritornello function contracts a habit, as a consequence of a change, and then subsists beyond this change, stabilising into a way of being. Contraction – passive synthesis – implies a response to the change that gave it birth, but also a stabilisation, one that can of course harden into a mechanism of reproduction, but that is first instituted by this virtue of response, transformation and change. The two aspects of time, rupture and duration, are linked at the core of repetition, as a cut and new departure consolidated through redundancy in a relative permanence, in a consolidation of coexistence and succession. Guattari approaches the problem of time through becoming, but he changes its frame: instead of investigating time in the order of thought of metaphysics, like Deleuze before their encounter, he approaches it on a plane that is practical, pragmatic, clinical and political, asking how we can change our habits, start the revolution, and transform our ritornellos.

The naïve example of the child struggling against her fear of the dark thus combines, on the same plane, the political critique of capitalist ritornellos and of their mode of reproduction; the clinical psychopathology of automatisms of repetition; the genetic analysis of the formation of the self, of play and of learning; and the ethology of dwellings – including those of animals and even plants. Schizoanalysis encompasses all of these aspects and articulates them in relation to this single question: how do we, as children and militants, birds and fish, psychotics and normopaths, assume consistency? Through the rhythmic game by which we extract a territory from a surrounding milieu, this being the only way we can consist as a centre, one that is not given in advance but is rather made up of ritornellos and is never isolated from the institution in which it shifts into phase (*dans lequel il prend phase*).

Ritornellos function in the orders of genetic psychology, politics and art. The rhythmic game of reassurance, in which music and art play the decisive role in the sensory-motor plane, sustains this uncertain consolidation of the self. Guattari always valorises this aesthetic dimension in terms of its capacity for rupture, and appropriates the power of repetition of play as the becoming, arranging and approaching of new universes, fostering an existential territory. Freud interprets the alternating, rhythmic game of Little Hans, who plays with his spool and cries 'Ooo' when he flings it away and 'Da' when he reels it back, as a conjuring ritornello that supports the absence of the mother and mimics her departure, symbolically filling that which good sense deems to be lacking. Guattari instead proposes to see in this ritornello an action conducted for itself as an affirmation of an individualising response of the child to his surrounding universe. The temporal entrance (breach) of the ritornello engages an entire controversy with psychoanalysis: the substitution of experimentation for fantasmatic interpretation and the substitution of the machine for structure. Little Hans's installation, just like the nursery rhyme chanted in the dark, presents a naïve and complete instance of this controversy.

> A child comforts itself in the dark or claps its hands or invents a way of walking, adapting it to cracks in the sidewalk, or chants 'Fort-Da' (psycho-analysts deal with the Fort-Da very poorly when they treat it as a phonologi-cal opposition or a symbolic component of the language-unconscious, when it is in fact a ritornello). Tra la la. (TP 299)

Instead of referring to the game as a repetition compulsion, as Freud does, one replayed incessantly and intended to deal with the departure of the mother (the pleasure principle tumbling into the abyss of the death drive), or locating in it a phonological scansion of the opposition between two phonemes, 'fort (away)-da (here)', Guattari observes that Freud assumes the role of interpreter, for whom the sound 'Ooo' has the value not of an interjection, but of 'fort', signifying 'away', for the German adult. Here, Freud pinpoints a masochism lodged in the heart of desire, a perplexing death drive obliged to repeat a loss in order to accommodate it. For Lacan, these repetitive games are significant above all in the order of discourse, the insemination of a pre-existing symbolic order to which the child submits while destroying the object (the mother, the spool) in the anticipatory provocation of her departure and return. The real departure assumes a body in the elementary ejaculation, 'Fort! Da!', a disjunction of phonemes by which the child catapults himself out of his miserable cradle into the signifying order by means of the system of discourse.[1] Schizoanalysis refuses to destroy the ludic apparatus of this little desiring machine by fixing it at a maternal-oral stage (an 'internal mini-cinema specialized in child pornography' [MU 9], as Guattari so aptly puts it), or at a linguistic stage, even if it participates in language without being reduced to it. Schizoanalysis promotes neither an eternal return of repetition nor psychic condemnation. As soon as we take the totality of the operation – spool, cradle, a child's nap and the gaze of the observer – into account, we realise that we are dealing with a ritornello that is 'probably happy', a child's game. The erudite mimicry of a Lacan, seduced by philosophy, in which the 'little man' eclipses the real in the symbolic by a tour de force that is specifically human, finds in this example a support for the sophisticated prevalence of death, a drive contrary to life, or an access to the symbol by way of the murder of the thing. The apparatus of such games is not so different from the installation of the bird, *Scenopoeetes dentirostris*, which turns leaves over to expose their pale undersides, vocalises by modulating the audible songs of birds and other species, and displays the coloured feathers at the base of its beak, arranging a total performance. Of course, the installations in the collective ritornellos of the child are not equivalent to the sexual displays of an Australian bird. Nevertheless, the child contrives to become *Scenopoeetes*, composing a scene with ready-mades, a new stage on which he seeks to distinguish himself. '*Fort* is chaosmic submersion: *Da* the mastery of a differentiated complexion' (C 75).

If it is indeed the case that Guattari borrows the term 'ritornello' from Lacan, he also erodes, bit by bit, the status of repetition in psychoanalysis, that of reproduction, and of the phallocratic anthropomorphism of any discourse that thinks a time in general for man in general. The entirety of schizoanalysis is inscribed in this political manoeuvre against the prevalence of the eternal, of a universal that is valid in all times and all places, in both practice and concept, in theory as in the clinic. Lacan uses the term 'ritornello' to name the stereotypies of the impoverished languages of psychotics, characterised by a mechanical (*scandée*), repetitive, stubborn and obsessional agrammaticality. As early as 1956, Guattari began to twist its usage in his clinical practice: in an early text, the ritornello indeed designates the impoverished song (stereotypy, protocol) of the psychotic R.A., but, despite that, it does not in any way act as the stable structure of the psychosis. Rather, it instigates a procedure devised by the analyst to propel the patient out of his torpor. This procedure consists of asking him to deploy all of his resources in recopying Kafka's *The Castle* in order to fight his compulsion with what is hoped will be a more fortifying repetition, but one whose aleatory and unforeseeable effects can only become discernible through a change in the clinical situation (PT 18–22).

Thinking repetition in terms of the ritornello in effect changes the situation. The differentiating return transforms the circuit of return into a departure from the self, a deterritorialisation. That a sense of self only emerges in this gap also changes the analytic clinic, the role of the therapist, and the status of the symptom, just as the way we conceive of identity, of the subject, of genesis, of time and of truth, overturns the theoretical apparatus of the sciences and of philosophy. The vital habit, or its more elaborate cousin, repetition, indeed acts as 'second nature', but this has nothing to do with a transcendent leap into the timeless universe of the symbolic. On the contrary, it concerns the temporal emergence of an initiative, however modest, to assemble forms that are already there, forms perceived to be menacing (or to be completed urgently), routines, or new and more beneficial rituals, even if the ritornello, as a line of flight, may turn into a ritornello of fixation, a line of death. The ritornello does not propel the 'little man', representative of the masculine in general, into the universal symbolic order, but instead traces a hesitant, wandering line, one that is ambulatory and mobile, rather than being exclusively linguistic. This territorial assemblage proves to be at work in the spheres of life (animals, plants), society (Greek nomes, social routines), and the mind, in accordance with the three intertwined aspects of ecology and without exempting the human from nature. It is characterised neither by the primacy of the signifier, either unconscious or linguistic, nor as a domain reserved for a human spirituality parachuted into nature as a theological exception. The fact that the child sings and gesticulates in order to conjure away her fear of the dark exempts this operation from language: although words are involved, they are not decisive. At base, what is crucial is the vocal rhythm, its motor aspect as much as its phonic one. These are highlighted as the crucial aspects of the anecdote in *A Thousand Plateaus*, which Guattari co-wrote with Deleuze a year later:

> A child in the dark, gripped with fear, comforts himself by singing under his breath. He walks and halts to his song. Lost, he takes shelter, or orients himself with his little song as best he can. The song is like a rough sketch of a calming and stabilizing, calm and stable, center in the heart of chaos. Perhaps the child skips as he sings, hastens or slows his pace. But the song itself is already a skip: it jumps from chaos to the beginnings of order in chaos and is in danger of breaking apart at any moment. (TP 311)

In this version, the song plays the principal role: the child 'takes shelter . . . with his little song as best he can'. The song serves as a gestural and motor outline, a dynamic schema, or a portable shelter. This outline traces out, abbreviates and condenses a reassuring centre, one that is not given but prospective, in the fashion of transitional space as Winnicott defines it, or of a line of flight that, for the autistic child, begins on a familiar path and then changes, effaces and overloads it (Deligny).[2] The self never establishes itself in the isolation of the signifier, but rather weaves its spatiotemporal web in a mode that is not ideational (mental), but practical, as an individuation that shifts into phase (*qui prend phase*) with its milieu by transforming it (Simondon). It is the song that creates the centre (and not the child), and this beginning of order marks a leap thanks 'to the song'. This leap does not indicate any opening to transcendence and is not exclusive to humans. Here, we do not enter the mortifying finitude of the Symbolic, but rather, through the viscosity of the song, create a mixture of the incorporeal universe and existential territory, which in turn compose a dwelling. The leap marks the movement from a pre-existing milieu, ultimately perceived to be chaotic or agonising, to territory.

NOW, WE'RE AT HOME

This example contains the three aspects of the ritornello: 'fort', the chaosmic dive; 'da', the mastery of a differenciated complexion, which, in *A Thousand Plateaus*, divides into two interdependent operations. Now we are at home, but 'home' did not exist in advance: it was necessary to constitute it, to trace a circle in order to constitute and institute a fragile, uncertain centre. Now, we open the circle slightly, not toward the side of chaos, but toward the new milieu constituted by the circle. It is not a question of three successive moments, but of three aspects drawn, that is, extracted or abstracted, from this territorialisation. It is not a question of remaining in these two 'nows', of maintenance, of holding on tightly, but rather of taking of a risk: leaving (parrying chaos), leaving (organising a limited space), leaving (propelling oneself outside to make it assume consistency). The procedure of the ritornello, which aims to explain consolidation, is achieved at the end of a cascade of deterritorialisations.

This procedure does not concern an origin, but rather a line, at the end of which a hesitant centre assumes form on condition that one leaves. The home indeed organises an identity, but one that is constructed ecologically, through the installation of a territory, an act of territorialisation. There is a crisis and a response, the organisation of a limited space, the preliminary condition that makes it possible for an uncertain and fragile centre to assume consistency, to progressively sustain an identity. This reflexivity, far from the reflexivity of consciousness or the identificatory jubilation of the mirror stage, is a gap produced though a circuit of displacements where that which will be reflected (the self) is not given as a point of departure. As François Zourabichvili observes, every beginning is a return, but the return already implies a difference and is not a return to the same (the origin) but a pathway (becoming).[3] The self is more of a signification that emerges when the ritornello relation has set down the self and its milieu at the two extremities of its circuit in an act that consists in territorialising oneself. In this instance, the ritornello appears to assume a sense that is more spatial than temporal. This is not surprising since lived time (*temps vécu*) arranges and organises the connected surfaces of coexistence (spatiotemporal simultaneity) and of succession (movements from one space to another, becoming, the transformation of milieus into territory) in a spatiotemporal block in a state of becoming. The leap thus implies the movement from milieu to territory, and this movement is produced semiotically by transforming selected qualities in the social milieu so that they can be reappropriated.

In the version of the story in *The Machinic Unconscious*, Guattari opposed the song to the fear of the dark, seeing it as an attempt by the child to regain 'control' (that dreadful term, as Lacan used to say, referring to apprenticeship in psychoanalysis that grants the analysand permission to assume the status of therapist or enter clinical supervision) over elements that, deterritorialising 'too quickly for her taste', proliferate on the side of the imaginary and the cosmos. This duality between the intimate domain (private fantasy) and the cosmos (surrounding order) no longer has currency: it is not as cosmos, but as chaos that a situation instigates the leap; chaos is not secondary, but rather the initial crisis to which the subject – still unformed, just threatened – responds by constituting himself. The threat is constituting; it is the threat that initiates the process in midst of a kind of crisis. But the child cannot accomplish it himself; it is the ritornello that territorialises him through its constituting process, exactly as Guattari asked his patient, R.A., to immerse himself in the postural choreography of a copy of a Kafka novel, itself routine and repetitious, to deterritorialise through it if he could in order to modify his existential territory by making his fixed ritornellos more flexible. With this asignifying, apparently nonsensical, act – the assignment to literally recopy a given text – Guattari was in fact inviting R.A. to deterritorialise. As in Borges's short story in which a literary classic, *Don Quixote*, is literally rewritten by an unknown contemporary, Pierre Ménard, and is completely transformed, R.A. transforms Kafka's *The Castle* by reproducing it word-for-word in its motor outline, not in imitating the meaning, but through gestures, through the motor routine of recopying the text. The copy neither imitates nor devalues its source, but instead transforms it. In the conclusion to the preface of *Difference and Repetition*, Deleuze observed of Borges's story that 'in this case, the most exact, the most strict repetition has as its correlate the maximum of difference' (DR xxii). All readings proceed in this way. Ritornellos do not begin in a vacuum: they are always ritornellos of ritornellos, a trajectory from one milieu to another. This was already the lesson of institutional psychotherapy.

The song is a vector; it is the song that territorialises the child, not the opposite, just as the copy transforms R.A., as the imitation creates its model, or as the *Scenopoeetes* bird modulates the markings of its milieu. It is a question of becoming, not of imitation or identification. The child comes after the song; she does not incarnate it: she follows it, and it is the song that grabs hold of the first sign of order from chaos. Of course, any ritornello can become hackneyed repetition as soon as it gives in to its tendency toward consolidation. But the rupture that makes ritornellos capable of encountering other possibilities in the milieu and of resonating in being transformed, which allows them to mutate, unleashes new ritornellos that in turn will carry the same risk of petrification. This rupture, this constituting cut, is always waiting, even though it is not always available. But where this rupture is engaged, it becomes available to a semiotic complex that assembles sonorous materials, motor postures, incorporeal universes (the song, going out at night; the parade, attracting a partner), semiotic mixtures specific to the child or to the bird, that encompass every living being in a distinctive way.

The ritornello performs the function of a territorialising, socialising and subjectivising cut, and does so by means of rhythm. The nursery rhyme of the child singing in the dark or the installations of a bird are indicative of the expressive mode of this subjectivising territorialisation, one that is operative once a living being works on (*agence*) expressive materials in order to consolidate his little self (*son petit moi*) as a 'home'.[4] The self is not pre-existent: it assumes form as an ethology of affects in accordance with the concrete ways we inhabit a milieu and transform it into territory. This dwelling is not exclusively human but operates through arrangements of signs, an entire opera of expressive materials, including sounds, colours, smells and other sensible markings, markings extracted from the milieu that are also operative at the level of animals or of life in general. Guattari stopped restricting the domain of signs to the signifying unconscious, to language, and to conscious signification. Rather, he understood semiotics to be rhizomatic, connecting diverse levels of material signals, biological codes and diverse indices to expressive signals that assume different linguistic or conscious forms of signification, but also opening them to an ecological mode involving an ethology of affects, of markings and periods. This is why it is just as productive to envisage this process at the animal level, beyond the added benefit of this having allowed us to dispense with the useless anthropomorphic cut, which assigns the setting into rhythm (*mise en rhythme*), and art as a whole along with it, music in particular, to the spiritual echelons of culture.

This ecology of territory, as a bioaesthetic and political act, encompasses a rhythmology that overturns concepts of rhythm, cadence and measure, as well as the status of politics and art. It also overturns the relation of nature to culture. Chaos, installation, territory: rhythm is understood to be a response of milieus to chaos, but these milieus are not unitary. Chaos becomes rhythm in this in-between space, not by necessity, but in order to create a path that crosses different milieus while simultaneously transcoding them. Rhythm thus exists as soon as there is heterogenesis between milieus, a difference between rhythm and the rhythmed. Rhythm is a phase between two or several milieus, between chaos and territory, and is therefore not patterned on a dogmatic measure. It is a critical rhythm, a rhythm in crisis, one that does not operate in a homogeneous space-time but rather between heterogeneous blocks of spatiotemporal duration. 'It is the difference that is rhythmic, not the repetition, which nevertheless produces it . . .' (TP 314). This conception of rhythm contrasts sharply with all theories of time and music that reduce rhythm to a schema of order, that measure rhythm according to established intervals or a stable structure, or that refer it to an originary, diastole-systole embedded in consciousness or in one's own body. Rhythm also has to do with becoming. It involves the cutting and mutant stabilisation of expressive materials.

These expressive materials are not found in the milieu but are emerging instead, through deterritorialisation: they are mobilised through rhythmic expression (an invention and not a measure) at the postural level, and generate a territorial expressivity (territorial 'signatures') applicable to all of the senses, to modes of sensibility no matter how diverse, and to the worlds that they produce, in the sense in which Uexküll speaks of animal worlds. Territory is defined by this emergence of expressive materials, which define a signature, such that it is the marking that constitutes a territory. These markings are already available; they are not created from whole cloth but rather redefined through a change in their function. Functional qualities become expressive components. They consist of indices borrowed from all milieus (organic products, states of membranes or skins, sources of energy, perception-action condensations), not because of an inherent quality or some property these components possess in themselves, but rather due to the act that deterritorialises them in the process of constituting a territory. For this to occur, it is not sufficient for these materials to be acted upon or reacted to; rather, they must assume a sufficient temporal consistency and spatial range without becoming dissipated as a reaction to internal or external release mechanisms that would determine them, whether these are related to instinct, to acquired behaviours, to hormonal maturation, to learning, or to a coming to consciousness of circumstances, all of which would act as 'good forms', structures that are already given. This transformation of functional qualities into expressive components takes place through the deterritorialisation of qualities, the converter of assemblages. Such an index extracted from the milieu becomes a marker. But what holds the assemblage together is the shift from the functional to the expressive, redefining a component that itself assumes the role of a specialised vector of deterritorialisation.

The possessive is thus revealed to be a consequence of the expressive, a proposition that has very powerful ramifications for politics, modifying conceptions of the proper, appropriation and property. The force of this analysis resounds in political philosophy as well as in aesthetics: if expressive territorialisation occurs by means of markings (qualities that are deterritorialised and taken up in a new assemblage), it is marking that creates the territory, which produces territory as the result of an act. Instead of assuming that what is proper (*du propre*) exists from the beginning – one's own phenomenological body, an anal synthesis of a sense of ownership achieved through toilet training – appropriative conceptions of the ego of identity, of one's own self and space (*du chez-soi*), and of property, all turn out to be the consequence of a marking: a particular signature, a profile of a political community. The expressive comes first and the possessive, which results from it, only has value in historical and determinate semiotics where science proceeds through defining properties or attributes and supports the law that guarantees private property. Such social semiotics single out, usually by way of contrast, only certain individuals as owners – usually those deemed 'normal' as distinguished from the psychotics, the autists, and so forth – or as possessors, by contrast with the day labourers, proletarians, illegal immigrants or aborigines. A political philosophy that requires a legal right to property depends upon a psychological conception of ownership. The ego (*moi*), the subject, the body, or private property all turn out to be the consequence of markings, of excretions that are otherwise rather dirty, signaletic and efficient. In one fell swoop, this transforms private property and the appropriation of the ego (*moi*), of the *cogito*, of one's own body, into a product of a specific semiotic, a specific composition of one's own self and space (*du chez-soi*). Instead of ownership being a point of departure, it becomes a hypothetical form in select modes of ritornellos.

This is why the analysis of ritornellos proceeds in directions that are usually isolated from one another: political analysis of modes of diverse social subjectivations, animal ethology, the schizoanalytic critique of psychological identity, and the change in the status of art. We should understand the aesthetics in question here on the plane of the esthesiology of territorial markings, the pattern of social interactions (the marking of distances), groupings of collective, existential territories that interpenetrate, one encroaching upon the other. Art fulfils a socio-expressive function that is instigated at the margin of a territorialisation – and it is thus relevant on the political plane as much as on the expressive or psychological plane – at the moment it has been established. This does prevent us from valorising what we deem a singular style in relation to the redundancy of stereotypical modes of expression. It all depends upon the scale or the perspective. If the perspective is sufficiently panoramic, territorial modes may appear to be essentially expressive, as, for example, in Marcel Mauss's total social fact, the style of an epoch or civilisation, wherein it is stereotypy that is valued as difference. We can also tighten the focus and zoom in, examining in close up the unusual emergence of a difference at the heart of redundancy, such as that which sets a Proust or a Kafka apart as exceptions from the average production of their era, or even selecting a certain fragment from their production as an exemplary success. In fact, it all depends on whether we value repetition from the point of view of redundancy, or from that of the singular cut. That boundary, that vibration, by which they pass from one to the other is what we call style.

The spatiotemporal bioaesthetics of ritornellos thus allows us to think about time in capitalistic ritornellos as standardisation (cadence), but also in terms of an extreme isolation of social biotopes. The social character of sensibility, in which time is not given 'in general', as an *a priori*, but is rather worked over by ritornellos of appropriation, allows us to enter political philosophy not from the angle of grand (historical) structures or forms of social models (fractures between industrial societies and societies said to be primitive), but rather by thinking through the ecology of the modes of dwellings by which we knit space and time together. This is not achieved abstractly, but through markings, buildings and pathways, through clothing and tattoos, or through a bird's calls and caws, all of these groupings becoming composed through interference, without being measured by a unitary rhythm.

Ritornellos thus propose a new model of consistency in which consolidation takes place through becoming settled, in the sense that in cooking or chemistry a mixture is said to settle. Such a conception makes it impossible for consolidation to be seen to operate in a linear fashion with a starting point, an inherent particularity (*un propre*), or a degree zero: mixtures are always implicated between differential levels, overlapping habits, and disparate rhythms not unified by a single measure. The isolation of ritornellos can only be achieved through abstraction-extraction, whereas they are in fact enmeshed – and are neither unitary nor homogeneous – in our bodies, our modes of dwelling and our rituals. They involve a provisional assumption of consistency, not an abstract beginning; an arrangement of intervals in which holes count as much as filled-in spaces; a superposition of disparate rhythms without the imposition of a cadence. Here too it is not a question of imposing a (good) form upon matter, but rather of elaborating consistencies whose densities neither pre-exist nor are referred to an eternal return, but rather fleetingly set up the operative and operational form of a style, of a signature that is itself spatiotemporal, singular and dated: a change, in history.

NOTES

1. 'For his action destroys the object that it causes to appear and disappear by *bringing about* its absence and presence in advance. His action thus negativises the force field of desire in order to become its own object to itself. And this object, being immediately embodied in the symbolic pair of two elementary exclamations, announces the subject's diachronic integration of the dichotomy of phonemes, whose synchronic structure the existing language offers up for him to assimilate' (Lacan, 'The Function and Field of Speech and Language in Psychoanalysis', *Écrits*, 262).
2. See Chapter 10 for an extended discussion of the work of Fernand Deligny. Translator's note.
3. Zourabichvili, *Le vocabulaire de Deleuze*, 75.
4. See Sauvagnargues, *Deleuze and Art*, and 'De l'animal a l'art', in *Philosophie de Deleuze*.

8. Guattari: A Schizoanalytic Knight on a Political Chessboard

Throughout his life, Félix Guattari worked to eradicate the identification of subjectivity with personal identity and to replace the classical subject, conceived of as a closed, personal monad, with collective and political modes of subjectivation. He thus proposed to rethink the productions of subjectivity from a clinical angle and to evaluate them as a function of their capacity to promote spaces of freedom. In doing so, he embarked upon a singular, philosophical enterprise, indissociable from the critical practice that he called schizoanalysis.

Of course, he was not the only thinker of the post-war generation to posit a subject that was the result of a social production, of an interpellation: Lacan, Althusser, Deleuze and Foucault all pursued their theoretical work under these auspices. But Guattari worked for the dissolution of any individual conception of the subject in accordance with a political and analytical axis that was not reducible to the principles of Lacan, from whom he clearly took a distance, or even to those of Deleuze, with whom he created a stunning collective work. In reality, Guattari opened up a problematic field with entirely new and singular conceptual operators, which brought into conjunction the contributions of Marx, Sartre and Lacan.

ECOLOGY AND TRANSVERSALITY

The problem Guattari addresses in *Schizoanalytic Cartographies* is how to describe such productions of subjectivity, especially in the case of contemporary capitalistic productions and as a component of the sociopolitical analysis of the present.[1] It is a question of developing the capacity to counter the toxic effects of the dominant system or to ecologically stimulate its beneficial effects. In all cases, we must define subjectivity, an unconscious production for which Guattari reserved the term 'collective assemblage', as plural, heterogeneous and machinic.

The later phase of his work hones in on the problem of the re-singularisation of the productions of subjectivity that we experience without always being able to decode or inflect them correctly. The most urgent task concerns the analysis of active machines of production of subjectivity in our societies. Since the end of the 1970s, we have endured Integrated Global Capitalism (CMI),[2] the last avatar of post-industrial, global capitalism, which increasingly decentres the seats of power of structures productive of goods and services, shifting them to structures that are productive of signs, of control over information (media, advertising, polls), and of subjective codings that Guattari terms 'semiotics' (TE 32).

This ambitious programme entails an entirely new political history of social assemblages, conducted from the point of view of their semiotic codings, which applies as well to previous formations, whether capitalist or not, as to contemporary formations, with their economic, juridical and technico-scientific semiotics that produce specific subjective effects with their own collective equipment (TE 32).[3] Through analysis of the current phase of capitalism, Guattari theorised the cognitive and subjective capital of societies in relation to the Earth, in its factual and singular existence. Human history concerns not an epic of spirit, but rather the adventure of the planet. Following Bateson, Guattari opens thought to ecology, freeing the latter term of its nostalgic connotation of preserving nature to instead initiate, with *The Three Ecologies* (1989), a veritable clinic of culture, an ethics of the Earth capable of reconciling the ecology of social bodies with that of mental states and environmental apparatuses (TE 28).

Guattari's theoretical operations, characterised by this diagnostic function, are veritable *coups de force* that leap and shift from one theoretical domain to another, in the manner a knight on a chessboard. These operations entail a new description of theory as well as new scientific practices that support Guattari's concept of transversality. Guattari developed this concept as early as 1964 as the discursive complement of his therapeutic procedure and to constitute the forefront of his theoretical offensive. Concepts and practices must renounce the discourse of the Master and the universalist ambition embedded in stable, immutable, static doctrines. There are no universal concepts, only theoretical takeovers (*coups de force*) that are a response to practical necessities and that are produced in the interstices of fields of knowledge, on their borderlines and at sites of fracture and renewal.

For Guattari, transversality first and foremost designates a practice, that of a kind of organisation (or group figure) that individuates and becomes organised by avoiding structuring, hierarchical and traditional connections of vertical submission and horizontal conjunction. Guattari opposes transversal, acephalous organisation, which proliferates diagonal connections with the strategic aim of undoing formations of power that so easily betray 'groups and groupuscules', both to the terracing of vertical levels structured along the lines of the command-obey relation, and to the horizontal conjunction of relays of the same order, which also assume the existence of hierarchical levels. Practically, this amounts to undoing formations of power; theoretically, it amounts to invalidating two master concepts: that of sovereign centralisation, justifying the exercise of power in the form of domination, and that of totalisation, a belief that determines the exercise of domination because it presides over the figure of a central, unique, unifying and centralising power. In other words, groups that resist oppression, especially groups on the Left, are not exempt from reintroducing, at the core of their modes of functioning, the very elements of domination they allegedly oppose. From this, Guattari extracts an operative distinction between subjected groups – groups functioning hierarchically – and subject groups – groupuscules experimenting with transversal operations, capable of auto-production in a singular mode by avoiding the mortifying effects of rigid hierarchies (PT 42–5).

Through the analysis of phenomena of power that work through subjected groups, Guattari, in synch with Foucault's analyses in *Discipline and Punish*, refuses the scheme of an auto-centred power exercising its mastery from a centre of domination. For Guattari the concept of transversality, formed through the practice of institutional analysis, is inherently political but practically concerns the political critique of the psychiatric institution, whose ostensible therapeutic vocation is inevitably thwarted by phenomena of practical domination (the institutionalisation of madness), and traversed by theoretical domination (the domination of the universal signifier). That Guattari, taught by Freud, but especially by Lacan, contests the representation of a power-individual, given as a constituted entity, is not at all surprising. We can see how his analytic formation led him to contest the unitary representation of the ego and thus that of the personal subject. But he extracts from this critique of the subject an immediate political consequence: if the critique of individuation is applicable to physical, psychical or collective individuals, it is also applicable to social, biological and material bodies. It contests, therefore, the very principle of centred organisation, and brings the critique of the unity of the ego to a political field in which power is at stake, at the core of theory. The polemic against the personal representation of the subject immediately branches out in the form of a political critique of centred organisations and an epistemological critique combating authoritarian conceptions of theory.

The concept of transversality, a practical concept elaborated to serve as a psychotherapeutic solution, turns out to be a war machine against rational and centred epistemologies. In applying a political critique to the epistemology of rational systems, Guattari contests the unitary, homogeneous and authoritarian model of organisation, and privileges instead a type of system with multiple, acentred connections. The behaviour of these systems – the tendency to privilege margins and hybridisations – bears witness to a new alliance between practice and theory. This is not surprising since the concept of transversality itself is the result of a hybridisation of discourses, of a pragmatic conception of theory as toolbox or *bricolage*. It favours the conjunction between a critique of the theory of the ego (psychoanalysis) and the practices of groups (sociology of power) from a militant perspective whose aim is precisely to deploy concepts at the forefront of an operational offensive. 'It is in this way that we can transmute concepts of different origins: psychoanalytic, philosophical, etc.', not out of a phoney humanist concern to create a panorama of culture, but in support of a guerrilla operation, to figure out how 'to escape when you've been cornered' (PT 42). This is how Guattari posits philosophy, in terms that are simultaneously analytical, political and ethical.

SCHIZOANALYSIS

The 'encounter between the psychoanalyst and the militant' (PT i) in a single person, Guattari, led him to place a direct analysis of the relations between power and desire at the core of a theory of the social.[4] Thought is practical and is provoked by real struggles. Guattari's immersion in a historical milieu is signalled by his use of a political lexicon, including in his research on psychotherapy. His interest in a critique of psychiatry and of asylums was a response to the militant and oppositional demand that fed the explosion of May '68 in which he was an active participant, and which, like a detonator, precipitated his thought from speculation toward real movements, political tensions and the concrete reality of madness in its institutional universe.

Guattari described himself as divided up among 'different places', a Marxist militant of Trotskyist inspiration, a Freudo-Lacanian at work, and a Sartrean in the evening when he theorised. His disparate references bring together the militant praxis of groups on the Left, institutional psychotherapy with Jean Oury at the La Borde clinic,[5] and analysis in the orbit of Lacan, who was his analyst and whose seminars constituted for him, as for a whole generation, a decisive laboratory for theoretical experimentation. At the same time, this heterogeneity cemented the need for the transversality of his procedures.

Engaged with Oury in applying analysis to the treatment of psychotics at the La Borde clinic, within the framework of institutional psychotherapy derived from the work of Tosquelles, Guattari conceived of the unconscious as a desiring machine, in direct contact with the political and historical dimension of the social.[6] This grafting together of psychoanalysis and politics, in accordance with Tosquelles' position – which prescribed walking on one Freudian leg and one Marxist leg – inscribed Guattari within concurrent attempts to bring together Marx and Freud. But in restoring a historical perspective to the unconscious, Guattari was quickly drawn into a radical critique of psychoanalysis characterised by a double movement of a transformation of analytic practice and an interest in schizophrenia, which opened the way to the invention of schizoanalysis, also developed in the work conducted with Deleuze, from *Anti-Oedipus* to *A Thousand Plateaus*.

Guattari absorbed this dual direction from institutional psychotherapy, which linked the care of patients to the reform of institutions – starting in the first place in asylums – in which they are subjects. Reducing the gap between the private dimension of the Freudian unconscious and the sociopolitical constitution of subjects, institutional psychotherapy acts upon actual institutions by reforming therapeutic structures. Its political dimension opposed it to psychiatry as practised in hospitals – administrative, juridical and medical management of the abnormal within the social body – but also to psychoanalysis, the analytic theory of the processes of the constitution of consciousness through unconscious flows.

We are faced with a Marxist-inspired analysis of the *psyché*. It posits consciousness within the material dimension of social production and historicises the Freudian unconscious, whose economy of the drives must be directly plugged into social assemblages instead of being maintained in a separate sphere as an 'empire within an empire'. It assigns to madness, maladaptation and psychosis a value of experimentation that has political stakes and cultural value: in accordance with Foucault and his analysis of madness as being situated at the border of Reason, the schizophrenic becomes, for Guattari, the operator of a transformation of the socius that reflects back on modes of social subjectivation.

Not only does schizophrenia in its usual sense indicate a pathology of capitalism, it also designates a hyletic process in which any society engages (*que toute société met en forme*). It also becomes necessary to correlate the sociopolitical analysis to a psychoanalysis that has exchanged its reference to a unitary and personal *psyché* for a hyletic flow, which in turn requires a new name: *schizo*-analysis.

Schizophrenia thereby becomes the generic term for diverse processes of subjectivation. This explains why schizoanalysis first engages in a critique of psychoanalysis and of its overly restrictive conception of the unconscious, wrongly reduced to a psychic entity or to a linguistic signifier,[7] even as it is concerned with a political analysis of mechanisms of production of subjectivity, particularly of those under capitalism.[8]

Nevertheless, schizophrenia also continues to designate the suffering schizophrenic Guattari sought to treat. It thus came to mean the maladaptation of a hyletic material to its assumption of form (*mise en forme*) in the social, and in this sense a failure or residual incapacity of another type, that of the catatonic insane person confined to a hospital. Schizophrenia thus functions at two levels: first, as a matrix of the process of subjectivation, it designates the hyletic flux present in any social formation; and second, as a blockage in the process of socialisation, it designates the individual despair of the schizophrenic, resistant to Oedipalisation. But it is necessary to see, and this complicates the analysis, that we cannot maintain the state of the schizophrenic as an individual, pathological given. It indicates the reaction between a state of desire and a state of social status that is conferred upon him by the type of 'care' imposed upon him.

The contemporary schizophrenic is not one by nature. He is rather an unhappy social actor, a defenceless patient who endures 'the alienation which, not the schizophrenic, but the people for whom it's a big deal simply to play cards in the presence of patients find themselves in [because the director of the asylum had instructed them not to do so]' (DI 241), that is, the psychiatric institution as a whole. It is thus necessary to distinguish schizophrenia as a process of desire and as a generic term for hyletic flux, and the committed schizophrenic, the patient produced by the repression of the asylum, 'therapy' and social normalisation.

THE PRIMACY OF PSYCHOSIS: LACAN AND GUATTARI

To comprehend the status of desire in Guattari's thought, to untangle the very particular connection he establishes between the clinic and social critique, and to understand how he manages to transform 'schizophrenia' into a name for a desiring machine irreducible to Oedipal social forms, we must return to the status of psychosis and the decisive influence of Lacan. It is because he was trained by Lacan that Guattari positioned desire on an impersonal plane that was collective from the very start, allowing him to avoid any synthesis between individual desire and social repression (or liberation), such as we find in Marcuse or Reich.

Guattari learned from Lacan that there is no individual desire, that the libido remains an undetermined flow as long as it does not become articulated in relation to a transindividual dimension, even if for Guattari this dimension does not consist of a symbolic signifier, but rather refers to real and variable relations of production for each society. Guattari's thought may thus be characterised as a Lacanian Marxism, which distinguishes it from previous efforts to join psychoanalysis and Marxism, and although he retains the goal of contesting the social order, he categorically refuses the principle of an opposition between the individual and social coding. Desire is not independent of the relation between hyletic flux and desiring machines that are always social; it is always related to the social and does not refer to a private, personal, individual dimension that we can relegate to the realm of the superstructure of mentalities and unconscious representations. If there is desire, it belongs to the regime of production, that is, to the infrastructure, to the material plane of effective relations of social production.

In Guattari's thought, desire is not hyletic flux itself, but, in conformity with Lacan, the assemblage of this flow. Simply put, it is in terms of this assemblage that their positions differ: both agree that desire involves a cutting of the flow, but for Lacan, this takes place in the form of symbolic structuration through inscription of the signifier, while for Guattari, it occurs by means of desiring machines and asignifying and material coding. To comprehend the divergence between the two, and further, to understand how desire does not operate at the level of individual spontaneity, but rather at the level of a machine that 'cuts', we must delve further into the Lacanian theory of psychosis and review its epistemological status and its articulation of desire to the Law, for which Guattari substitutes the social production of desiring machines.

Guattari retained from Lacan's teaching the idea that psychosis is not a deficiency, but rather a process that is perfectly independent of neurotic repression, and even more suitable than the latter for providing information about the unconscious syntheses that constitute the subject. Psychosis functioned as the problematic field in which Lacan situated his 'return to Freud' as a 'beyond Freud' based on the two following points: the signifying assemblage as a symbolic order and the place of the father as a master signifier, the Other that founds the symbolic order. Guattari paid close attention to this theoretical position, but displaced and critiqued it in turn.

Without doubt, Lacan also contributed to disengaging modes of production of subjectivity from any reference to an act of individual consciousness. In articulating the Freudian unconscious to the findings of linguistics in order to accentuate the rhetorical character of the primary process, Lacan disentangled the symbolic plane from any subjective intentionality. The unconscious symptom, the entire unconscious, must be considered to be 'structured like a language',[9] which does not mean that Lacan applied linguistic analyses to the rhetoric of the unconscious, but on the contrary, that the distinction between the signifier and the signified in Saussure, or the theory of shifters in Jesperson and Jakobson, can only become effective starting with the unconscious, which is constitutive of the differences of language as well as of the structuration of the subject.[10]

Lacan thus appropriated the Saussurean analysis of the signifier and the signified, as well as its adaptation by Lévi-Strauss:[11] the signified is a continuous, amorphous flow that can only make sense from the moment it is cut by a signifier, which confers upon it its binary coupling term for term with related signifiers to which the chain of signifieds begins to correspond. The master signifier cuts the amorphous mass of floating signifieds, and constitutes them in their position as signified, becoming 'the point around which all concrete analysis of discourse must operate'.[12] Lacan calls this the quilting point (*point de capiton*) in reference to Plato's comparison of discourse to cloth, but which is no longer produced through weaving (braiding of threads, continuous weaving) but through upholstering, an activity that gathers together a continuous fabric by means of an external pin or fastener, and violently and extrinsically imposes a topological structure upon it that twists it into a fold of a determinate subjectivation.

This signifier-quilting point exceeds the domain of linguistic reference: non-linguistic, extra-propositional and psychic, it is from the quilting point that the floating lines of signifieds and symbolic signifiers, among which figure other linguistic signs, can become articulated. Lacan names this the master signifier, the phallus, or the Name of the Father.

Guattari takes up the quilting point, but decisively transforms it by collapsing the ordered chain of signifiers and signifieds, refusing the authoritarian cut of the master signifier, for which he substitutes, with a dash of humour, the transversal minority of the desiring machine, which also cuts the flows, but which does not function in the signifying order of the symbolic or of discourse. Hence the opposition between structural, signifying semiologies and machinic, asignifying semiotics: term for term, Guattari opposes the machine, in the social order of production, for structure, in the symbolic order of significance. In short, Guattari operates with Lacan just as Marx did with Hegel: he puts Lacanian theory back on its feet by reversing it from logic to the Real.

The decisive point of Lacanian theory concerns this redoubling of the signifier, appearing once in the chain of relative signifiers, and once as the big O signifier. Here is the second point at which Lacan's return to Freud constituted a transformation of Freudian theory. Lacan slanted Freud in favour of a preponderance of the paternal function, the guarantor of sexual difference, the bearer of the phallus. The phallus is not anatomical but signifying. In short, Lacan transposes the second Freudian topography (id, ego, superego) – too anatomical for his taste because it posits already-totalised objects – onto a structural grid that allows him to transform parental points of identification (the superego) into signifying tensors – logical and topological sites – that converge on the site of the phallus. This is the great Freudian heritage that his followers have covered up, according to Lacan, because they remained focused on the object relation when they weren't busy transforming analysis into an exercise in the adaptation of the ego. For Lacan, what matters is avoiding the object relation that privileges the imaginary position of the fantasm and finds its axis in the mother-child relation. Only the phallic function permits this. These analyses of the paternal function, the redoubling of the signifier, accompanied by the absolute transcendence of the master signifier, are made possible by psychosis and imply at the same time the relativity of the Oedipus complex, now revealed to be applicable only to neurosis.

The analysis of psychosis reveals the quilting point. In other words, more neatly than neurosis, psychosis indicates the structuring power of a signifier irreducible to the order of discourse, but it does so negatively. Psychosis is the structure wherein there has been a failure to introduce a signifier. The remarkable feature of psychosis is that the structuration of the signifier has not played its role. What indicates psychotic foreclosure is that the quilting point has been eluded or missed. The Oedipus complex affects the imaginary, signifying structuration of the neurotic and does not concern the psychotic: Lacan's 'return to Freud' proves to go 'beyond Freud', and for this reason Guattari is the successor of Lacan, not Freud.

Guattari derives two major conclusions from this. First, the primacy of the signifier implies the relativity of the Oedipus complex because it is not functional except in the name of a signifying structure, for a subject who has already been articulated by triangulation and submitted to the symbolic order, but not for a subject foreclosed from it. Oedipus is not operative for the psychoses. This in turn indicates a historicity of the Oedipus complex that Guattari applies to the signifier itself. Guattari absorbed from Lacan's teaching the need for a critique of the Oedipus complex, which he performed with Deleuze in *Anti-Oedipus* in 1972.

MARX AGAINST LACAN: THE PRIMACY OF THE SIGNIFIER AND THE PLACE OF THE FATHER AS FIGURES OF SOCIAL DOMINATION

But in pursuing the Lacanian path, Guattari establishes his distance from Lacan and turns to a critique of the signifier itself. The phallus imposes the Law that sustains and animates desire. Lacan only reduced the imaginary complex of individual desire in order to posit the symbolic signifier as the phallus in the order of sexual difference, the symbolic Law in the imaginary order of desire. Oedipus only has purchase in so far as it inscribes the place of the father, which is not that of the man, but that of the master signifier that binds the floating chains of signifiers and signifieds to its structuring lack, and organises desire in relation to the signifying lack of the Law, imposing the symbolic order that the psychotic lacks. Lacan proposed that Freud found the Oedipus complex everywhere because 'the notion of the father, closely related to that of the fear of God, gives him the most palpable element in experience of what I've called the quilting point between the signifier and the signified'.[13]

Like Lacan, Guattari recognised the urgency of critiquing Oedipus, but he approached this critique in a radically different way. Lacan reduces Oedipus to a false step in the symbolic topology of the constitution of the subject, while Guattari understands its reduction as a liberation of desire, which would have been laughable to Lacan if Guattari hadn't also proposed, like Lacan, that there is no such thing as a spontaneity of desire or a desire anterior to its social coding. But the two authors stake out different positions on this coding, as well on the transcendence of the Law, which targets this liberation. This is already indicated by the fact that Lacan oriented his clinic to the treatment of paranoia, while Guattari oriented his toward schizophrenic depersonalisation, characterised by a militant suspicion with regard to the power of the Law. Guattari felt the urgent need to escape the Lacanian position. But he did not limit himself to the Deleuzian critique of the Law as a transcendent invariant and of desire as lack; he understood the Law as a positive structure of social domination, a perspective lacking in Deleuze. It is through Marx and his critique of the law and of rights that Guattari recognised the need to take up the critique of the signifier. From this perspective, the literary analysis of Kafka implies not only a contestation of the Oedipal status of literature – Kafka, like Proust, considered one of the great Oedipalists, who falls back so easily upon the neurotic relation to the Law – but also a refusal of any Oedipalisation of literature or of art. It implies especially a direct confrontation with the transcendent position of the Lacanian Law, and the term 'minor literature' encompasses a critique of the master signifier.

Lacan thus plays an important role in the theory of the desiring machine: he made it possible to think of the object of desire as a 'nonhuman "object," heterogeneous to the person, below the minimum conditions of identity, escaping the intersubjective coordinates as well as the world of meanings' (AO 360). The second pole, that of the Other signifier, contributes to the theory of the desiring machine, which directly takes up the function of cutting and coding flows as operations *constituting* desire. But the Other signifier must be subjected to the same critique as that applied to Oedipal structuration; its socio-cultural attraction is comparable to that which allowed Lacan to mock Oedipus.[14] It must thus be subjected to the same materialist and political examination instead of being positioned as an expression of culture. Lacan seemed well disposed to an approach that put the unconscious in relation with history and politics, but he did not pursue it.[15]

Guattari's critique of Lacan thus proceeds by way of a Marxist analysis. The signifier itself is also historical; it has not been given for all time to human constitution. Lacan is indeed correct to deal with the Oedipus complex as an Imaginary myth, and he does not hesitate to destroy the pretensions of fantasy in favour of (collective) symbolic structure. But in introducing the phallus as an ahistorical master signifier, he did not see that he was constructing an even more destructive myth, the efficacity of the phallus installing in every subject the existence of a complex analog, fabulated no longer upon parental figures (to marry Jocasta, to kill Laius – to read Sophocles) but upon castration, the anguish of being produced as a socially sexed being who inscribes desire within the Law: there is no transcendent phallus without the agony of castration. Guattari deals with the agony of castration as a complex comparable to that of the Oedipus complex. Once the reduction of the phallus to the castration complex has been accomplished, the critique that was applicable to the Oedipus complex as imaginary identifier must also apply to the castration complex, and Lacan did not follow his analysis through to its conclusion.

Second, the signifier now assumes, according to Guattari, a determinate historical inscription: it refers to despotic social formations, and its very historicity invalidates Freudian analysis, which is not applicable to a universal psyche, but only to the specific social formation of *fin de siècle* Austria. Once Guattari reduced Oedipus to the literate fantasy of the Viennese bourgeoisie, it was not difficult to pursue the analysis and invalidate the master signifier as an even more archaic structure of domination. It is henceforth its role as a marker of power – a consideration completely absent in Lacan – that will polarise all of the critiques. The Lacanian determination of psychosis as foreclosure not only functioned to reveal the insufficiencies of Oedipal psychoanalysis; it also condemned the primacy of the letter and the Law that theoretically define foreclosure, most notably its use in interpretation. It led Guattari to separate himself once and for all from psychoanalysis (AO 90–1).

DESIRING MACHINES AND THE REFUSAL OF FREUDO-MARXISM

Guattari thus operated a double displacement: he opposed the machine of real production to symbolic structure, and distinguished between social realities, productive realities (machines), and products (structures). Next, he defined oppressive structures and assigned an 'anti-productive' value to the results produced. The libidinal reality of desire permitted it to be classed among productive forces, while the family – as a social form historically linked to property – is not only an anti-productive residue, but is also a structure defined as oppressive: it is not content to give shape to desire, but subjugates it in a form of social domination. Guattari thus transforms psychoanalytic theory using Marx, since structures depend on anti-productive forces of subjugation, and the unconscious on real forces of production. But, at the same time, he opposed the Marxist gospel of a separation between material infrastructures and superstructural representations.

In separating subjectivity and individual existence, Guattari connects Marx to Lacan in a singular way. Subjectivity is not an ideational effect of a structural or signifying kind; it is manufactured, it is machinic. This is the polemical sense of the concept of the machine that Guattari proposed very early, and which he opposed to Lacanian structure, conferring upon it a pragmatic effectivity that is clearly politically engaged, in line with his militant activity. For Guattari, it was never a question of sequestering himself on the intellectual plane. Deleuze attaches 'a particular importance' to this text (*Psychanalyse et transversalité*), which signals the failure of the concept of structure due to its abstract formalism.[16]

In this way, Guattari dissociates the concepts of the individual and of subjectivity. Corporeal individuals undergo modes of social subjectivation such that the body of a material individual is always the site of different modes of subjectivations that are often concurrent, disparate and heterogeneous, but which converge with more or less harmony or inadequacy to produce social individuals. The individual is thus the result of social subjective modes of production. The example of language clearly demonstrates this: all human individuals-subjects socialised by language have submitted to the coding of a language that subsists exterior to individuals; even if it does not exist outside of speakers or outside the set of material apparatuses that code it, the written traces thanks to which it subsists are deprived of living speakers. The individual-subject thus finds himself positioned in relation to unconscious subjective formations as a result or product, but also as a terminal, to use the superb expression Guattari introduced in 1984: if it can justifiably be said that an individual corporeally exists, this individual only functions by means of transindividual programmes that inform it, educate it and govern it, and with which it interacts. It is necessary to conceive of the individual as a terminal. The individual terminal is thus a consumer of subjectivity. We must conceive of the relation between the individual and the unconscious social mode of subjectivity in the following way: the individual is modelled by modes of subjective production. These are not ideational, as the structuralists assume; they may not be reduced to effects of language, of significations, or even of signifiers. They are rather of the order of asignifying material production. 'Subjectivity is manufactured just as energy, electricity, and aluminum are' (MRB 47).

NOTES

1. Guattari, *Schizoanalytic Cartographies*.
2. In French, *Capitalisme Mondial Intégré*. See Guattari and Rolnik, *Molecular Revolution in Brazil*.
3. Deleuze, Guattari and Foucault, 'Chapitre V: Le discours du plan', in *Recherches* 13 (1973): 183–6.
4. Deleuze, 'Trois Problèmes de groupe', Preface, *Psychanalyse et transversalité*.
5. On La Borde, see 'Sur les rapports infirmiers-médecins' (1955) in *Psychanalyse et transversalité*, 7–17; *Molecular Revolution in Brazil*, 135–7; and Oury, Guattari and Tosquelles, *Pratique de l'institutionnel et politique*.
6. It was François Tosquelles who, in the 1940s, having withdrawn to Saint-Alban due to the war and participating in the Resistance, founded institutional psychotherapy. Ten years later, after the somewhat artificial tumult concocted by the experience of the Resistance and of Liberation, Jean Oury moved to La Borde and took up Tosquelles' experiment with a small group of around forty people, including patients. On institutional psychoanalysis, see Oury, Guattari and Tosquelles, *Pratique de l'institutionnel et politique*. On La Borde, see Polack and Sivadon-Sabourin, *La Borde ou la droit à la folie*.
7. Guattari, *Les Années d'hiver, 1980–1985*, 274.
8. It is apt in this context to recall that *Anti-Oedipus* and *A Thousand Plateaus* have as their subtitle, 'Capitalism and Schizophrenia'.
9. Lacan, 'The Function and Field of Speech and Language in Psychoanalysis', *Écrits*, 223.
10. Lacan, 'On a Question Prior to any Possible Treatment of Psychosis', *Écrits*, 479.
11. Lévi-Strauss, *Preface to the Work of Marcel Mauss*.
12. Lacan, *The Seminar of Jacques Lacan, Book III, The Psychoses*, 267.
13. Lacan, *The Seminar of Jacques Lacan, Book III, The Psychoses*, 268.
14. 'Yet the Oedipal show cannot run indefinitely in forms of society that are losing the sense of tragedy to an ever greater extent.' Lacan, 'The Subversion of the Subject and the Dialectic of Desire', *Écrits*, 688.
15. 'I have only been able to briefly mention the cultural history of this signifier, but I have sufficiently indicated to you that it's inseparable from a particular structuration.' Lacan, *Seminar III, The Psychoses*, 267.
16. Deleuze, 'Trois Problèmes de groupe', Preface, *Psychanalyse et transversalité*, xi.

9. Symptoms are Birds Tapping at the Window

Slips of the tongue, bungled actions, and symptoms are like birds that come and tap their beaks on the window. It is not a question of 'interpreting them.' It is a question of situating their trajectory to see whether they are in a position to serve as indicators for new universes of reference that could acquire sufficient consistency to bring about a radical change in the situation. (MRB 328)

With this elegant formulation, Guattari proposes a new theory for addressing the unconscious and the symptom such that they no longer refer to the personal interiority of a subject or even link up to the symbolic order, a theory that treats them, as Deligny does, as the emergent point of a line, a dynamic trajectory that begins to be traced with the tapping of the beak on the window, an air current, a shock wave.[1]

All the elements of this apparatus powerfully – and, as always in Guattari's thought, concretely – condense the means by which he intends to free psychoanalysis from currents he deems reactionary through the cartographic method of schizoanalysis. This formula, contagious in its pedagogical clarity and poetic power, contains a radical critique of personalist and familialist forms of the cure centred on the normalisation of the patient, and condenses at least three principles. First, the nature of the symptom changes, as does the clinic at whose core it functions as an indicator of the psychic state of the patient. When viewed as a rupture, as a crisis that 'assumes' consistency in the present of the analysis, the symptom is inscribed in a critical conception in relation to psychoanalytic processes that understand it as a representative of the work of the drive, that depict it fantasmatically or structure it symbolically. It is these two variants of interpretation, imaginary and symbolic, that Guattari dismisses.

Second, Guattari makes precise use of an image to explain the work of

the unconscious and the way the primary process emerges in consciousness. It is not a question of a metaphor, of a transfer of a proper meaning
to a figurative one that in turn must be translated into a more adequate
formal language, as if Guattari himself was unable to propose a clinical,
scientific formulation. The theoretical image necessarily changes its status
at the same time as the clinical symptom, and can no longer be understood
as a manifest content whose latent content must be restored to it. It is not
a question of an allegorical figure, wherein a concrete image disguises
a proper meaning and demands that we re-establish its formal, literal
meaning, or its symbolic, signifying structure: it is this double model of
interpretation that Guattari's whole enterprise contests, proposing instead
to shift to a kind of experimentation that requires a paradigm that is more
aesthetic than scientific. In this instance, the symptom becomes an event
and assumes meaning in a concrete assemblage, one that opens it to an
experimentation with a future and not exclusively to an interpretation of
the past. Once this has been established, the vocabulary of metaphor can
be preserved, as Guattari does occasionally, on condition that it be understood in terms of metamorphosis, a displacement that produces at the same
time a prospective reconfiguration of the sense produced by the symptom.
But for political reasons this transformation of the status of interpretation
necessarily calls for a new, engaged clinical practice.

For, third, Guattari indeed aims to reform the relations between the
clinical and the political, opening psychoanalysis to schizoanalysis, to reinforce it and thereby transform it into a component of the social order. At
the same time, this indicates his militant confidence in analytic, therapeutic
practice, for which his engagement at La Borde provides sufficient evidence.
It nevertheless seemed urgent to him to put the analysis of unconscious and
therapeutic practice on new foundations through a critique of psychoanalysis that is simultaneously clinical and political. This is demonstrated by the
use he makes of a poetic image to transform the theory of the symptom.

SYMPTOMS

The bird tapping at the window draws attention to itself behind the glass, a
plane of separation but also a surface of appearances between the analysand
and analyst, a membrane of contact and two-way mirror. Like any other sign,
a symptom becomes individuated through its enigmatic effect: it becomes
actualised, drawing attention to itself by means of an asignifying rupture,
because it has no signification determined in advance, and because it does
not refer to a latent content that it supposedly manifests. Analysis does not
consist of substantialising these birds, of naming them, or of capturing or
opening them up to see what they contain, like soothsayers who predict the

future by reading entrails. Here, the bird plays the role of a random figure (*un figurant quelconque*) of the symptom and does not in itself have any signification. It is thus not necessary to focus the analysis on the bird, for it only assumes meaning as a function on its plane of actualisation, just as a word composed of asignifying elements is only actualised in the sign system of a given language. With this formula, Guattari distanced himself equally from a Lacanian position that would refer the symptom to the symbolic system that structures the unconscious 'like a language'.

For Guattari, the unconscious is not structured like a language because it is not possible to impose the model of a unitary, linguistic formalisation upon it, just as, for that matter, it would be unsuitable to impose such a model upon language itself. Guattari does not conceive of language as a closed system, referring only to itself, but in terms of a semiotics always in contact with other, non-linguistic semiotics, whether they be social, political, biological or material: 'languages wander all over the place' (MU 13, with modification), and scientific language is no exception to this rule. The ideal of order and of exhaustive, systematic formalisation is not theoretically operative because it ignores the plurivocity of its object, for language as well as for the unconscious. This ideal answers to a pragmatics of knowledge, a micropolitical strategy of domination and repression, which nevertheless can never be achieved, even in the University or in any 'School' whatever – Freudian or Lacanian – but which is always active when we elevate a single theoretical model and when we enclose theory within abstract universals, cutting it off from pragmatic assemblages. So Guattari does not oppose the existence of a theory of the unconscious, but he does oppose the attempt of a theory to dominate with regard to other attempts at formalisation. He especially resists theory's tendency toward idealising abstraction and toward the refusal to open structure to its concrete historical milieu. 'The structure of the signifier is never completely reducible to a pure mathematical logic; it always has a part that is linked to a diversity of repressive social machines' (RM 231, my translation).

Guattari explains this at the beginning of *The Machinic Unconscious*, a work dedicated entirely to emancipating the practice of the unconscious from the tutelage of linguistic formalisms or topological mathemes: the unconscious should not be considered 'an unconscious of the specialists of the unconscious'; an 'internal mini-cinema specialised in child pornography or the projection of fixed archetypal shots'; 'an unconscious crystallized in the past, congealed in an institutional discourse, but, on the contrary, an unconscious turned towards the future' (MU 9–10, with modification). He proposes a 'machinic' unconscious and not a structural one, an unconscious populated to be sure with images and words, but also with the mechanisms of reproduction of these images and words. This unconscious is thus not representative or expressive, but productive.

Because the unconscious is production, Guattari advises that 'the inventiveness of treatment distance us from scientific paradigms so as to bring us closer to an ethico-aesthetic paradigm' (C 7–8, with modification), oriented toward actual praxes instead of toward regressions in the past. This entails a relinquishing of the dualism conscious/unconscious of Freudian topographies, as well as of all binary oppositions that correlate to Oedipal triangulation and the castration complex. The schizoanalysis that Guattari proposes is no longer centred like *psycho*-analysis on the analysis of a given *psyche*, as if the unconscious was only an individual given that could be known in itself. He conceptualises subjectivity as the unconscious and language in a collective, impersonal mode, such that the unconscious implies multiple heterogeneous strata of subjectivations whose consistency and extension vary, and which cannot be reduced to the authority of a dominant determination according to a univocal causality. This 'schizo' conceptualisation of the unconscious and of analysis neither consists in imitating the schizo, nor in valorising the madman, but in observing that Oedipal familialism, valid only for neurotics, cannot be considered a coding that is universally explanatory in itself.

THE SCHIZO VERSUS OEDIPUS

The schizoanalytic conception of the unconscious entails a critique of the Oedipus complex: it must no longer be considered a natural property of the unconscious, just as the libido is not a private, individual sexuality, coded solely by the family. We must open the unconscious to the entire social field, a move implied by the term 'desiring machine'. At the same time, the Oedipus complex no longer has the status of an unconscious structuration of individual desire, and emerges instead as a determinate social production, the form that it takes when desiring machines are moulded by processes of social normalisation typical of the European bourgeoisie of the end of the nineteenth century and the beginning of the twentieth. Its operativity is limited to this field and cannot unconditionally be exported to different cultures. Most importantly, its effectiveness within this field is a product of social repression and is not in any way a formation of the unconscious. This does not mean that symptoms cannot be found here or there that assume the form of the Oedipus complex, but rather that it is not an invariant of human nature or a universal at work in all cultures. Oedipal triangulation is thus not the ahistorical nature of the unconscious discovered by analysis; it is, to be precise, the socio-historical mould in which interpretation smothers unconscious syntheses. If psychoanalytic interpretation can operate this flattening out of delirious productions onto familial persons, it is also a relay for the process of social normalisation at work in society.

Guattari and Deleuze thus recall that *Anti-Oedipus* marked 'a rupture that occurred by itself' with respect to classical clinical conceptions. Two principles followed from this. First, 'the unconscious isn't a theater but a factory, a productive machine' (N 144); it is not an unconscious that is representative or expressive of an individual libido. Second, 'the unconscious isn't playing around all the time with mummy and daddy' but only with 'some social frame' (N 144).

As early as 1965, Guattari had insisted upon the following: the unconscious does not work on givens that are exclusively familial, but is rather active in the totality of the social field:[2] the castration complex cannot be reduced to an individual locus, and the Oedipus complex demands that the social situation – with its spiralling social signifiers – be taken into account. This constitutes a Marxist critique of psychoanalysis, for Guattari applies Marx's critique of commodity fetishism to the Freudian unconscious: the forms assumed by the unconscious are determined by a social process that is in no way imaginary; the social form of unconscious work is too often mistakenly seen as a property that it possesses naturally. Failing to understand its real operation, the unconscious is thought to be representative or expressive. The Marxist analysis of commodity fetishism is applicable to the work of the unconscious: it is Marx who substitutes the notion of real metamorphosis for that of an expressive metamorphosis in his analysis of the commodity. The commodity form appears to be mysterious only as long as we fail to identify the relations of domination of concrete, social labour that are crystallised within it, just as Oedipal familialism transcribes real complexes of social domination as if they were figures of the Imaginary.[3]

Freud's interpretation of symptoms in terms of private parental figures provides an additional justification for our suspicion that analysis is an institution of social normalisation, which found its footing in the era of development of a bourgeois society that it accompanied and reinforced. The second moment of this critique of psychoanalysis is supported by the critique of psychiatry in *The History of Madness*. Foucault demonstrated that psychiatry, as a normative discipline speaking in the name of Reason, authority and law, in its double relation to the asylum and to the law court, contributed to the rise of the bourgeoisie and inserted itself into a specific social process. The development of psychiatry participates in the development of the bourgeois family and its social policing that assigned madness a place on the margins of justice, binding medical expertise to the elaboration of penal law. Psychoanalysis is inscribed in the extension of this movement and ultimately links madness or psychical trouble to the institution of the bourgeois family in thinking madness in terms of 'endless attacks against the Father', the head of the family exercising his authority over wife and children.[4] This is why Deleuze and Guattari conclude in

Anti-Oedipus that psychoanalysis does not participate in 'an undertaking that will bring about genuine liberation' but instead 'is taking part in the work of bourgeois repression at its most far-reaching level, that is to say, keeping European humanity harnessed to the yoke of daddy-mommy and *making no effort to do away with this problem once and for all*' (AO 50).

Hence the strong critique of psychoanalysis involving two principles that are developed over the course of *Anti-Oedipus*: first, the unconscious is not representation but production; second, it does not code the structures of the private and imaginary family, but instead codes the actuality of social history, which is real and collective. The clinic is thereby opened to politics: from the start, this was the principle of institutional psychoanalysis conducted at La Borde.

The castration complex, to which the Oedipus complex refers, cannot find a satisfactory solution as long as society confers upon it an unconscious role of social regulation and repression, and as long as psychoanalysis functions as the unconscious organ of the normative ideal of social adaptation. Deleuze and Guattari summarise their critique of Oedipus accordingly: 'whether in its domestic or analytic form, the Oedipus complex is basically an apparatus for repressing desiring machines, and in no sense a formation of the unconscious itself' (N 17).

We thus shift from the theatre to the factory: the unconscious does not express itself as a fantasmatic scene onstage, in which the actors in a bourgeois drama (daddy-mommy) give a performance for an audience consisting of the mystified analysand and the knowing therapist. The primary work of the unconscious does not sequester itself in this fictional space, bathed in footlights, emerging as in a dream in the form of imaginary fantasms or real symptoms, the performance delivering its symbolic message, carefully maintained at a distance by the apparatus of the scene, the theatre, the acting – without also taking into account the real, non-fictional character of the theatre as a social apparatus. The unconscious must be thought in terms of the real frame of a factory of social production in which desire is manufactured, given form, and transformed from primary matter (hyletic flow) into a product of consumption. It does not function, therefore, according to a regime of imaginary representation, but instead as real production; it is not expressive but productive, open to the entirety of the social field and not just to familial figures. The destruction of expressive pseudo-forms of the unconscious in turn disqualifies the regime of interpretation in the treatment if statements are cut off from their collective assemblages of enunciation, which are the primary concern of treatment, but also from other assemblages that are simultaneously at work. Connecting the unconscious to the political real entails seeing it as a productive machine, not as a theatrical performance (AO 167).

For his part, Lacan also critiqued the universality of the Oedipus complex by according primacy to the psychoses and by recommending a return to Freud that remains hostile to any centring of analysis on the ego and its adaptation. In effect, Lacan's return to Freud drew the work of the primary process of the unconscious toward a structural operation of a linguistic kind in order to de-psychologise the symptom. He conjugated the Freudian unconscious with the findings of linguistics to extricate a symbolic plane from any individual intentionality: 'it is already quite clear that symptoms can be entirely resolved in an analysis of language, because a symptom is itself structured like a language: a symptom is language from which speech must be delivered'.⁵ Lacan does not adhere to displacement and condensation like Freud, but rather relies on the structural analysis of meaning resulting from the correspondence between signifiers and signifieds, an approach inspired by Saussure and Lévi-Strauss. He takes up this conception of the symbolic, but thinks of the articulation of floating lines of relative signifiers and signifieds in terms of the symbolic introduction of a master signifier, the Other or Name of the Father, which violently introduces the subject to the symbolic order and to structure as a remainder. It is thus the signifying process of language that can no longer be comprehended outside of the imposition of an unconscious symbolic order, a master signifier, the phallus, or the Name of the Father. It is that which separates, and creates, through its act of cutting, the order of significations, including linguistic ones.

Lacan thus orients Freud toward a primacy of the paternal function with his conception of the Signifier, guarantor of difference between the sexes and bearer of the phallus – a phallus that is not anatomical but signifying, a symbolic lock (*verrou*) marking the difference between the sexes, for men as well as for women. From Lacan's teaching, Guattari concludes that a critique of the Oedipus complex is necessary (AO 53; 174–5), and resolutely selects psychosis as the theoretical object capable of clarifying unconscious syntheses: 'In some ways Freud was well aware that his real clinical material, his clinical base, came from psychosis, from the work of Bleuler and Jung. It's always been like that: everything new that's come into psychoanalysis, from Melanie Klein to Lacan, has come from psychosis' (N 15). But, if Guattari absorbed from Lacan the urgency of critiquing Oedipus, he provides a radically different version of this critique.⁶

SCHIZOPHRENIA AND POLITICS

Lacan reduces Oedipus to a false step in the symbolic topology of the constitution of the subject; Guattari understands it as a sociopolitical assemblage that codes desire. For both Lacan and Guattari, in contrast to

Freudo-Marxists like Marcuse or Reich, there is no spontaneity of desire, no desire anterior to its social coding. Nevertheless, the two authors differ on the nature of this coding. Guattari did not limit himself to critiquing the conception of the Law as a transcendent invariant and of desire as lack: he understood the Law to be a positive structure of social domination, a perspective completely lacking in Lacan.

It is thus through Marx and his political critique of the law and of rights as social institutions that we need to resume the critique of the signifier and of the Lacanian symbolic order. It is no longer a question of interpreting, but of experimenting, in accordance with the elegant formula that Guattari and Deleuze articulate in *Kafka*: 'We believe only in a Kafka *politics* that is neither imaginary nor symbolic. We believe only in one or more Kafka *machines* that are neither structure nor fantasm. We only believe in a Kafka *experimentation* that is without interpretation or significance and rests only on tests of experience' (K 7).

This formula, cited and analysed many times in the context of critiques of literary interpretation, must also be considered in its clinical and political dimensions. This reveals how an aesthetic paradigm can turn out to be more effective in exposing the complexity of the unconscious than a scientific paradigm. Neither psychotherapy, with its analysis centred exclusively on the familial scene, the castration complex, or the Oedipus complex, nor symbolic structure, with its despotism of the signifier and its logico-scientific formalism, is sufficient. In addition, abstract formalisations of metalanguages always pragmatically play the role of guaranteeing assemblages of power, and, first and foremost, that 'of its pundits and scribes' (MU 14). Schizoanalysis first turns critique against itself: therapists are necessarily inscribed within the structure of the institutionalisation of care (which Guattari in no way opposes, being himself at La Borde – admittedly an alternative structure), but he advocates great caution with respect to the mechanisms of reproduction of domination that inevitably work through institutions and their actors.

The psychotic delirium thus turns out to be world historical rather than a private mania, as Guattari affirms as early as *Psychanalyse et transversalité*: 'the subject is blown apart to the four corners of the historical universe, . . . he hallucinates history' (PT 156, my translation). In other words, the delirium is not about the Name of the Father, but about all the names of history, and the father only finds himself in the despotic position because of the specific assemblage in which the symbolic is inscribed.[7] This is why Guattari, writing *Anti-Oedipus* with Deleuze, articulates the analysis of schizophrenia in relation to that of capitalism.

This explains the distribution of the concept of schizophrenia in accordance with two thresholds, that of the molecular processes of desire and that of the psychotic collapse of the committed patient, which is ascribable to the molar process, to the mode of capitalist subjectivation. From the molecular angle, schizophrenia in *Anti-Oedipus* designates the process in general, the indeterminate name for flows to which the desiring machines give form, positively defining its active value, while the artificial 'schizo' is only assigned his role of suffering individual, as socially maladapted, from the molar angle of group phenomena, in so far as he succumbs to the reactive affections of capitalist codings. In this context, Artaud the Schizo turns out to be an experimenter in the social: he 'breaks through the wall of the Signifier', but the anomalous, extreme and perilous position that he occupies vis-à-vis social coding allows him to simultaneously denounce the fabrication of the patient in the psychiatric hospital alongside the Oedipalisation of literature, or of subjects in general.

Guattari thus does not oppose the revolutionary flow of desiring processes to the fascism of reactionary investments in a binary fashion, but rather insists on the necessity of the social critique of psychosis, and on the permanent risk it runs of reaching a standstill. 'Schizophrenia is at once the wall, the breaking through this wall, and the failures of this breakthrough' (AO 136). Schizophrenia reveals how desiring machines either submit to or don't submit to modes of unconscious codings and modes of social subjectivation. This is why it signals the process of the coding of desiring machines (the wall), as well as the breaking through accompanied by its possible new codings, but also by their possible failure leading to a catatonic collapse. It thus takes into account social coding where it experiences failures. Like the symptom, art and various social practices have the ability to break through, tracing out lines of flight that do not consist only in eluding a given assemblage, but in constructing an alternative: this, however, does not always succeed and sometimes results in a line that is more unfavourable than the initial wall. The whole difficulty in valorising schizophrenia derives from this double status: it offers an alternative to Oedipalisation as socially adaptive coding and indicates an alternative social production of desire, all the while remaining the name of a psychic disturbance that Guattari dedicated himself to treating at La Borde.

CLINIC

In this way, the symptom, slips of the tongue, bungled actions, or any manifestation of the unconscious need no longer be understood in terms of language, comprehended as symbolic signifiers or analysed as individual fantasies. Guattari enlarges the punctual actualisation of the symptom to encompass the staging of its drama, its trajectory, the tapping of the beak, and the resolution, no longer restricting the tapping to the bird. Dilated in its temporal dimension, the symptom is no longer referred exclusively to the past and instead becomes the instigator of a crisis, of a something = x that can only be grasped in terms of the shockwave that it provokes, beginning with the initial shock, *Kairos*, the decisive instant of actualisation, which unleashes (or not) the turning point of a situation. The symptom should therefore not be translated as a map of the past in accordance with the reductionist modelling of psychoanalysis, but instead be made use of to experiment with becomings, to explore cartographies of a possible future. Schizoanalysis not only takes the beak of contact into account, and the indeterminate and necessarily unknowable bird, but its trajectories and the entirety of its assemblage as well.

The trajectories are not themselves given as an outline, but as a 'wait and see' programme, one that is ludic and conditional – for 'to wait and see' is to be unsure – on condition that they may '*serve as indicators of new universes of reference that could acquire sufficient consistency to bring about a radical change in the situation*' (MRB 328). Analytic work, now a kind of experimentation, comes down on the side of practice and becomes defined as prospective and adventurous, not as a deductive, defined, exact science. All of the components of analysis are thereby transformed.

The first decisive consequence of this is that the symptom assumes a signification that remains in the order of experimentation. Signification will emerge when we are able to observe the kinds of pragmatic changes produced in the situation. It is thus not a question of a given signification, but of an effect of sense that is programmatic, since it is to come, and pragmatic, in that it is in contact with its collective assemblage. It is not a threat to analysis if it is not known where the bird is coming from or where it is going, for in treatment this is always the case. Viewing the symptom as a given essence from which one can exhaustively extract the content by redirecting it toward its supposed origin – whether that origin be traumatic and temporal (the 'origin' of the fantasy) or structural and signifying – refers to imaginary and structural modes of interpretation that Guattari opposes.

It is also not a question of projecting the symptom to a point of resolution in an assumed future (the cure) that would orient it teleologically. It has neither cause nor end. It does not matter if the symptom, a kinetic fragment, does not tell us where it is going and where it came from: for its operative role is not linked to the static terms of its path – departure and arrival – adhering to an obsolete conception of movement that reduces it to its stopping points; it is trajectory, becoming. The symptom is always plural and as such is an assemblage, a kinetic fragment, a point of view that opens the way to a reconfiguration of territory: it is a crossroads.

The second, equally decisive consequence is that no symptom, dream, lapse, or other formation of the unconscious has a sense outside of the assemblage of treatment or any other context in which it appears. Its actualisation always sets a relation to work; it refers to the external cartography of its real actualisation, to the situation in which it emerges and assumes sense, tapping against the window of the distracted, wandering ear of the psychoanalyst. Because it concerns an assumption of pragmatic sense in a defined assemblage, which depends on its pre-individual milieu, we could say that the same symptom will assume different senses in different assemblages. But in reality, there is no 'same' symptom because the symptom does not have in itself an existence outside the shock, the crisis, the enigmatic effect of appearing at the window. Far from being reducible to a signifying capsule indifferent to its context of enunciation, the symptom thus assumes sense as a function of its capacity for reconfiguration, for the production of nodal turning points or vectors of transformation capable of changing the situation. The symptom confronts us with 'a multiplicity of cartographies', those of the analyst as well as those of the analysand, but also those of the family, the different spaces it traverses without an *a priori* formalisation of these spaces being possible or even desirable. Beginning with the initiating, asignifying rupture (the tapping of the beak), it emerges at the crossroads of retrospective and prospective lines. It is the symptom that creates its time, its before and after: 'Analysis is no longer the transferential interpretation of symptoms as a function of a preexisting, latent content, but the invention of new catalytic nuclei capable of bifurcating existence' (C 18).

NOTES

1. For a detailed discussion of Fernand Deligny, see Chapter 10. Translator's note.
2. Guattari, 'La transversalité', *Psychothérapie institutionelle* 1 (1965): 92.
3. Karl Marx, *Capital*, Volume I, Chapters 1 and 4.
4. Foucault, *History of Madness*, 490.
5. Lacan, 'The Function and Field of Speech and Language in Psychoanalysis', *Écrits*, 223.
6. See Chapter 8 for further discussion of Lacan's critique of the Oedipus complex through his theorisation of the psychotic structure. Translator's note.
7. This is a response to Laplanche's *Hölderlin et la question du père*, and to Foucault's 'Le "non" du père'.

10. Deligny: Wandering Lines

In a May 1961 journal entry, Fernand Deligny described the meanderings of a piece of charcoal that he held perched between his fingers. As
he rubbed it across the paper, the shape of a goat appeared, 'tied to her
manger, the flesh of her stomach stretched [*outre de chair distendue*] . . .'[1]
'This line has a long history. If I recounted it, all at once, without interrup-
tion, it would take thousands of pages', he wrote, adding, 'I will not have
lived for nothing' (O 16). This Leibnizian hallucination already condenses
the whole story: the transformation of a hand-drawn, errant line into a
seismograph, a complete *transcript* of an existence, bound together by the
chance encounter, on a rocky plain, between a surprised goat and an artist
(*dessinateur*) as vagabond as his subject.

This proposition does not conceal any will to totalise the real. What
Deligny calls a *transcript*[2] – a bold contraction that turns the line into
the participle of the gesture, the unfolding of an act – is derived from the
network (*réseau*), which does not 'represent' anything, but which has the
value of an undertaking (*tentative*). In this instance, writing is brought to a
transversal relation to language, eating into the tracing (*tracé*), a ridgeline
that divides the symbolic domain of the hand from the motor gesture, simple footprints. The transcription of a tracing involves the improvisation of
a way of writing in which writing reaches its graphic status. Deligny has
produced mixed writings like these all his life, alone or collectively, assembling the apparatus of wandering lines in order to bring the trajectories of
autistic children into visibility: their meanderings and loopings around a
few points of attraction on a communal landscape, points of reference that
only emerge with the orbital repetitions of specific trajectories.

Such tracings do not have any features that would assure us of a unitary
content or establish features of an identity or of a personal profile. Rather,
their lines proliferate into a vertiginous bundle of opportunities, branching
out in all directions, unravelling the fabric of existence into zigzags and

curly-cues, the starting points of a tornado of possibilities. Everything is contained in the *transcript*, in an impersonal mode. Deligny explains this with his customary precision: 'to trace is to act' (*tracer est d'agir*).[3]

Examining what constitutes a line and a network allows us to define Deligny's wandering lines more precisely. Two magnificent books make them available to us, thanks to the initiative of Sandra Alvarez de Toledo, who in 2007 published (under the auspices of her publishing house, given a Delignian name, *L'Arachnéen* [*The Spider*]), a large volume of *Works*, followed in 2008 by a thin collection, *L'Arachnéen*, which summarises Deligny's conception of the network. However dissimilar, the two books go together: the enormous yellow book and the small grey volume. Between the sun-yellow covers of the former, de Toledo has compiled dreams, experiments, turning points, and abrupt movements – the living lines of Deligny's preoccupations. The second volume, scintillating in its sense of actuality, presents a singular, stimulating overview of the network (*réseau*) and of the fabric (*toile*). This two-volume set is remarkable, providing a critical apparatus that anticipates the questions of the everyday reader along with an erudite apparatus to satisfy the specialist.

The experience of reading this scholarly edition is akin to that of turning the pages of a children's book: you skim it in wonderment, turning the pages with your eyes as much as with your fingers. Its onion skin paper trembles with the slightest breath. It has been laid out with meticulous care and inventiveness: writing, painting, and transcriptions of thought in the form of lively notations, barely set down on paper, are all juxtaposed. Deligny's writing wavers, jumping about the page in a distracted arpeggio, frequently running right into an image, drawing, photo, or photogram. Even when the pages are only covered with text, the writing goes its own way; often the lines, due to the strain of effort, warp or collapse under pressure, and the letters that are legible retain the character of words scrawled in chalk on a blackboard, reminding us that Deligny's first job was as a schoolteacher. Above all, the tracings of wandering lines constitute a fascinating, collective work. These tracings, transcribed by adults who superimpose them upon the directionless paths of children, radiate neural maps and ethological paths, thereby opening new pathways to thought.

POLITICAL CLINIC

In Deligny's work and practice, two lines of force converge, reinforcing each other: first, clinical and political action on the side of childhood (and we are tempted to say instead, at the 'underside' [*à l'envers de*] of childhood), including its relation to the institutions, knowledges, and practices that sustain the massive apparatus of ideologies of childhood; and second, a different thread intimately related to the first, the invention of modes of expression that resist analytic or therapeutic practices – as well as poetic and theoretical ones – dominated by language.

Deligny is a man of the network and 'the network only exists in the infinitive' (A 95). This explains his suspicion of and indifference toward the position of the author and preference for collective production (reviews, wandering lines, films, dwellings). In 1981, Deligny clarified his conception of the network, of the *arachnéen*: it is collective and never driven by personal will, even in terms of language.[4] It can eat away at institutions, as occurred early in his career, and always follows transverse lines that resist institutions, as well as incomplete lines that are contingent, emerging in the aleatory mode of an encounter.

The network is endowed with an ecological competence, one that involves selecting elements in the surrounding milieu as a means of devising experiments; for social humans, this involves an engagement with the obligatory or social milieu; for a spider, it might involve the corner of a wall. The network is a kind of resistance woven in response to and disappearing along with a threat. It thus is secondary. 'We should not be too surprised if the obligatory is the necessary support for the unfinished lines of a network' (A 25). Nevertheless, although the network is secondary, it is not necessarily true that it requires a threat, which would turn it into a counter-power, nourished only by that which it contests. Rather, and in this it comes close to Guattari and Deleuze's lines of flight, it introduces play into the surrounding real. In this sense, the network always involves a milieu, and is also always prospective. Any network acts upon existing assemblages and plays with them. The second main characteristic of the network is that it is never of the order of consciousness, will, calculation, or even of unconscious or sexual signification. It is lodged deeper, in the vital and the ethological domains, where experiments endure or fade away depending upon circumstances, chance, or a propitious moment. This is why it must assume form by straddling codes and institutions that already exist.

In this sense, the *arachnéen* has nothing to do with 'the being conscious of being, completely woven of sex and language' (A 24). It is not anthropomorphic. This is why it is difficult to theorise this reserve (*ressource*), which is permanent rather than eternal, precarious in all circumstances because defined by the experiment. The network must necessarily fail. This is one of its most propitious traits and should not be seen as a lack: it is provisional. According to Deligny, we must take into account the full sense of the ambiguity of the term 'completed': a network that is completed becomes institutionalised and dies. Networks are sketches that must remain incomplete because if they are completed, they become institutionalised and end. Or, better yet, they offer a stable support or enveloping milieu to new undertakings, new fabrics being woven or stitched together, taking them upon itself or unravelling them.

RESISTOR

The infinite network is a response: this clarifies Deligny's experiments, which are always collective and are grafted to the irritable tissue of social institutions and increasingly resistant to institutions dealing with children. Deligny inserts himself into the social fabric at the point where justice, education and psychiatry intersect and interfere with and define one another. He intervenes directly at the point where the police, the school and the asylum meet, always with an incisive diagnosis and always with a focus on the same problem: children who fall outside of the normative parameters of childhood.

At the beginning of his career, he held numerous positions within these apparatuses of control, following a trajectory that took him from educational institutions to working with children labelled delinquent, deficient, maladjusted and incurable. He quickly began to operate outside the institution, relying upon increasingly *arachnéen* networks: doubling, mending and openly questioning institutional action, honing in with ever greater precision on the creation of group homes where adults with different livelihoods no longer pretend to care for, reform or transform autistic children, but rather just live with and among them, in their milieu.

Initially a schoolteacher in Paris – on the *rue Brèche aux Loups*! (the wolves' clearing) – and then a special education teacher at the IMP (Institut médico-pédagogique) in Armentières, responsible for children deemed maladjusted and delinquent, he turned down the position of director of the prevention of juvenile delinquency for the North region, offered to him by the Vichy Commisionarship of the Family in 1943. He founded ARSEA, the regional association for the protection of childhood and adolescence of the North. At the time of the Liberation, he became the director of the first Centre of Observation and Triage (COT) of the North, but he conceived of this centre as an open site, recruiting monitors from among the workers, unionists and unemployed of the region, weaving another social network, parallel to the institutional structure, one which wove the existences of adolescents together with those of social workers and families in the region. This project continued for a time but reached a turning point when Deligny, a Communist, neglected to uphold institutions by keeping the strategic position of director, as the Party recommended, and went elsewhere.

He took a divergent path in 1947 by becoming involved with a new kind of organisation, one that was more relaxed, less centralised, associative more than administrative, built upon the dispersed nodes of the youth hostels. With the help of activists involved with popular education movements and youth hostels, Deligny envisioned a network that would assume responsibility for delinquent and emotionally disturbed adolescents. The network would welcome young people, but would also send them away for experimental stays throughout France. These are the principles of the Grande Cordée, an association whose statutes were established in 1948, supported by Henri Wallon and Louis Le Gaillant. It functioned until the early 1960s.

Another turning point occurred in 1965 when Jean Oury and Félix Guattari invited Deligny to La Borde. Despite the obvious affinities between his work and that of institutional analysis, Deligny, neither a psychologist, analyst nor psychiatrist, was not a supporter of the psychoanalytic exploration of the unconscious. He started a small school and a painting and woodworking studio, and although these years were productive – Deligny participated in the writing of the clinic's journal, *La Borde-Éclair*, mimeographed Lacan's seminars, published articles in the first editions of the review *Recherches*, and directed, from conception, to layout, to mimeographing, the first three *Cahiers de la Fgéri* – La Borde did not suit him.[5]

Significantly, in 1966 he met a ten-year-old child diagnosed with severe encephalitis by Professor Duché at the Salpêtrière in Paris. He was confided to Deligny's care by the boy's mother. With this encounter, Deligny achieved a regular rhythm of activity within a restricted community, and then reached yet another turning point.

Beginning in July 1967, Deligny initiated another undertaking around this child, whom he named 'Janmari' to express that 'speaking, he is not', so that this name does not designate him 'in person'. From this point on, Deligny narrowed the focus of his action to

> a small network of rest areas, that is, four or five dwelling places. In these places, there is a persistent presence of children who, lacking language, are not subjects. Here, the breach in all apparatuses of power becomes visible. In the place of the great political cut [between those with power and those without], another appears: the cut between acting and doing (*agir et faire*), between reacting and wanting. (O 1398)

MILITANT

Deligny mercilessly tracked down the well-meaning anthropocentrism of any educational or therapeutic position, all of which ultimately embrace this dictate: 'that they should become like us' (A 196). This position encompassed the critique of the apparatus of power that filters childhood through its sieve, the critique of institutions and of their apparatuses of power, including their facilities, their educators and personnel. He addressed this leitmotif to all well-meaning people who only want to help, or worse, to love: 'Help them; don't love them' (O 207).

He was even more hostile toward the neutrality of knowledges than he was toward devotion: he battled against disciplines that target the child, the pedagogies that bombard the child, that correct him, and that push him toward work and social happiness (Makarenko). He resisted psychologies that submit children to batteries of tests and that classify them according to age, stage of development, or stage of unconscious maturation. His refusal of these knowledges is not due to an irrational valorisation of lived experience or of a Rousseauistic liberty anterior to the social contract. Quite simply, these sciences are not sciences: there is no such thing as 'a' child, one that is closed and unitary whose nature could be known. If such knowledges do nevertheless exist, in effect, it is because they pursue the aims of legitimation and not of knowledge: they reinforce, legitimise and make possible the very existence of educational institutions by fabricating an abstract child, categorised according to age, whose deficiencies and progress can be evaluated. These knowledges pretend to objectify the abstract child that they themselves, in reality, constitute.

With Deligny, 'psychology kicks the bucket', as Pierre-François Moreau observed.[6] His surprising tactics exasperated the guardians of psychology on the right who were ready to shoot him, but he also troubled those whose objectives seemed to be more in line with his, but who remained mired in structures of treatment and of childhood, and who maintained the status of the signifying subject.

This becomes more comprehensible if we keep in mind the two-pronged fight in which he was engaged: first, that against the apparatuses that control (*quadriller*) and correct childhood; and second, that against any psychoanalysis, psychology or mode of care centred on the linguistic subject, a consequence that emerged and developed rationally, albeit very gradually. The great political breach was no longer between the reformers of the left and the social police, but with anyone who ignores the fact that power is lodged in the production of a human speaking subject, a subject *subjected to* a mode of subjectivation that interpellates and constitutes it as a speaking subject and as a willing and autonomous citizen. With his austere and methodical inclinations now running counter to the views of militant reformers, who in his view did not decisively change the traditional ways of training (*dressage*) children, Deligny found himself objectively to be more and more isolated.

Deligny's struggle against the powers that control children diagnosed

the solidarity between progressive forms of knowledge and apparatuses
of repression with remarkable precision: he ultimately opposed the theses
of Communist educators (Freinet, Makarenko), practising psychologists
(Wallon), psychoanalysts (Lacan), and institutional psychotherapy (Oury),
all in the name of the same principle, that these sciences and forms of
knowledge become apparatuses of repression as long as they maintain the
essential aspect of the product of their action: the child, subject of and
subjected to language and to the unconscious signifier. The child that they
promise to liberate, cure or reform is in reality a product of the scholarly,
social, normative institution. To Janmari or other humans who do not lack
language, but are outside of it, these disciplines do not apply.

From this point on, everything is transformed. Alienation results from
desire and language, and from the social straightjacket that transforms
us into speaking beings, or, at the very least, into signifying beings. For
Deligny – ricocheting from 'experiment to experiment', from maladapted
childhood to the solitude of the Cévennes – investigates the outside of language, what remains of the real for those who 'speaking, are not', a saying
he frequently uses to emphasise the degree to which we, speaking beings,
are prisoners of the signifier, of spoken language, of the symbolic, blind to
the alternative networks and full modes of life that may be constructed,
even at the heart of communities based on language and social complicity.
This is the basis of the radicality of his approach, one whose scope is as
much clinical and political as philosophical.

ETHOLOGY OF THE NETWORK

Deligny resolutely dismisses the status we grant to speech or thought as
adorning the real with a layer of intelligibility, a layer that we imagine to be
of another, superior tenor to the real. It is precisely this anthropocentrism
that Deligny combats in his position as a proletarian educator and sounder
of the psyche (*sourcier du psychisme*). But he wages this battle – yet another
aspect of the radicality of his position – without confronting contested
knowledges with another knowledge or renouncing a singular intelligibility, one which he produces on the margins of language, in the poetic and
practical mode of a writing of the trace and of the gesture in his numerous
works, poems and films, a writing that always takes its point of departure
from or within the dispersed sites of life (*lieux de vie*), the concrete, empirical ground 'where the presence of children persists, children who, lacking
language, are not subjects' (O 1398).

For science concerns the subject and speech. Deligny combats this
latent anthropocentrism, a position that, rather than leading him outside
of knowledge, instead requires that he engage the most pressing theses of

his day, those of structural anthropology (Lévi-Strauss), political ethnology (Clastres), psychoanalysis (Lacan) and ethology (Karl von Frisch). He thus proposes a new galaxy of knowledges to study the everyday human who persists or insists in the breaches of the socio-symbolic empire, and explores this by means of the pen and the gesture. He revolts through practice, by maintaining precarious sites of life (*lieux de vies précaires*) and through writing, which granted him the strange position of being a resistant writer – celebrated by Chris Marker in 1947 – one who uses writing to resist language.[7] Deligny pursued the transformation of writing and political action against the well-meaning motives of instruction, of special education, and of the therapy of children falling outside the norm, all at the same time. This combat, even in the milieu of the child who 'speaking, is not', was never solitary, but was conducted collectively. It is a combat against the myth of the autonomous, speaking, willing individual, and this practical combat, engaged on behalf of childhood, led him to develop a thought on the collective, innate human, that is, an ethology of the non-speaking human.

AGAINST THE SYMBOLIC

Deligny affirms a profound Spinozism: we believe that we are the free cause of our actions, which in reality are woven in the continuous web of the real, in the ethology of their milieu.[8] Deligny explains that the problem is that 'the being conscious of being' cannot believe that things 'happen' (*que les choses se fassent*), and 'prefers to believe that he does them in full knowledge of cause and effect' (A 14). Hence the critique of a subjectivity that positions the self as a cause, accompanied by a vigorous calling into question of the personological aspect of language: the pronouns and the nouns, the 'I' or the 'Me', written with capital letters to emphasise the status of the personal subject as an illusion, one who is the cause of his actions, capable of mastery and finality, imposing his conscious plans upon nature and upon other humans. Here, Deligny shares – even while he transforms them – the struggles of a whole generation of thinkers who oppose the primacy of the subject, including Lévi-Strauss, Lacan, Althusser, Foucault, and Deleuze and Guattari. But he formulates the stakes differently, opening up a radical line of fracture.

To the Spinozan motif of the illusion of being free or a cause, Deligny adds (but also transforms) stakes that come from Lacan. Will and desire are effects of language; they sustain the illusion of a sovereign, distinct consciousness (being an author). If consciousness is produced through the play of language, it results, like language itself, from a collective, unconscious structure that inscribes us as speaking subjects. Refusing the dominance of will, of free and autonomous consciousness, steers the critique back to language, and consequently, to the empire of the signifier, of which the symbolic order itself is a product. Lacan demonstrates how linguistic structure depends upon the symbolic that produces the subject as a remainder, such that the subject is nothing other than the result of the imposition of a master signifier. Submission to the master signifier propels us into the linguistic, cultural, symbolic order, an order from which autistic persons and psychotics are foreclosed. In alignment with Guattari, Deligny mounts a political critique against the Lacanian signifier.

The brutal imposition of the symbolic order does not result from a timeless signifier, the anthropological indicator of the human unconscious for all eternity, as Lacan maintained, but rather from a mode of subjectivation (*subjectivation*) that is a mode of social subjection (*assujetissement social*). Henceforth, the status of the signifier changes: it becomes a vector of alienation, an auxiliary of processes of human domination. It is the signifier that must be reduced in order to refuse the right of one person to dominate another. It is thus necessary to apply the political critique formulated by La Boétie to the Lacanian signifier: the entry into the symbolic constitutes 'voluntary servitude' not only because humans fight for their servitude as if for their freedom, as Spinoza said, but more radically, because the entrance into the symbolic produces this servitude, fabricating the illusion of a conscious and personal mode, of an ego that makes modes of social subjectification possible.

Deligny thus does not disagree that the speaking subject can be considered the product of the imposition of the signifier, as Lacan maintained, with the exception that the symbolic is not a universal, indicator of the eternal nature of the human being; rather, the symbolic is a cultural construct. The universal markers on which anthropology is based – such as the prohibition against incest, the identification with the other, the entry into the symbolic – in reality reduce childhood to a stage in the development of the normal human, or the non-European human to a stage in the development of the white man. In opposition to Lévi-Strauss and Lacan, and with the amiable collusion of Clastres, Deleuze, and Guattari, Deligny refuses the portrait of the policed human, an identity card that in reality legitimises processes of domination of non-industrialised humans. The cut thus occurs within the symbolic – the universal human for some, social domestication for others – and it is political.

Deligny also combats the symbolic in the name of a rational issue, one which refers neither to a Rousseauist utopia nor to a Robinson Crusoe-type fantasy embodying the pious wish to escape civilisation, but to an empirical fact that anthropocentric theories are incapable of explaining: the existence of non-speaking humans. Deligny returns obstinately to this fact, his Archimedean anchor, and to the case of Janmari: 'we live in the midst of children who are not children', those for whom 'the behaviour that comes to them does not proceed from any will' (O 1393). Psychiatry has nothing to say about such cases and it is thus not sufficiently theoretical because an empirical fact exists that it does not account for.

These children are not lacking the symbolic; nor are they outside the human. Connected to water and the making of bread, keepers of goats and other companions, they tranquilly bear witness to the fact that humanity is not exclusively linguistic and is not defined in its essence through its cultural inscription in a symbolic order, in which the will is policed and organised language is symbolically mastered. Other modes of life exist that cannot be swept under the rug by deeming them deficient in relation to normed social humans.

THE ARACHNÉEN

Such is the *arachnéen*, whose relation to the vital order is becoming clearer. The human is not separated in essence from the kingdom of other living beings thanks to his speaking mind and his social culture, properties that exist naturally and that mask the *arachnéen* without substituting themselves for it. Other orders exist for the human besides the symbolic; Deligny names them innate, nature, species, common, accepting the risk of appearing to side with instinct or human nature, he who had, on the contrary, just demonstrated the limits of anthropology. In reality, he was seeking points of reference in the realm of ethology, of custom, not in order to cure, but in order to live beside, exploring the immutable *arachnéen*.

If we feel threatened by the assertion that the symbolic is not a unique human order, Deligny observes, it is because 'we have been holding onto a position' (A 46). This position is that of subjectification, in language, the obligation to the sign, our 'cadastral universe under the sign of property' (O 675).

Deligny's powerful, anti-anthropological theory – which he pursues methodically, with means that have nothing to do with a theoretical order centred on the symbolic – follows from this. We can organise the strands of his position in a few principles, which summarise his conception of the *arachnéen*.

First principle: the symbolic is not the universal nature of humans, but a political order of subjectification. 'If the symbol is the sole master, its reign is established to the detriment of the *arachnéen*, which only exists to be silent, to always remain at a distance from the represented' (A 68). Thus the *arachnéen*, the communism of the network, a life raft of experimentation, opens the way to an alternative community, one at the very heart of the

social, where a fragile and obstinate common life develops that serves as
an observation post for this asymbolic life. Here, the autistic child does
not assume the position of the Other (*Autre*), as Deligny observes jokingly,
mocking Lacan, but 'between Others' (*entr'Autres*) (O 844): one among
us. The autistic child should not be absolutised in his difference from
speaking humans according to the figure of the opposition I/you; he is one
between an other, a living being among others, and not centred on the self.
A being of the milieu, between being, the autistic child is not centred on
his ego and thus stands beyond representation. This silent one, apart from
representation, is not acting only on behalf of autistic children, but equally
on behalf of speaking beings, and it is here that Deligny finds his political
inspiration, through a call for a common ethology, always persisting in
the lacuna, the interstices, the cracks in the instituted, and in which the
smallest revolt is reinvigorating. A 'fossil' communism, persisting and not
primitive, anterior, or first, but given, incessant, and 'tough': a communism
of the life raft, which takes on water on all sides but cannot be eradicated
by the social order; a communism of the network, resistant and perpetual;
an ethological communism (A 68–80). Despite his suspicion with regard
to the forms of the Party, such as membership cards, he still claims to be
a member of this Party (A 134), the only one capable in his eyes of leading
the struggle against class domination in capitalist society.[9] Deligny insists
repeatedly: the State, as the government of persons, will only perish when
attention is paid to the person herself, woven of language, sex and will, in
her struggle against the symbolic.

   Second principle: it is not a question of turning the social into a *tabula
rasa*, but of awakening and constantly inciting the *arachnéen* within the grid
of the instituted, whether it is a question of the alienating social institution or
of ordinary social life. If we look at the beginning of his career in Lille and in
the North, Deligny performed his interventions in an institutional fabric that
was irritable and contractile, one that reacts to intruders by first absorbing
them, trying to integrate them, and then expelling them at the end of a variable period of time. But his work never begins at ground zero in the style of
utopianists. It is thus not a question of making a clean sweep of the social, but
rather of contradicting it through gestures that endeavour to materialise on
an existing structure while troubling it. The network is thus involuntary and
exists only in the infinitive, avid for coincidences ('nevertheless it is necessary
that, in the surroundings, there be something' [A 49]).

   A milieu is always a prerequisite; but Deligny encodes it in a new and
creative way, without relying upon constituted structures or having *a priori*
confidence in specialists, instead making use of what he finds, what is available, by chance: thus, the unemployed hanging out on the corner, the wives
of the guards in Armentières, various adults involved in the networks of

the Grande Cordée, and, in the hovels of the Cévennes, adults encountered by chance, sometimes concerned with disabled children, sometimes not. Deligny cuts new configurations in the social tissue, indifferent to positions, diplomas or powers, always remaining on the margins but never outside or hostile to the existing, concrete milieu, with which it may be possible to compose (*composer*). This subtle destabilisation of normed functions can be compared to infiltration or guerrilla tactics, directed against regular State armies: 'I had in mind and in outline a schema of dispersal, guys who succeed in infiltrating themselves into everyday life',[10] evoking a memory of the Resistance; Deligny thereby reveals the arc that runs in France from the Resistance, to the post-war period, to May '68.

Third principle: the *arachnéen* proposes an ethology of the network, which disturbs our usual boundaries. In the first place, the act itself does not count; all that counts is its ethological milieu. Instead of correcting the child, Deligny transforms his conditions of life, indifferent to well-meaning institutional tendencies: his ethological comprehension of the act functions in a mode that is strictly operational. The act thus does not refer back to a person, to his nature or will, or even to an isolated signification, but only becomes individuated in a milieu in which it is 'taken up', and only as a function of this milieu. In accordance with Spinoza, an act is neither good nor evil, but rather favourable or unfavourable, not to the isolated individual, but to his ethos, in the ethical mode of the encounter. Deleuze signals his proximity to Deligny when he writes of Spinoza that ethics consists of 'organizing good encounters, composing actual relations, forming powers, experimenting' (SPP 119).

Consequently, if we transform an act's milieu of insertion, it changes. An act has no sense in itself because it does not exist in an isolated, individual, separated state. This is the source of Deligny's maxim when he was a teacher: 'Protect living beings. If life, for them, consists of stealing, teasing, or destroying, simply seek out direct or indirect complements for these verbs that will make them imperceptibly derive their force from acts that are worthy or useful' (O 139). We need to understand that this is not to change the act itself (by prohibiting or rewarding it), or even to transform the child's will or his act, arriving at the magical transformation of the infraction into a 'worthy or useful' action. The act has no moral or psychological value in itself, and becomes exclusively a function of the ethological milieu, in which it can be made to resonate favourably by transforming a few components of the milieu.

The act is thus sensitive to its milieu, being swept along with its entourage, entirely constituted by its complement, the milieu. The social (or moral) colouring of an act may be modified by transforming its complement. Deligny – in this sense very close to Deleuze and Guattari

– transforms the philosophy of action, and politics, in demonstrating that the act is not the product of a sovereign consciousness. There is neither an act, nor an individual will, but only 'opportunities' and thieves, thieves that dance before the opportunity. If the action functions in the mode of thief-opportunity, it is because it must be understood in terms of the collective mode of the network, which is resolutely non-anthropological and anti-humanist, and refuses to fetishise the will (but cannot be considered dissident either, because this would attribute too much activity to the will). The act is just resistant, obstinate in favouring experiments in spite of existing stratifications.

We need to avoid another misinterpretation, which would be to believe that the network would be 'good' for the child or for society, that it would incite liberty or good will. A few teenagers abruptly reinvigorated before one's very eyes: this would prove the presence of a network. But what project are they concocting? With perfect moral neutrality, Deligny suggests knocking off an old lady for whom one of them had worked. What reinvigorates them is not the perspective of killing the old lady (in accordance with a morality of perversion or vice), but only the possibilities that this act automatically unleashes and with which it shares no essential link, such as alleviating the boredom of the asylum or finding money to go to Dunkirk or Calais to get on a boat. The network is neither good nor bad: it instigates a functioning. If someone had given these teenagers the means to go to Calais, the dissolute crime could have been avoided, but the network would not have been constructed, for in that case the trip, now controlled by the institution, would have become obligatory. The network thus develops on the elastic surface of experiments, where they gain a hold on the real in order to transform the situation in an involuntary mode, one that is not symbolic, but real (A 27).

Fourth principle: it is not a question of eradicating the social to create a space for the *arachnéen*, but rather of perpetually reanimating the aleatory and provisional web of undertakings that persist, extinguished by language. And it would be wrong to conclude that we can consciously promote the *arachnéen* in our societies, because 'consciousness is in no way capable of mending, stitching and repairing the damage which it would be erroneous to believe it had provoked; it provokes it incessantly' (A 82). This is the reason why it was possible to take Deligny for a psychotic visionary, a solitary monk preaching a religion of silence and incest, 'to the point that one of us heard a psychoanalyst say: "But how come you don't go crazy?" It was a mystery to her' (O 972).

Deligny does not combat the enormous privilege of the institution and of language directly, but rather deflects them, just as he does with the rules of cultural orders, whatever form of obedience they entail, instead placing confidence in what he calls an innate nature, which consists of the ethological relations of the milieu.

In defiance of the algebras of language (O 939), he plants himself in things as they are, on the terrestrial globe, in the ecology of the real milieu, in a concrete ethology. The reference to the spider is not fortuitous, for this species becomes for Deligny that being for which 'consciousness of being' is excluded.[11] A confidence, therefore, in nature, since Deligny refuses all Lacanian terminology – in one blow, both consciousness and the unconscious – and he remains indifferent to the spiritual break instituted between culture and nature. Henceforth, the network is vital and terrestrial, and in these terms we can expect as much from the spider, the azote or the tree, as from ourselves.

We cannot interpret a spider's web as a conscious project, any more than the invention of fire or of writing may be considered the result of an individual project or will. This does not prevent us from referring to the will and to language, which we do constantly, but it overturns the status of intentionality: the plan seems to be the goal, while it is only 'the pretext, or to put it another way, an opportunity' (A 27). If the 'being conscious of being' puts all of his hope in will, will kills the network.

> The network is not to be made (*de faire*); it is deprived of any intention (*de tout pour*), and any excess of intention (*excès de pour*) tears it to shreds at the very moment when the excess of the plan is inserted into it. (A 20)

> The slightest desire to make use of the *arachnéen* – for any purpose whatsoever – would make it disappear. (A 33)

Another misinterpretation to avoid: Deligny does not act outside of the social, does not demand any utopia, any outside, beside, or before the social state. He does not valorise disability or autism as more natural or superior human states than ours, and does not extol muteness or solitude. The network is neither outside of nor before the social: it is collective. Hence Deligny's political project and his unwavering support for Communism (though not in its party form) are comprehensible in the mode that, with Guattari, we may term transversal. Deligny writes against bosses and heads, against the Man, which corresponds to the practical and theoretical struggle against centralised, personal, hierarchical organisation. To counter the latter, in theory as in practice, Guattari in 1964 proposed the practical concept of transversality: against vertical hierarchies subordinating the lesser to the greater, against horizontal conjunctions of the same order that also assume the existence of hierarchical levels, Guattari counter-posed the acephalous, transversal network that propagates diagonal connections with the strategic aim of liberating groups from the formations of power of the command-obey type, as well as bodies from the conception of the organism as a centred organisation.

Deligny is in alignment with this struggle, which he terms the *arachnéen*, and which demonstrates the same insistence upon transversal coincidences, the same critique of unity and identity, the same attention to connections and heterogeneity. No doubt his thought exerted an important influence on the conception of the rhizome, and we should think of him when Guattari, with Deleuze, presented its six principles, demonstrating that the rhizome, an ethological principle of connection and heterogeneity, just like the *arachnéen*, is characterised by asignifying cuts and multiplicity.[12] Finally, it is a map and not a tracing, an explicit reference to Deligny's wandering lines and to his practice of experimentation over and against interpretation.

LANGUAGE LYING DOWN/WANDERING LINES

If the symbolic is now no longer the exclusive order of the human or the universal reserve of our nature, language becomes a social phenomenon. Perfectly in synch with Guattari's analyses conducted with Deleuze in *A Thousand Plateaus*, Deligny analyses grammaticality and linguistic communication as an order word (*mot d'ordre*). An apprenticeship in linguistic signs is a matter of social domestication, and the sign, for Deligny, is an indicator of a brutal and obligatory training process. 'Our cadastral universe under the sign of property' (O 675) – the notion of personal ownership, the subject subjected to modes of State domination – is fashioned through the very structure of language, with its personal pronouns, its conjugated forms and its declensions. This political analysis of the constituent social function of language does not imply any demonisation of grammar or advocate taking any refuge in muteness: 'words are not the worst enemy of reality; they create it, and we are creatures of this creation' (A 170).

Here, Deligny places language within a general theory of signs, in which linguistic signs are no longer predominant but rather coexist with nonverbal semiotics. All of his research from this point on focused on this 'nonverbal language'. He did this by a meditation on the proximity between writing and image, and by turning language against itself through poetic expression: in art, whether or not it concerns speech, the effect produced is not signifying or subordinated to linguistics. Hence the clinical and political value of his writings, which he piled in a box, likening them to 'leaves fallen from a tree' (O 148), but which also catch the wind like a kite, 'disparate proposals', as he calls them (O 149):

> If once, having been read, a few of my propositions tremble joyfully in the sky of a few memories, all the better; that is their very *raison d'être*. But the reader who wants to use them or apply them in some way will immediately

see what they are made of: fragments of pages pasted to and dangling from supple and light branches, sprung from the particular kind of enthusiasm that surges each time a child approaches me. Something that has been sawed and felled a thousand times, but whose stump never stops growing shoots. (O 149)

Deligny has his own way of unfolding the sinuous pathways of his thought, which scintillate in an accumulation of words chiselled as close as possible to the real: reading him, we always find ourselves laughing, stupefied, in coming across the clinical picture that he draws of our society: 'a feathered hat that I will never forget, even if I lived fifteen years with the Kanaks'; the centre 'cleaned by a simple current of girls'; 'a centre where "maladjusted children" live should be a little factory of the unexpected' (O 187, 199). This is the way Deligny writes. Short phrases brusquely intertwine with long, harsh ones, hammered with italics and capital letters. His verbs move closer and closer to the infinitive and toward semantic invention: to trace it, to locate it, to swing it, to silence, to 'commune' (*communer*), to 'camera' (*camérer*): these describe our existence better than conjugated verbs, with their turn away from the possessive toward the impersonal infinitive.[13] His writing is marked by swirls of discourse and by the enmeshing of slices of life in the impersonal, for Deligny does not filter out the theoretical argument from the sensible affect, placing on the same plane the door before which the child hesitates on the point of crossing the threshold into his first kindergarten class; or the examination of autistic children's extreme susceptibility to doors; inscribing the story of his enlistment in the military, a faraway policeman holding his hand high to indicate to him that his number has just been called at the lottery for the war; or he himself, a teacher, raising his own hand to teach children to master the number '5', with its small hat and fat stomach. Deligny refuses to neutralise the affective in the theoretical, not caring at all about our codes of scientific respectability, insisting by contrast on writing as he thinks, with his whole experience. This could create the impression that he succumbed to writing pleasant autobiographical notes, he who, on the contrary, practised an impersonal documentation. Rather, Deligny respects the randomness of thought, and its variable anchorage, sometimes in affect, sometimes in discourse, considering equally active an impersonal crystal of lived experience, a philosophical aphorism, or an image. Without devaluing the poetic in relation to the theoretical or by purifying thought of its affective flows, Deligny mixes styles and modes of discourse.

In other words, Deligny does not conceive of his writings as commentaries, but as part of the pursuit of his experiments; his writings are not superimposed on them as a form of intellectual translation, but instead connect to clinical practice in its singular mode. 'Writing is taken up in the doing', it's 'the artillery: it makes possible, it defends, it protects' (O 1095).[14] Writing overturns reality and makes possible new undertakings; it bombards fortifications: art of attack and escape, it shoots its bullets, printed characters, against social fortifications in accordance with a constructive function (to allow, make possible), a mode that is simultaneously defensive and protective: making possible always opens a breach in social defences.

Writing must help. Deligny's writing is thus plural, experimental and theoretical, with its suitcase words, its scansion that approximates speech, its singular slang: he carries language to the margins of the symbolic. We must observe that his undertakings act in a mode that is 'mécreatur': creative in the sense of artistic attempts, with a zest of disbelief directed at given certitudes. In these writings, the autistic child is not 'the representative in person of the human', but a simple 'cleavage', opening a path toward a mode 'which for us is covered in sand' (O 950). The same goes for our words, and Deligny frequently consults the dictionary to reconstitute their wandering lines, because they are choked with meaning, like a seashell with sand after its occupant has left: simple shells, then. If autistic children lack engines to propel them into the symbolic, their example helps us recharge language with affect and sensibility:

> And you borrow my word *wander* which I happened to find lying around, on some beach of my memory, the wave of language having deposited it there. But what you need to understand is that, when I gather a word shell, it is because it is empty. If I say it is rich, it is because it is richly adorned, as sometimes happens to be the case with shells. If you put the shell to your ear, a thousand and one meanings start jumping around, with which the nearby language supplies itself. (O 974)

We thus need to understand wandering lines in this sense: to 'trace', we need a little 'free time' (*temps de séjour*) (O 949), a topos to rival the ancient, mythological entities dear to experts in psychoanalysis: Eros and Thanatos, Oedipus and Narcissus. Deligny only needs a little space and time, a topos. This topos may not be said, but traced, with wandering lines. Hence the humorous opposition between orating (*pérorer*) (in the manner of the Lacanians) and locating (*repérer*).

This tracing, this transcript, 'comes from afar'. The first sentence of his *Journal of an educator* announced in 1965: 'the slightest gesture has a history' (A 11). He recounts in *Les enfants ont des oreilles* how he came to pay attention to the drawings of children: 'A child's drawing is not a work of art: it is a call for new circumstances' (O 212). He said this not to minimise their value, but to keep a sketch from being used as a measure of a child's performance, or worse, for an interpretation of her past. Improvising based on the tracings (*tracers*) of children does not involve commenting upon the tracing. Besides, the child no longer expresses himself. The tracing is left to its capacity for wandering: 'A drawing can be questioned, but not a tracing, which, it should be understood, doesn't *represent* anything, whatever the intentions of its author' (O 353).

Thus the poetic, the image and the tracing do not represent anything: they are imprints, well-worn paths that the gesture impresses onto the page. It is not a question of having wanted to do something, but of acting. Wandering lines happen by chance. These maps first served as a crutch, a support: Deligny had first suggested doing a tracing to an adult who had shown some dismay when confronted with the wanderings and curly-cues of autistic children, proposing that he transcribe the lines so that they would stop being disturbing and become familiar, from a distance. They first served as a crutch for speaking adults before becoming maps of intensity, as Deleuze described them in a text consecrated to Deligny.[15]

This is why Deligny specifies that these maps are not instruments of observation but of evacuation:[16] they support the struggle against the 'interpretosis' (*interprétose*) of psychoanalysis. In addition, we should not underestimate their importance for the invention of the rhizome and of cartography in Deleuze and Guattari, and of their struggle, in solidarity with Deligny, to replace interpretation with experimentation: 'Nothing is more instructive than the paths of autistic children, such as those whose maps Deligny has revealed and superimposed with their customary lines, wandering lines, loops, corrections, and turnings back – all their singularities' (CC 61). They are not made to be interpreted as a function of a family experience or of a past story; they sustain a simple topological and ethological relation with their trodden milieu (*milieu parcouru*).

Deligny proposes the topos as a version of living together, and this comprehension of enlarged, corporeal space includes children as well as adults, but also the landscape, with its heavily travelled zones, its notable immobile entities (the mountain, the path), the 'ultrachose', as Wallon termed it. This cartographic conception should be distinguished from the archaeological conception of psychoanalysis, which links the unconscious to the memory of the subject, attaching him to a commemorative conception of the family, to parental or personal authorities, whereas maps trace the prospective lines of a milieu. Psychoanalysis turns the mind of the subject in the direction of his signifying past; Deligny's cartography locates motor habits in a full milieu, each map distributing openings and holes, thresholds and poles: ribs of a cathedral ceiling, black flowers positioned where they cross, where they insist, where the feet return obstinately, 'there' where thresholds and bifurcations open up.

The wandering lines traced by artists are of the order of locating, not pronouncing. They do not inscribe the detours of children in a system of translation that would uncover their signification or flatten them on the signifying order. They remain resolutely empirical and subject to chance. They are collective works consisting of the pathways of children transcribed by adults (anyone takes responsibility, anytime [O 821]), these maps that assume an ethological sense. The signs on the maps are not signifying: in order to be able to trace, what is needed is a little 'free time' (O 949), time that is also space, such that customs are necessary: they do not serve either for observation or for interpretation, but rather as an accompaniment to mapping; they are not addressed to us (O 863). They served to modify the gaze upon autistic children, but also on the milieu and on the customary, ornamented with ways of being (O 1149). They move outside, for inside is the place of the subject: they trace pathways, not projects or subjects.

In the space emptied of language, 'we have taken a position':

> language has disappeared
> as we would say
> of the sun.

What remains are the glimmering and provisional lines on the tracing, and words, at the border between saying and tracing.

Thus, the place of artistic experiments in Deligny's clinic becomes clearer: any experiment is a political act, but where political action initiates projects and becomes prepared to direct initiatives, art skips out, taking detours for no reason, expressing itself in hesitation. For Deligny, the experiment, a political act, is thus expressed in an artistic act, where politics gets refracted, laterally, to bring our asignifying affects to visibility. Thanks to him, 'the human appeared as that which remained, a bit frayed, of the *arachnéen*, traversed by the blind meteorite that is consciousness' (A 81). This is why Deligny's action is ethological. Guattari explains this clearly: 'Fernand Deligny does not repress and does not interpret: he worked so that the disabled with whom he lived would begin to experience other objects and other relations, and begin to construct another world' (RM 288, my translation).

NOTES

1. Deligny, *Oeuvres*, 16. (Further citations will be abbreviated as 'O', and inserted directly within the text. All translations are mine. Translator's note.)
2. *Transcript*: a substantialised participle, thus: *trans* in writing (*dans l'écrit*), in the function of recording not what is verbal, but rather a marking (*trace*), including a graphic marking.

3. Deligny, *L'Arachnéen et autres textes*, 75. (Further citations will be abbreviated as 'A', and inserted directly within the text. All translations are mine. Translator's note.)

4. The French 'arachnéen', denoting that which is proper to a spider, or spider-like, will be preserved. Translator's note.

5. Along with others, Guattari founded the journal *Recherches* in 1966, and accompanied it by the *Cahiers de la Fgéri* (the Federation of study groups and of institutional research), satellites of the journal, which aimed to collate the work of its different groups (see O 637–47). The *Cahiers* were published from January 1968 to March 1970, and Deligny edited the first three, reproduced in O 647–71.

6. Moreau, 'Quand la psychologie passe l'arme à gauche', 23.

7. Chris Marker reviewed *Les Vagabonds efficaces* in *Esprit* 48: 434–5. He hailed Deligny the writer, observing that the text was a chronicle of a struggle revealing a new kind of educator (*le Vagabond efficace*) and a new kind of writer.

8. Spinoza, *Ethics*, III.

9. 'I had been a member of the Communist Party numerous times' (O 1123) Deligny said, specifying that 'it was impossible for me to erase the card that Henri Wallon and Louis le Gaillant and others gave me in 1947' (O 1124). 'If I am always and again a Communist, it is as a dissident against the thousand and one reasons to not be a member' (O 1124). He showed no obedience to the Party, but was a faithful fellow traveller with the militants. Thus, he was on the side of the Communists, but '*I never took the Party to be someone*', and 'I was more of a fellow traveller than a member' (O 1207).

10. Deligny, cited by Moreau, *Fernand Deligny et les idéologies de l'enfance*, 91.

11. 'Human is the name of a species, a species that has disappeared so that man could take his place' (A 22).

12. See Deleuze and Guattari, *Rhizome*, taken up in *A Thousand Plateaus*.

13. See the excellent commentary of Sandra Alvarez de Toledo, O, 680.

14. See also Moreau, in his superb book, *Fernand Deligny et les idéologies de l'enfance*.

15. Deleuze, 'What Children Say', *Essays Critical and Clinical*, 64.

16. *Recherches* 24 (1976), *Cahiers de l'Immuable* 3, 39.

PART IV: MACHINES AND ASSEMBLAGES

II. *Machines: How Does It Work?*[1]

Technics is long way from explaining what is at stake when we speak of machines since Guattari uses this term to specify how an assemblage works, the kind of assemblage that he calls 'machinic'. Of course, the first kind of machine that comes to mind is one that is a fabricated, material apparatus, machines as they are ordinarily defined: technical entities distinguished from tools, the latter set in motion by human muscular force, while our industrial machines engage tools through automation, regulating their temporality and their energy in the repetition of their performance of work.

When we define technical machines in this way, we turn them into artifacts that are more complex than tools, situating them on an evolutionary timeline of culture leading to an industrial capitalism that integrates calculation and technics (engineering). A rupture with the simple tool set in motion by human motor and informational energy, the technical machine 'combines solid elements functioning under human control in order to transmit movement and execute a task', capturing a kind of energy that is biological or natural.[2] According to this definition, machines only exist in the industrial age of capitalism.

TECHNICAL INDIVIDUALS AND
MACHINIC ASSEMBLAGE

Henceforth, the machine is no longer understood as a subset of technics and certainly does not represent progress vis-à-vis the tool. In the sense in which Guattari uses the term, it is instead the problematic of technics that is dependent on 'machines': the machine is a prerequisite for technics, not an expression of it. Drawing upon historians and philosophers of technics, including Leroi-Gourhan, Détienne, Mumford and Simondon, Guattari proposes that a technical entity – a tool or a machine (for example, a hammer or an airplane) – should not be studied in isolation without taking into consideration the milieu of individuation that surrounds it and allows it to function. No machine or technical tool exists by itself, for these artifacts only function in an assembled (*agencé*) milieu of individuation, which constitutes its conditions of possibility: there is no hammer without a nail, and thus the interaction between a multitude of technical objects makes the fabrication of hammers and nails possible, while also forming the conditions of their utilisation and the practices and habits associated with them. Simondon explains this succinctly: any technical entity refers to an associated technical system, which functions as a transcendental condition of possibility.

At the same time, this condition is not limited to the technical domain, for the hammer and nail presuppose the hand that holds the hammer to pound in the nail, that is, the mobility of the gesture, the definition of the worker, the division of labour within the system of production, all in addition to the wall, the wood and the surface into which the nail is hammered: the operative context of the becoming of a motor gesture in its existential, cultural territory, which implies its specific assemblage of production. The technical object and the social arrangement in which it is inserted are in no way independent of one another. Moreover, it is the social arrangement that determines technics, not the opposite. Détienne formulated this clearly: 'technics is, in a way, internal to the social and mental'.[3] We thus cannot analyse the most humble technical object – the hammer or the airplane – without taking into account the social montages that make it possible.

MACHINE: CONCEPTUAL OPERATOR OF ASSEMBLAGES

Guattari thus urges us to expand the 'limits of the machine, *stricto sensu*' (the technical entity) to include 'the functional ensemble which associates it with man' (C 34), though it would be better to say with humans, men and women socialised in diverse assemblages. With this formulation, the concept of the machine is completely transformed: it no longer concerns the technical entity, but instead the social assemblage that tools and machines require as an operative condition. The machine henceforth serves to define the conditions of possibility of technical works (*mises en oeuvres techniques*), explaining how cultures modulate the biological, the sociopolitical and the material in their assemblages. This new transversal conception turns the machine into an operator-concept that aims to explain real social processes, an operator of individuation, and an operator of social assemblages.

Lewis Mumford, who first integrated the term 'machine' into the analysis of societies, proposed the concept of the human collective machine to analyse the architectural accomplishments of preindustrial societies in the Copper Age, which channelled enormous quantities of human labour into collective machines. These machines extend beyond technical entities because they define the organisation of labour in terms of a 'social machine' that assembles humans together with materials and other living beings to perform this work (large-scale collective productions) under human control, a power exercised in a coercive, motor form (for example, through guards and soldiers) through the neuro-motor transmission of information (which in turn implies writing, teams of scribes transmitting orders from the summit to the base). For Mumford, the social apparatus manifests itself as an information machine, transforming muscular energy into social labour, requiring a division of labour whose huge differential dissipates enormous quantities of energy in the form of inequality.

Deleuze and Guattari retain from Mumford the extension of the concept of the machine to the social, but they extend it to types of organisation for which the notion of labour remains alien because they do not manifest the statist conditions of class division. Societies said to be without a State, studied by Meyer Fortes, Evans-Pritchard and Pierre Clastres, exhibit social machines that are different but nevertheless operative. Machines are thus social before being technical, not only because any technical entity refers to a social machine, but also because the concept of the machine makes it possible to integrate the Marxist problematic of the analysis of modes of real production into structural conceptions of the social provided by ethnology, sociology or history. Viewed from this epistemological perspective, the concept of the 'machine' proposes nothing less than a transformation of the social sciences in accordance with a philosophical method that opens symbolic structures or logics to real modes of production. 'Machine' in this second sense defines the operativity of the social, not in general, but on a case-by-case basis.

Guattari thereby extends the analyses of *A Thousand Plateaus* by distinguishing three different kinds of social machines that correspond to different social states: the Neolithic machine, or writing machines linked to the emergence of urban megamachines (Mumford); nomad machines, involving the collusion of metallurgical machines and war machines; and capitalist machines. The concept of the machine thus defines a historical and social machinic assemblage, an assemblage of enunciation, and a machinic assemblage of bodies, which concerns the operativity of singular social functioning. The machine thus authorises both a new philosophy of history, which is empirical and not linear, and a political philosophy that refuses to cut theory off from its social conditions of realisation. It also calls for a conception of the interaction between thought and matter as a cutting of flows, and a social conception of the desiring individual, no longer solitary but 'machined', which Guattari terms a 'desiring machine'.

THE SIX MACHINIC COMPONENTS

In *Chaosmosis*, Guattari attempts to construct the concept of the machine by proposing at least six simultaneous components, which together contribute to its definition (C 33–5). The first three primarily concern actual individuation, while the last three refer to modes of subjectivation, in accordance with the systematic distinction that differentiates the individual from modes of collective subjectivation, which are largely unconscious and which transform the individual into a subject.

First, Guattari considers 'material and energetic components'. His materialist commitments motivate him to take this empirical condition of actualisation into account above all else, and in post-Einsteinian physics, matter is composed of energy.

The second component concerns the semiotics – noetic more than mental – that play a part in the fabrication of every technical object. With regard to industrial technology, these 'diagrammatic and algorithmic components' – plans, formulas, equations and calculations – play a role in all manufacturing. An industrial, technical machine can never be reduced to its material components. It entails complex noetic data, including calculations, programs and algorithms that turn any industrial, technical machine into a theoretical object. In effect, these technological machines require the contribution of engineers, not only with calculations – equations put to work through their functioning – but also, in the preparatory phase of their elaboration, scientific research, industrial applications and private or State laboratories. The industrial machine is built on a scientific machine with a cognitive output. This scientific machine capitalises on the cognitive factor from elementary school to the university, according to complex networks (*arborescences*) of teaching, research, laboratories, institutes and companies, as well as circuits of finance, research funds, foundations, economic investment in education, research, production and commercialisation. These elements not only make the fabrication of artifacts possible, but even more, they make them profitable by producing humans capable of using them and especially of purchasing them.

Consequently, it is impossible to deal with technological machines by relying on a Cartesian description of thought penetrating into mathematicised matter. It is not a question here of individual thought, but rather of a collective assemblage of enunciation, which articulates an entire civilisation of technological industry. Pure thought demands a sociological analysis, which in turn leads to a politics of its industrial operations. Thus, the mention of the matter or energy of technical machines is perhaps a prerequisite to their concrete existence, but it is not sufficient, for these machines also involve semiotic components that are clearly of the noetic order and doubtless put a kind of thought into play, but a thought that is not necessarily conscious, or even human or mental.

These codings and numerical applications in effect depend on semiotics, but only by automation, by an artificial intelligence that is neither conscious nor mental in the sense of an act of consciousness that takes place in a human brain, but which is rather performed by motors of computational calculation and other technical machines, recalling Leibniz's claim that every machine entails machines of machines. The functioning of any machine, an airplane for example, additionally requires diverse, discursive semiotics: written codes, printed marks rather than speech, assembly instructions, schedules and instructional diagrams, which are also non-discursive (figures, sketches, measurements), as well as patents, instructional manuals, security warnings, treaties, industrial and State conventions, and a variety of laws which encompass, permit, configure and regulate these industrial productions.

These diagrammatic and algorithmic functions thus refer to semiotics, calculations and to language, but may not be attributed to an original author, to a human individual who thinks them or produces them under his or her proper name. We are very far from Descartes.

Third are 'components of organs, influx, and humours of the human body' (C 34). Here, we are on the plane of human individuation, that of the constituted individual: you and me. While we may have surmised that the organs disappeared with the body without organs, in this instance the organ becomes a machinic organ, blinking on and off with impulses and humours; it is not an abstract organ, but rather a body being traversed by flows that precede the material and the cognitive. These material and noetic components are not arranged according to an evolutionary timeline, the energetic-material component serving as the basis for the noetic component. The first two components must not be understood as two stages that progress toward a successive assumption of cultural form. On the contrary, Guattari makes it possible for us to recognise their 'heterogenesis', their becoming active (*prise en acte*), their mutual consolidation.

This, then, is what a machinic assemblage consists of when it individuates a singular body – a human body or technical machine – within a collective assemblage of enunciation and a machinic assemblage of bodies. More precisely, a machinic assemblage 'consists', assuming a provisional consistency in individuating, not from matter in general or from pure thought, but as cerebral individuation, a corporeal organ blinking on and off, which becomes extended by cutting through material and noetic flows. *An* organ, certainly, but this organ does not have any more existence than the machine on the plane of its actualisation alone: vibrating with chemical and electrical impulses, with affects, we are indeed situated on the plane of the body without organs, because the brain is no longer centred in terms of a sovereign organisation, but open, in machinic connection with flows and humours.

We must then define the machine as what connects us, not as a technical object we can hold in our hands and turn on and make work with a button, lever, throttle or screen, or as something we insert our bodies into. The machine is no longer a technical object, but is rather the operative philosophical concept that explains how three components – matter, thought and brain – may function together while remaining heterogeneous. As stated in the first and second principles of the rhizome, the principles of connection and heterogeneity, to connect is to produce (and not reduce) heterogeneity.

MACHINIC ASSEMBLAGES, DESIRING MACHINES AND ABSTRACT MACHINES

But, this analysis is still not sufficient. These components, after all, explain nothing and have already been discussed for a long time: what philosopher has not attempted to consider the material, the cognitive and the affective together? Nevertheless, everything changes when we conceive of their mode of composition as machinic. According to this new definition, the machine only exists in the plural, as the cutting of flows, a machine that cuts a flow in turn gets cut by other machines, as we have just seen in the case of the body, which cuts material and semiotic flows. This becomes clearer when we approach the three final components of subjectivation.

The fourth component consists of 'individual and collective mental representations and information' (C 34), a formulation that may trigger worries about the reappearance of strata of ideology or of the sphere of communication, which have been justifiably criticised. On the contrary, what is at stake is a collective assemblage of enunciation, which does not refer to an individual's use of thought or of speech, but consists of the semiotic layers of mass-mediatised information, of the industry of social and commercial order words (*mots d'ordre*), order words that also emanate from every sphere of local or professional expertise or social situation. Every machinic assemblage includes a collective assemblage of enunciation, which must not be confused with the structure of a spoken language (French or English, for example), or with a technical, formal or scholarly language. In accordance with the critique of structural linguistics performed in *The Machinic Unconscious* and extended in *A Thousand Plateaus*, a language may no longer be considered a closed and homogeneous structure. Language does not belong to any one of us, and is rather positioned between us, as a plane of enunciation for which we are only individual terminals. Language does not function as a system centred on its own grammaticality but is rather constantly set into variation, thrown off course by singular usages that set it adrift. Even defined in this way as heterogeneous, such a language remains an abstraction. The assemblage of enunciation is not only of a linguistic order, but is also semiotic, mixing levels of disparate languages with order words, images, fictions, information and representations relayed by an industrialised mass media that inundates us, as well as by all of the multiform, contradictory discourses to which we are exposed and that we in turn help circulate, following the diversity of our affiliations – both private and public – including those that are professional, convivial, local, amorous and social. This whole cacophony of discourses precipitates into enunciations, projecting modes of representation that norm our perceptions and thresholds of tolerance.

This fourth plane of information and representation cannot subjectivate us without a fifth component: 'the investments of desiring machines producing a subjectivity adjacent to these components' (C 34). It is indeed our investments, composite as well as massive, economic as well as desiring, that allow the preceding components to assume consistency. 'Desiring machines': the term 'machine' reappears here, no longer to define a collective assemblage of enunciation, but as that which makes it possible for an individual human body – mine, yours – to be subjectivated by a social machine, all the while that it is feeding into it. There is no longer any spontaneism of desire; the desiring machine is constructed by social coding through and through. For this reason, it is called a 'desiring machine', a coding of flows. Lacan demonstrated how desire is coded by the unconscious, which functions like a language. Such an unconscious is thus not private but social, and is also not familial, constructed around the parental figures of a given individual. On the contrary, Lacan proposed an unconscious caught up in a mode of subjectivation that is not individual but implicated in language, which is both collective and unconscious. But, following Marx and against Lacan, language is not sufficient to code the unconscious. In the first place, any language presupposes a regime of machinic production, not one that is symbolic or structural. At stake here is the polemic against structuralism, which completely opposes Lacan's theory of the signifier. The machinic unconscious does not express itself in abstract mathemes or in any kind of language of the unconscious defined by specialists. On the contrary, it is produced, historically singularised, within a specific, determinate social assemblage.

This fifth condition encounters the subtle and decisive difference between the terminal individual and the collective mode of enunciation that subjectivates us, codes the unconscious, and moulds consciousness. In *A Thousand Plateaus*, Guattari calls them, with Deleuze, strata of significance and subjectification, advocating that we liberate ourselves from our Oedipalised unconscious and our consciousness programmed to make us good citizens by viewing them as capitalist codings, not as human nature.

But collective assemblages cannot work without the investments of desiring machines, 'which produce a subjectivity adjacent to these components'. It is crucial to observe that subjectivity thereby intervenes laterally, by becoming detached: subjectivity is not the abstract sum of our desiring machines but instead their condition, which we can transform if we make an effort. Socially produced, artifactual, subjectivity acts as an always-open possibility, not as a causal result. If our desiring machines produce 'a subjectivity in adjacency', their investment thus also contributes to transforming it. This open and dynamic relation, rendered possible by the mode of consistency of concrete, machinic assemblages, whether we are speaking of social, capitalist machines or other social assemblages, explains why societies change.

In order to insure this becoming, the sixth component, doubtless the most decisive, intervenes: 'abstract machines installing themselves transversally to the machinic levels previously considered (material, cognitive, affective and social)' (C 35). Abstract machines hold together the five heterogeneous components that we have just analysed.

Abstract machines must be absolutely distinguished from desiring machines. First and foremost, they are created at the moment they are set in motion by a concrete assemblage as that which makes it hold together and gives it a provisional consistency. As always in Guattari's thought, consistency proceeds through deterritorialisation, not through an identificatory binding together: abstract machines operate within concrete assemblages through points of decoding and deterritorialisation. It would be wrong to consider them an essence, a reason behind the assemblage, or a kind of structure that evaporates from the real: there is nothing eternal about them, as they are positioned precisely in the interstices of components that they deterritorialise by connecting. Presupposed by the assemblage that they explain, they operate in this assemblage as its condition of possibility, neither exterior, nor anterior, but strictly coextensive with its empirical existence.

An abstract machine is thus not a thing or a Platonic Idea, any more than it is a structure of an assemblage. Transversal to different components, it carries them along in a functional arrangement, which works through breaking down and through deterritorialising. There are thus as many abstract machines as machinic assemblages. Since an assemblage is not given, any more than an individuation is fixed on the plane of the human body (but instead concerns a bottle of water, an eyelash, an electron or the Earth), the same goes for the abstract machine, which is a diagram of an assemblage. The abstract machine operates at whatever fractal level you want and enables you – as a variable in your possibilities of analysis, of your capacities to invest reality – to produce new modes of subjectivity. Any given assemblage engages its 'extracted machine' – points of deterritorialisation, non-formed materials, non-formalised functions – which causes it to hold together. This is why the machine works by breaking down.

AESTHETIC PARADIGM

This reveals the extent to which the concept of the machine is operative in relation to structure. We may think that the machine and structure are equivalent at the level of abstract machines, but structure thinks the abstract machine as a system of ideal relations, perhaps defined at the level of reality, but nevertheless frozen in the eternity of its logical consistency, whereas the abstract machine pushes us to think an operativity that is not closed on itself or eternal, but given in the variable course of its real and provisional operativity. This is why, once again, a machine only works by breaking down.

Contrary to structure, the abstract machine is, according to Guattari, traversed by a desire for abolition. It is a question of becoming, of a little lucky charm that goes 'poof', not of a death drive. The desire for abolition only has mortifying connotations for those wedded to the schema of identity. But when the abstract machine functions, it fails, it always fails, it necessarily fails, because any functioning involves the provisional singularity and uncertain contingency of a force that becomes exhausted right at the moment it gets going.

Failure is thus decisive for an understanding of machinic operativity. The machine fails in functioning. It fails at all possible levels of its structure. This failure concerns its operativity, and it is here that Guattari replaces what he calls the scientific paradigm with his aesthetic paradigm.

The scientific paradigm corresponds less to the actions and imaginations of real science than to the representation we make of it. It defines the operativity of science as the discovery of an explanatory structure, lodged in an eternity that necessarily looks longingly to the past because it presents itself as the stable essence of a reality, sufficient in itself. The aesthetic paradigm, open to the future, conceives of explanation as a risky endeavour, like a diagnostic construct. While the scientific paradigm would like us to believe that in order to understand our societies, our political action, our ways of thinking, we should find truths, the aesthetic paradigm – which does not oblige us to be artists, to put flowers in our hair, or play the flute in our bare feet – enjoins us to think about the operativity of our concepts in a prospective, uncertain and unhinged way, in order to decide whether, yes or no, it works.

NOTES

1. The agrammaticality of this title is intentional and meant to call attention to the new conception of the 'machine' being put forth. Translator's note.
2. According to the kinematic definition of Franz Reuleaux, director of the Berlin Industrial Academy, author, in 1875, of *The Kinematics of Machinary: Outline of a Theory of Machines*, trans. Alexander B. W. Kennedy (Mineola: Dover, 2012). My translation.
3. Détienne, 'La phalange, problèmes et controverses', in *Problèmes de la guerre en Grèce ancienne*, 134. My translation.

12. Desiring Machines and Social Codings

TECHNICAL MACHINES AND SOCIAL MACHINES

The conception of the machine deployed in *Anti-Oedipus* takes up work Guattari had pursued since 1969. The machine is opposed to structure in terms of its vitalist, mechanistic and historical character: it is not structural and auto-regulated but rather historic and open to the exterior.[1] Guattari assigns to the term the typically Lacanian function of 'the operation of the detachment of a signifier as a differentiator',[2] but he gives this operation a social existence by drawing on the work of Leroi-Gourhan and especially Lewis Mumford, who inaugurated the term 'social machine' in an article that appeared in a French translation in the journal *Diogenes* in 1966.[3] In this article, Mumford reflects on the technological accomplishments of strongly centralised early empires from the perspective of their great architectural accomplishments (for example, Egyptian pyramids and Mesopotamian ziggurats). Beginning with a somewhat traditional analysis of despotic architecture, Mumford transforms the analysis by describing the constructive efficacy of this mode of social production at the level of a kinetics of forces. Gigantism – the Promethean character of these collective creations – requires that we see this kind of social organisation as a 'megamachine'. Here, it is indeed a question of a machine in the technological sense of the term. Mumford relies upon Reuleaux's classic definition, which defines the machine as a 'combination of resistant parts, each specialized in function, operating under human control, to transmit motion and to perform work'.[4] Mumford's innovation was to go beyond the frame of the technical object (a simple or complex machine as an individuated artifact) and to apply this technological definition to the social body itself. The mechanical goes beyond the artifact – the machine entity constructed by the human hand – but is always characterised in terms of a relation of force/displacement, transmitting a force and executing a task under human control. Simply put, it is a question of a 'human machine',[5] a *mega*machine because it goes beyond individual machines and takes into account the organisation of labour at the level of the social body itself, articulating solid elements (materials and humans) to transmit a (muscular) movement and execute a task (great, collective creations) under human control (despotic power exercised in armed, muscular form, as well as in neuro-motor form through the transmission of information). Mumford thus applies the term 'machine' to the social machine. According to him, 'the collective human machine came into existence roughly during the same period as the first industrial use of copper', and was transmitted by the intermediary of human actors for 5,000 years before assuming the 'non-human' – but also 'despotic' – form that characterises modern technology.[6] Before the appearance of water-powered mills in the fourteenth century, the megamachine or human machine ('royal machine') with its muscular motor had no equal in terms of realising the capacity for production. Even if it functioned through political coercion and class division,[7] dissipating enormous quantities of human suffering in horrendous social conditions, its efficacy on the plane of construction is undeniable. For Mumford, it is no longer technics that appears as the social apparatus, but the opposite. It is the social apparatus that manifests itself as technological in the strong sense of the term: an information machine transforming muscular energy into labour accompanied by a significant dissipation of social energy. We thus cannot be satisfied with the classic definition of the machine as 'the support of a tool' nor with a genealogy that makes it the heir of the tool:[8] the machine is from the start a carrier of the human, which it arranges (*agence*) in accordance with a constraining mechanism with the purpose of channelling collective energy for the execution of a social task. Mumford thus proposes a theory of civilisations that takes into account their technical apparatuses, calling for a veritable history of technics from a technological, scientific and social perspective. It is indeed from Mumford that Deleuze and Guattari derive their concept of culture as a 'social machine' (AO 33).

But their extension of this theory leads to its transformation. Mumford limited his definition only to those archaic kingdoms and empires in possession of enormous reserves of manual work, which he called 'royal machines'. Deleuze and Guattari refuse to limit the range of his analysis to this sociopolitical form, which corresponds to what they call 'the barbaric, despotic, institution', instead extending it to all social bodies. From the definition of the machine that Mumford adapted from Reuleaux, Deleuze and Guattari retain only the functions of capture, division, coding of a flow and the mechanical transmission and production of a social energy. Mumford's definition, which focused on a building machine and a sociopolitical State dependent upon the kind of social organisation characterising despotic empires and producing work, represents only one application under determinate conditions. There is nothing determinant in itself about the architectural vocation and the diagram of forces extracting labour; these may take other forms. Specifically, some social machines prove to be inept at producing work because the conditions (those having to do with a State) are lacking.[9] The labour function and the mode in which it is exercised are not determinant. The machine is what makes it possible, under determinate conditions, for the social apparatus to assume the technological form of either the 'royal machine', as Mumford describes it, or of societies that lack or are characterised by a State, by industrial capitalism, or by recent technology. Deleuze and Guattari retain from Mumford the extension to the social; labour and the tool become variables of the machinic phylum upon which social machines depend. 'Before capitalism, there are indeed technical machines, but the machinic phylum does not proceed by means of them because it is content to "machine humans and tools".'[10] These modal differences do not affect the definition of the machine as that which produces a social assemblage, in the very general sense of productive syntheses defined above.

The 'machinic phylum' (TP 349–403; 406–11) prepares the ground for the definition of the 'assemblage', a term created by Guattari but adopted by Deleuze and used by him in his reading of *Discipline and Punish*, which he read as a confirmation of the theses on the machine in *Anti-Oedipus*. The machine includes the technological apparatus without being reduced to it; it is the technological apparatus that is assembled (*agencé*) by the social machine. Mumford's social machine is thereby radicalised by way of Foucault's analyses. For Mumford, it is the society that turns itself into a *mega*machine, integrating its members with a goal of realising an *ergon*. For Foucault, it is the exercise of power that becomes technological, which displaces the problem: it is not the society that assembles (*agence*) and articulates its members within a system of forces that depends upon an immense machine. It is the manner in which power socialises and differentiates its members that depends upon the technological. For Foucault[11] demonstrates that the 'discipline' that defines societies, beginning in the eighteenth century, cannot be identified with a specific institution or with a determinate apparatus, but 'is a type of power, a technology, that traverses every kind of apparatus or institution, linking them, prolonging them, and making them converge' (F 26): the same 'parts', in the physical sense of the term, the same 'wheels', belong to the State or to the prison, and this theory of mechanisms of power justifies Foucault in speaking of a 'machine-prison'.[12] If 'technology is therefore social before it is technical' (F 40), this is because machines refer to the 'collective machines' that encompass them.

This confirms the analyses that Foucault devoted to limited technological series like the rifle,[13] as well as his approach to architecture in his analysis of Bentham's panopticon in *Discipline and Punish*.

This analysis of the integration of technics and the social thus converges with the work of Leroi-Gourhan and Simondon on the history of technics,[14] as well as with the decisive work of historians including Vernant, Détienne and Braudel, who articulate material history to the history of institutions.[15] Deleuze and Guattari rely heavily on this work,[16] and *A Thousand Plateaus* confirms the importance of these analyses (TP 399–400). In the first place, the technical object (tool or machine) only exists, as Simondon showed, in a 'technical arrangement' that defines its machinic existence. We should understand this as a social apparatus in the broadest possible sense. Simondon's analysis of 'the mode of existence of technical objects' does not account for the economic and cultural aspects of the social that determine it. It is in Braudel's magisterial history of capitalism that Deleuze finds confirmation of this: 'the tool is the consequence, not the cause'.[17] It is in Détienne's work that Deleuze found the analysis of hoplite arms,[18] and in White's work the analysis of the stirrup. These systematically return in the analysis of the assemblage because they connect the technical object (stirrup, hoplite shield with two handles) to a complex and rigorously connected social apparatus, such that the (technical) object can no more exist outside of its milieu of (social) constitution any more than a society can assume its specific form in its absence ('The famous two-handled shield of the hoplite reform, which soldered together human chains' [TP 391]).

> Historians have often been confronted by this requirement: the so-called hoplite armies are part of the phalanx assemblage; the stirrup is selected by the diagram of feudalism; the burrowing stick, the hoe, and the plough do not form a linear progression, but refer respectively to collective machines which vary with the density of the population and the time of the fallow. (F 39–40)

Historical analyses of technical apparatuses, which stress the importance of a cultural history of social technology, indicate in addition that they do not always constitute linear progressions, even though one assemblage abolishes another (the steel sword wiped out iron, just as iron wiped out bronze). There is thus a history of technics that is just as fascinating and complex as the history of political institutions or of art. In addition, these three forms are indissociable. Hence the importance of a study of 'technological lineages', of the machinic *phylum*: there is a technological *continuum* that distinguishes, for example, metallurgy from basket weaving (expressive forms of a material), but there are also historical connections (the propagation and diffusion of a technique) that make the history of technics, here, radically indissociable from the history of art, opening the ground for experimentation within history (TP 405–6). But before establishing the position of the arts in social technics, it is first necessary to demonstrate that there is no independence of what Simondon calls a 'technical individual' – the rifle, the burrowing stick, the stirrup – from the technical arrangement in which it is inserted.[19] Détienne sums this up succinctly: 'Technics is, in a way, interior to the social and the mental.'[20] It is the social assemblage that determines technics and not the other way around. Deleuze and Guattari are in complete agreement with this conclusion: 'Weapons and tools are consequences, nothing but consequences' (TP 398). With 'weapons' characterising, in their view, nomad societies, and tools referring to sedentary societies, they aim to cover the entire field of available technical objects. Our analysis of technical objects must therefore take place on the technical level of the assemblage, of the 'concrete machine' that puts them to work, and conversely, the analysis of a social body must not omit the weapons and tools integral to it. In this way, analysis resituates the technical object in the social arrangements that made it possible.

At the same moment, Foucault was taking the analysis in the opposite direction, showing that it is impossible to analyse a modality of power and to assess the extension of disciplinary methods without taking into account the development of technologies classed within that culture, such as agronomy and industry, a list that may be extended to other forms neglected until now. Thus, Bentham's panopticon is assigned a 'technological' value: 'But it must be recognised that, compared with the mining industries, the emerging chemical industries or methods of national accountancy, compared with the blast furnaces or the steam engine, panopticism has received little attention . . . And yet this represented the abstract formula of a very real technology, that of individuals.'[21] Doubtless, Foucault hesitated to consider Bentham's project a technical apparatus, properly speaking: 'But it would be unjust to compare the disciplinary techniques with such inventions as the steam engine or Amici's microscope': they 'are much less; and yet, in a way, they are much more'.[22] If Foucault hesitated on the one hand to grant such procedures the consistency of determinate, technical inventions, on the other hand he credited them with 'much more' because they are diffused throughout society and thereby indicate that it is necessary to stop limiting technology to the analysis of the technical entity, and rather to think it in terms of a relation to the social entity. This entails a change of domain. Deleuze, along with Guattari in *A Thousand Plateaus*, and on his own in his review of *Discipline and Punish* and in *Foucault*, infers from this analysis a strong connection between social machine and technological machine.²³ The technical assemblage connects signs, devices, technical mechanisms and relations of powers. Any society is thereby characterised by the 'concrete machines' that it invents: thus, the school-machine or Foucault's prison or hospital machine,²⁴ but also the weapons and jewellery of nomads, the signs and tools of sedentary societies, the plough, the stirrup, the rudder or the computer.²⁵ These devices, these technical entities, depend upon 'concrete machines' that assemble (*agencent*) them and that connect knowledge to technologies of power. They do not have a technical existence that is isolated from the milieu in which they become established.

> But the principle behind all technology is to demonstrate that a technical element remains abstract, entirely undetermined, as long as one does not relate it to an *assemblage* it presupposes. It is the machine that is primary in relation to the technical element: not the technical machine, itself a collection of elements, but the social or collective machine, the machinic assemblage that determines what is a technical element at a given moment, what is its usage, extension, comprehension, etc. (TP 397–8)

From this point of view, the panopticon refers to a concrete machine, even while it may not be considered a technical element: a plan, a blueprint, or a simple design, can very well become determinant in a given constituting assemblage into which it is introduced. This is what occurred in the case of Bentham's panopticon. Referring to Foucault, Deleuze called these concrete machines 'biformed apparatuses' in the sense that they assemble (*agencent*) a form of visibility (the 'effect' in the perceptual sense analysed in *Difference and Repetition* and *Sacher Masoch*) and a form of knowledge through an articulation to a power (a relation of force).²⁶ These concrete machines thus indicate differences of culture, and a given isolated tool only assumes social consistency when it refers to a concrete machine.

> Even technology makes the mistake of considering tools in isolation: tools exist only in relation to the interminglings they make possible or that make them possible. The stirrup entails a new man-horse symbiosis that at the same time entails new weapons and new instruments. Tools are inseparable from symbioses or amalgamations defining a Nature-Society machinic assemblage. (TP 90)

But if 'technology is social before being technical', it is not only because power articulates tools in modes of realisation that are at the same time modes of expression of relations of production. The concrete machine refers to an 'abstract machine' or a 'diagram', to use Foucault's term,²⁷ that is, to a relation of forces that is 'inter-social and caught up in a process of becoming' that characterises a historical society, a 'spatiotemporal multiplicity'. The abstract machine is the correlate of the desiring machine in *Anti-Oedipus*; only sketched out in the analyses in Part 3, it is fully developed in *A Thousand Plateaus* in the analyses of technics in the 'Treatise on Nomadology'. With this definition of the abstract machine, the desiring machine and unconscious machine of *Anti-Oedipus* are replaced by a stronger and empirically more detailed analysis of the machinations and mechanisms that work through the social body. '[T]here are as many diagrams as there are social fields in history . . . every diagram is intersocial and constantly evolving' (F 34–5).

MACHINIC ASSEMBLAGE: CONCRETE MACHINES, SOCIAL MACHINES, ABSTRACT MACHINES

It is now possible to reconstruct the line of development that goes from the machine in Guattari's work to the machinic assemblage in the work of Deleuze and Guattari. The machine is not a structure. We cannot reduce it to a technical entity or to an abstract or symbolic relation. The machine involves a 'supple and transversal' alliance that defines a 'practice', which is at the same time a physical procedure and a social strategy 'distinct from any single combination' that forms 'an unstable physical system' (F 35–6). It is in the process of becoming, subjacent to the material, vital and social relations that characterise a social state. The technical-historical analysis of the specific kind of assemblage that characterises a given social state is thus superimposed onto the desiring machines of *Anti-Oedipus*. The assemblage, the concrete machine, including such combinations as stirrup-feudalism or hoplite weapons-phalanx, are open to an analysis that reveals the 'relations of forces' that constitute the mode of power articulating forms of knowledge and regimes of social visibility. Deleuze and Guattari name an analysis of this kind a 'diagram' in homage to Foucault. The diagram 'acts as a non-unifying, immanent cause that is coextensive with the whole social field' (F 37). As such, a diagram is also what Deleuze and Guattari call an 'abstract machine': 'For a true abstract machine pertains to an assemblage in its entirety; it is defined as the diagram of that assemblage' (TP 91; see also F 38).

The 'abstract machine' is thus the 'map of relations of force' that occur 'not above' social assemblages, or below them, but transversally. In Deleuze, an immanent cause always signifies a cause that becomes actualised in its effects (F 36; see also EP): the diagram, or abstract machine, is not reducible to a transcendent Idea, an ideological superstructure, or an economic infrastructure. Instead, in accordance with analyses in *Difference and Repetition*, it is an actualisation, a differenciation:[28] the diagram is thus the differentiated relation of forces that presides over a given assemblage, and which is neither anterior nor posterior to it, but which is rather virtual

and immanent, an empirical encounter that emerges from the 'coadaptation' of a given form of power with a given form of practice. The diagram
is not an archive but rather an intensive map of relations of force that
assemble (*agencent*) humans and materials, techniques and institutions.
'[T]here are as many diagrams as there are social fields in history' (F 34).
The diagram thus occupies the position of the differentiated virtual, which
in *Difference and Repetition* Deleuze called an Idea. We may call it a 'cause'
of assemblages on the condition we specify that it concerns an immanent
cause, at the same level of the assemblage, one that is non-unifying and
coextensive with the assemblage, consisting of a complex of singularities
that become actualised in all of the assemblages that differenciate it. This
does not denigrate other, concurrent abstract machines that may be operating simultaneously. Thus, to return to Foucault's example, the encounter
between the visibilities of the prison and the statements of penal law
differenciate the diagram of confinement (F 39). But the diagram is given
nowhere other than in the empirical encounter between the form of the
prison and penal form.

> There is only a relation of forces which acts transversally and finds in the
> duality of forms the conditions for its own action and realization. If there
> is such a thing as coadaptation of forms, it arises from their 'encounter'
> (provided the latter is forced), and not the other way round: [here, Deleuze
> cites Foucault] 'the encounter is justified only by the new necessity it has
> established'. (F 39)

Such is Deleuze and Guattari's machinic assemblage. It entails a dis-
sociation between tool and machine (technical objects), between the
machinic (social and concrete machines effectively existing in given empirical assemblages) and the abstract machine (the diagram of the assemblage),
all of which are realised in specific assemblages, and which differenciate
societies: yams and rice, easel paintings and frescos, do not belong to the
same diagram.[29] Foucault 'reserves the term mechanisms' for concrete
assemblages (F 37). The diagram is the Idea of the assemblage, neither
transcendent nor exterior, but given in a 'forced' encounter, through the
force of a state of fact. Its necessity is retrospective: it is the 'new necessity'
produced by the encounter that retrospectively justifies the empirical existence of it. Hence this montage characteristic of Deleuze's work: 'There is
a history of assemblages, just as there is [becoming] in the diagram' (F 42,
with modification).

Deleuze thus finds in Foucault a confirmation of the distinction between
technical entity, actual assemblage and virtual diagram, and he integrates
the Foucauldian theory of the diagram into his own theory of capture
and coadaptation, which in this instance serves to underline the empirical

character of the encounter between prison and confinement. Power coordinates knowledge and visibility because they are two disjointed forms (F 39). Capture, the outcome of the encounter between the orchid and the wasp in Proust, theorises the fortuitous encounter between disjointed forms, one which produces a 'symbiosis' that, as soon as it is produced, acquires its immanent necessity in the form of a virtual diagram. In other words, it is not the diagram, or abstract machine, that confers a necessary consistency upon the assemblage. The social machine captures forces – in a 'transversal' relation of forces (F 39) – that constitute a symbiosis, an alliance between two heterogeneous forms, as in the present case of the prison and penal law, or the vegetable series of the orchid and the animal series of the wasp. These symbioses – in the domains of technics and of human cultures, as well as on the plane of life – assemble (*agencent*) elements from disparate series and cause them to enter into an improbable, unstable alliance that transforms them: the domestication of plants and animals also acted as a differenciating culture with respect to humans, causing them to enter into always singular alliances (horse or llama, wheat or maize). These captures are not limited to biological individuals but rather concern any kind of semiotic link – living, technical (shield, stirrup), material (thermal or solar energy) – as, for example, in the case of the human-silicon assemblage that characterises the contemporary era of control, which Deleuze frequently mentions in his interviews.[30] What is at stake is a capture of forces, a composition of forces that enters into a relation to compose a given form that did not pre-exist it. At the level of capture, this brings us back to Simondon's notion of molecular modulation. The encounter between two heterogeneous forms becomes stabilised in an 'alliance', which Deleuze calls a coadaptation, that is, a double becoming or an aparallel evolution; the last section of chapter 2 of *Foucault* is devoted to the theory of capture, transferred from the domain of animals to that of social assemblages. We will return to the theory of capture by examining why this conception of the social machine invalidates any distinction between the organic and the technical, the vital and the social, and how, in the domain of art, it implies a shift from resemblance to becoming.

The definition of the assemblage articulated in *Anti-Oedipus* and *A Thousand Plateaus* corresponds to the 'political anatomy' defined by Foucault in *Discipline and Punish*. 'One would be concerned with the "body politic," as a set of material elements and techniques that serve as weapons, relays, communication routes and supports for the power and knowledge relations that invest human bodies and subjugate them by turning them into objects of knowledge.'[31] As we shall see, the mixed semiotic, adapted from Markov, is a response to this 'anatomy of the political body'. The mixed semiotic assures the correlation, the 'capture', between disparate series of technics, lives, communications and forms of knowledge. If the assemblage shares the Foucauldian goal, it does so neither from the same perspective, nor with the same theoretical stakes.

> We will call an *assemblage* every constellation of singularities and traits deducted from the flow – selected, organized, stratified – in such a way as to converge (consistency) artificially and naturally: an assemblage, in this sense, is a veritable invention. Assemblages may group themselves into extremely vast constellations constituting 'cultures', or even 'ages'; within these constellations, the assemblages still differentiate the phyla or the flow, dividing it into so many different phylas, of a given order, on a given level, and introducing selective discontinuities in the ideal continuity of matter-movement. (TP 406)

This allows us to measure the proximity and distance between the Foucauldian approach and Deleuze and Guattari's notion of assemblage. First, Deleuze returns to the 'ideal' continuity of 'matter-movement', which situates the hyletic flow of *Anti-Oedipus* on the vital and social plane, but now without giving pride of place to the thematic of desire.[32] This hyletic flux, thought of as matter and movement (exactly what Deleuze will explore in his work on cinema), is the plane of immanence that diverse assemblages differentiate. Deleuze thus adds the Bergsonian accent of creation, of a vital differentiation, to Foucault's political anatomy. We can understand the history of cultures in terms of diverse modalities of assemblages, some being *phylogenetic*, drawing a line of *longue durée* between the 'cooking pot' and the (combustion) 'engine', and others, ontogenetic, translating the extremely varied speeds of diffusion of technical objects moving from one assemblage to another, often by changing nature (for example, the horse-shoe, which slowly spread in agricultural assemblages, or the difference between the iron sword, emerging from the dagger, and the steel sword, emerging from the knife).[33]

This articulation of the social and the technical is of great importance to the philosophy of art; Deleuze does not provide an analysis of a specific artistic assemblage, such as the 'easel painting'. Rather, he either works on more general series – so, with Guattari, the 'nomad' assemblage of 'arms and tools' as compared to the sedentary assemblage of 'signs and tools' – or on more specific series, such as the analysis of Bacon's work. In *The Fold*, he outlines the Baroque assemblage and characterises it by its trait (of expression): the fold going to infinity. But he does construct the theoretical frame of the argument, even if he himself does not explore its historical and technical realisation (for example, a technological history of cinema, or a precise analysis of the historical conditions of realisation of the still life in Flanders). Of course, Pierre Francastel demonstrated the solidarity between the technical form and the ideational mode in the creation of space, using the example of the visual cube of Renaissance perspective.[34] But he maintained a relative separation between the conditions of production and the expressions of art. Deleuze locates in Foucault's analyses of architecture the conditions for a more decisive articulation, one that no longer treats art as an expression derived from the social body. Statements are indistinguishable from the 'regimes', and visibilities are indistinguishable from 'machines' (F 58, with modification). It is not that every machine is 'optical', but every machine is a phenomenal production of actions and passions. Art is thus indissociable from a theory of social production. Foucault paved the way with his analyses of *Las Meninas* and *Don Quixote* in *The Order of Things*, but his analysis of architecture in *Discipline and Punish* introduced a new element. The prison is not just a 'figure in stone' (F 57, with modification) but is rather defined by a visual assemblage (surveillance) and a luminous milieu (rendering the prisoner asymmetrically visible, such that he is completely visible without himself being able to see) that characterise the abstract machine of panopticism: the guards see without being seen, the detainees are visible without seeing (F 32).[35] Materials are assembled (*agencés*) to respond to social imperatives that are directly expressed in textures, such that it is not a matter of imposing a form upon matter, but of assembling (*agencer*) matters of expression that assume consistency in a determined assemblage. 'If different examples of architecture, for example, are visibilities, places of visibilities, this is because they are not just figures of stone, assemblages of things and combinations of qualities, but first and foremost forms of light that distribute light and dark, opaque and transparent, seen and non-seen, etc.' (F 57)

These forms of light are creative in themselves. Architecture is the first art and indicates a correlation between art, technics and life: art first fulfils the pragmatic function of an expressive dwelling, a territorialisation: this is the 'ritornello'.[36] With the social machine, the sociopolitical apparatus, the assemblage of techniques and modes of reception, habits and knowledge become an integral part of aesthetics in Deleuze's work. This has two consequences: first, vitalism, which thinks the assemblage in terms of the continuity of a dwelling and positions art in continuity with animal ethology; and second, the determination of the assemblage itself as creative, as a social and technical invention, producing multiple humanities in no way reducible to a chronological sequence or to a development. Henceforth, Deleuze will no longer deprive himself of the resources of the socio-historical milieu, and will always take into account the correlation between artistic production and the machinic assemblage to theorise creation, as demonstrated by the analysis of the Baroque.

MACHINES AND CODES: MARKOV CHAINS AND THE THEORY OF SURPLUS VALUE

The 'machine' is neither reducible to a State nor to a technical entity. It is a social assemblage and thus designates the combination (assemblage or *agencement*) of material elements. The concept of the 'social machine' serves to reduce the opposition between the mechanical and the biological starting with a single theory of the vital articulated in relation to a mode of social production, one in which Marx's influence is always discernible. Even if we agree that the technical object only exists in its mode of social assemblage, this does not explain the expression 'desiring machine', or how we can, without metaphor, apply the concept of the machine to the capture of forces. We thus must explain the functioning of the machine in terms of the cutting of flows and coding.

We have seen that the desiring machine functions through fragmentary cuts but is never itself a closed unity: just as it is always open to flows, it is also always a machine of a machine, a Leibnizian theme[37] that rejects the separation of the organic and the mechanism in favour of a dynamic vitalism that invalidates the distinction between the mechanical and biological. For Leibniz, organisms are machines from start to finish. Similarly, for Deleuze and Guattari, there is no antinomy between flow and cut, not because these modes are equivalent, but because their difference is a matter of perspective: that which in one place cuts a given flow can elsewhere appear as that which is cut (AO 36–7).[38] The machine cuts and codes, but then becomes a flow for another machine, not necessarily homogeneous to the first: thus, the schizophrenic regime cuts into Oedipal machines and vice versa, as a function of the relations of force that affect them. Different technological regimes can coexist: a flow is nothing other than another 'machine', captured as a matter of determination and not as an element of coding. The machine acts as a cut in relation to that which it connects, and itself has the status of flow when it is taken up by a relation of forces: machine and flow are thus relative to the actions of cutting and coding. The machine is the operation of coding that confers form upon a material, and coding is a capture of force that transforms (whatever) material by causing it to enter into (whatever kind of) assemblage. And this apparatus is applicable at every level since it does not define individuals, but materials and forces, and thus works indifferently on all bodies (crystal or membrane, global capitalism, amorous relations, wasp and orchid).

What does this action of the machine – this capture and coding – consist of now that it can no longer be based, as in Lacan, on a typically human, symbolic articulation? Here, code is thought as a Markov chain: it is 'jargon', not a language,[39] a 'capture' of code. If 'we owe to Jacques Lacan the discovery of this fertile domain of a code of the unconscious' (AO 38), we owe to Ruyer the demonstration of the fecundity of Markov's analyses, which allows us to think of code as a statistical 'jargon' of elements through an iterative (automatic) procedure and not as a language: it is from Ruyer that Deleuze and Guattari borrow – without citing him – the use of Markovian chains that, on a decisive page of *Anti-Oedipus*, enables them to shift from the signifying symbolic of Lacan to statistical computation, just as applicable to life as to culture, and through this, to overcome of any difference of nature between vitalism and mechanism (AO 38).

Markov, a Russian mathematician, studied the partially dependent, aleatory phenomena that characterise the structure of languages in particular, and believed that it is possible to statistically determine the variables that regulate the use and succession of semantic, syntactic or phonological elements, and to apply them to an iterative, simple, artificial procedure (code) that would make it possible to 'automatically pastiche' a language.[40] Markov provided proof in a demonstration using Latin. Such a statistical procedure remains independent of any signification, but nevertheless reproduces characteristics of French, for example, where q is always followed by u, h is preceded by c in 50 per cent of cases. Second, this jargon is applicable to all linguistic entities in a culture – language, style, idiolect (through a study of key words) – by taking into account only real occurrences and not their significations. Since he deals with linguistic signs on the plane of the automation of data, this is also applicable to all kinds of signals, and is also applicable in the domain of the living being. Ruyer created the expression 'biological jargon' to indicate the 'semi-fortuitous enchaining of themes'[41] evoked 'without a total plan, according to the demands of the preceding phrase',[42] through non-significant iteration, to determine the linkages (morphogenetic or behavioural) that do not answer to the unity of a form developing in accordance with a global theme. Ruyer uses Markov chains to theorise a mode of 'open formation', which is aleatory and iterative in opposition to a 'thematic' development, and which is occurring at all levels of form. The open, Markovian formation allows us to understand a host of phenomena, from the 'Markovian keyboards' of cultures, to historical contingencies, to biological mutations, and Markov does not fail to indicate that parasitism, symbiosis and commensalism are the most striking examples of it.[43] For Ruyer, Markov chains thus determine the mode by which forms communicate, a mode that is non-final but also not lacking in order: in this way, an animal allows itself to be taken in by pastiches of the stimuli-signals that it finds interesting, something hunters know very well. Ruyer's use of Markov turns out to be decisive for the theory of coding and the capture of code on three points: first, because it makes available a theory of order that is neither continuous nor determined; second, because the linking of signals is indifferent to signification as well as to the homogeneity of its elements; and third, because it encompasses a theory of 'pastiche'.

The Markov chain transforms the Lacanian signifying chain on the level of both its articulation and composition. The coding of a flow is neither symbolic nor signifying. It does not answer to any linguistic rule, whether symbolic or signifying, and yet it is not completely random. Rather, it is likened 'to the lottery drawings that sometimes cause a word to be chosen, sometimes a design, sometimes a thing or piece of a thing, depending on one another only by the order of the random drawings' (AO 309). It produces the semi-aleatory order (a drawing of lots) that Deleuze interprets as 'a throw of the dice',[44] a 'mixture of the aleatory and the dependent' (F 86) that allows us to think order without submitting it to a continuity, but without succumbing to disorder either. The Markov chain thus serves as a model for all problems that concern order at whatever scale one is situated: material, biological, cultural, historical:[45] it presents a model of becoming as an 'emission of singularities'. For Deleuze, what is at stake is thinking a mode of linkage that is not aligned on a causal or final succession, or on an Idea or a structure: Markov furnishes the concept for such a 'linkage', as far from an absence of order as from a continuity:

> Not that anything can be linked up with anything else. Instead it is more like a series of draws in a lottery, each one operating at random but under extrinsic conditions laid down by the previous draw . . . like a Markov chain . . . Things are not joined together by a process of continuity or interiorization, therefore, but instead they rejoin above and beyond the breaks and discontinuities (mutation). (F 86)

With Markov, Deleuze maintains a dimension of order as an aleatory operation, through discontinuous junction, including cuts, but also determinate sections. In Deleuze, therefore, the nature of order is semi-aleatory. In addition, the elements thereby linked are assigned two essential determinations: they are neither signifying nor homogeneous. In other words, they are asignifying and heterogeneous. What is therefore linked in a section of order are 'mobile stocks' of information that fit together through a system of 'switches and drawing lots', a writing that is not discursive but rather 'transdiscursive', as Deleuze and Guattari write, rediscovering Simondonian transduction to describe a process taking place 'at the level of the real'. Markovian jargon thus permits the articulation of heterogeneous signs, attaining value uniquely by their position in the code. But, in contrast to the structural series that Deleuze assesses in *The Logic of Sense*, their composition is heterogeneous: a word has the same value as a drawing or a thing. On the one hand, articulated signs are of 'whatever nature'; on the other, 'the code resembles less a language than a jargon', an 'open-ended formation' – this is a textual quotation from Ruyer (AO 38). We can still talk about 'signifying chains', as Lacan does,[46] on condition that we specify that they are signifying because they are made of signs, but that the signs in themselves are not signifying. This is the essential determination of a theory of the sign that is not indebted to the linguistic sphere. Unconscious, machinic coding opens the way to an asignifying semiotics, which enables us to think the articulation of a plural and discontinuous order.

> The code resembles not so much a language as a jargon, an open-ended, polyvocal formation. The nature of signs within it is insignificant . . . No chain is homogeneous; all of them resemble, rather, a succession of characters from different alphabets . . . Each chain captures fragments of other chains from which it 'extracts' a surplus value, just as the orchid code 'attracts' the figure of the wasp. (AO 38–9)

The Markovian 'code' (Guattari), the Markovian 'jargon' (Ruyer), is 'mid-way between order and disorder':[47] here we return to the theory of the transversal fragment that allows us to present the theory of machinic production more precisely. The machine is a unity of functioning that codes, but also detaches, extracting other fragments and codes, doing so on an organic plane (genetic code) as much as on a neurological or social one.[48]

> In this sense it was possible to insist [an allusion to Ruyer] on a common characteristic of human cultures and of living species, as 'Markov' chains: aleatory phenomena that are partially dependent. In the genetic code as in the social codes, what is termed a signifying chain is more a jargon than a language (*langage*), composed of nonsignifying elements that have a meaning or an effect of signification only in the large aggregates that they constitute through a linked drawing of elements, a partial dependence, a superposition of relays. (AO 289)

The Markovian code allows Deleuze and Guattari to break out of the enclosure of the human symbolic world and gain an entryway that allows for the unification of the new molecular biology and the discovery of the genetic code with economic theories and the cultural order in general, in a free enough variation that mixes political economy, the science of coding of flows, and especially, the Marxist theory of surplus value, freely interpreted as 'surplus' and 'capture of code'. Operating between heterogeneous chains, it introduces a semi-aleatory order across disparate regions, which Deleuze and Guattari will soon describe as different 'strata' of the material, of the vital and of the cultural. The code allows us to think phenomena of order in the physico-chemical, chemico-biological and neuro-biological domains, such that the cultural no longer appears to be an isolated domain,

but rather fully depends on the vital one, in conformity with an enduring aim of Deleuzian philosophy. As a determination of a linkage that is
neither determinate nor fortuitous, it enters into the constitution of the
concept of the *rhizome* in 1976, as well as into that of the *assemblage* in
1980. For as a logic of real multiplicities, the rhizome possesses as its first
characteristic two connected principles (in the plural): '1 and 2: principles
of connection and heterogeneity' (TP 7). There is connection, a unifying
link, but this connection is immediately pluralised by the second principle
of heterogeneity. Heterogeneity concerns both modes of encodings and
linked semiotic elements. As an articulation of differenciated signals, it
entails a multidimensional semiotic that requires abandoning the primacy
of linguistics, since one cannot 'make a radical break between regimes of
signs and their objects' (TP 7), as we saw in the case of the Markov chains.
From this perspective, the unconscious is no longer a local agency. What is
achieved with the second synthesis of inscription is a theory of code freed
from structuralism and the signifier. This provides theoretical support
for the definition of the rhizome, which is characterised by the connection between 'semiotic chains of any nature'. They are indeed semiotic,
and have the value of signs, but they do not belong to a unitary order of
significations: the plurality of regimes of signs emerges from this, as does
the transversal connection between signs and states of things, between
discursive and non-discursive statements. 'On the contrary, not every trait
in a rhizome is necessarily linked to a linguistic feature: semiotic chains
of every nature are connected to very diverse modes of coding (biological,
political, economic, etc.) that bring into play not only different regimes of
signs but also states of things of differing status' (TP 7).

To pursue the analysis of the rhizome, and to better define coding, we
need to consider the different kinds of movements that affect it: the 'code'
is modulated through operations of 'coding', 'decoding' and 'overcoding',
which entail the definition of the line of flight as well as that of movements
that affect territories: deterritorialisation and reterritorialisation.

The theory of asignifying, molecular coding assures the communication
of the vital to the social. It is only when we conceive of the machine as
an individuated object, a global and separated object, when we confer
upon it a structural unity, that we split the world of the living and the
social world off from the technical artifact. To grant the machine such a
structural unity entails in turn that we grant a biological unity to the living being. But with the notion of the social machine, technics is not only
extended to the social, but also to the processes of life (coding). Technics
is porous on two fronts: to social assemblages that diffuse it in the social
body, and to codings and vital flows that render it indiscernible from
vital mechanisms.[49] That which allows the extension of the machinic to

the social calls at the same time for its extension to the vital, to molecular *engineering*, an expression borrowed from Jacques Monod (AO 289).[50] We need to see an allosteric protein as a specialised product of molecular engineering, allowing an interaction to be established between bodies lacking chemical affinity and thus serving any reaction whatever, including 'the intervention of compounds that are chemically foreign and indifferent to this reaction' (AO 288): thus, for the biologist, the domain of 'chance', of real disorganisation, serves 'large configurations' that reproduce by drawing lots chained together in big sets. Monod can speak of a 'microscopic cybernetics' and see biochemical syntheses as operating on chemical signals of whatever kind, completely indifferent to the substrate, but in such a way that the first serendipitous choices constrain the unfolding of the rest of the process, which Deleuze and Guattari compare to Markov chains. It is thus a vitalism that is machinic. But reciprocally, the world of technics may only be seen as a closed, human domain, an 'empire within an empire', a cultural pocket within nature, when the historicity of the existence of real machines is turned into an abstraction. Here, Deleuze and Guattari refer to a new version of capture, this time provided not by Proust, but by Samuel Butler. In *Erewhon: The Book of the Machines*, the opposition between natural vitalism and cultural mechanism only holds if we have not posed the question of the reproduction of the machine, a question that explodes the abstract thesis of the machine's structural unity. The machine does not exist on its own. It assumes an external agent who fabricates it, maintains it and repairs it. Butler uses the example of the symbiosis of red clover and the bee to demonstrate the real indistinction between the mechanical and the vital. 'Does any one say that the red clover has no reproductive system because the humble bee (and the humble bee only) must aid and abet it before it can reproduce? . . . We are misled by considering any complicated machine a single thing; in truth it is a city or society. . . .'[51]

In the case of machines, the external agent of reproduction is the human, and the technological lineage, the *machinic phylum*, should be understood against a background of machinic vitalism and molecular *engineering* (AO 284–5). The red clover and the bee, the orchid and the male wasp that it attracts, which it intercepts by 'carrying on its flower the image and odor of the female wasp' (AO 285): this *mimetic* symbiosis cannot be explained in terms of resemblance, which would assume the intervention of an exterior finality, but should rather be understood as a 'capture of code', proceeding in fragments, a part of the orchid integrating into its system a fragment of the code of the wasp, capturing 'within its own code a code fragment of another machine' (AO 285), which is the definition of 'the phenomenon of surplus value of code' (AO 285). Markov chains provide, with their determination of pastiche – the fact that a given code can be identified easily, just as one 'recognises' French or as the duck allows itself to be taken in by a decoy – an important support for the theory of becoming that in *A Thousand Plateaus* replaces the theory of imitation. This is why the example that emerges in Deleuze and Guattari's writing to explain molecular coding is that of 'capture', by which the genetic code of the orchid 'extracts' the motif of the wasp. This is a definition of capture as double-becoming, which is applicable here for thinking not the identity of man and machine, but rather an 'assemblage', a double-becoming that transforms domesticated material as much as it contributed to the transformation of animal and vegetal species that have entered into a human assemblage (Neolithic agriculture and breeding).

> At *this point of dispersion* of the two arguments, it becomes immaterial whether one says that machines are organs, or organs, machines. The two definitions are exact equivalents: man as a 'vertebro-machinate mammal', or as an 'aphidian parasite of machines.' . . . Once the structural unity of the machine has been undone, once the personal and specific unity of the living has been laid to rest, a direct link is perceived between the machine and desire . . . the machine is desiring and desire, machined. (AO 285)

The machine is thus not a development of the tool; it is an organic and social machine. A difference doubtless exists between a virus,[52] a biological organisation, different societies and an economic axiomatic, but all of these phenomena may be seen as codings of flows and desiring machines.

NOTES

1. Guattari, 'Machine et structure', 241. Originally published in *Change* 12 (1969) and reprinted in *Psychanalyse et transversalité*, 240–8. Page numbers refer to the latter text.
2. Guattari, 'Machine et structure', 243. This formulation connects the Lacanian 'signifier' to the 'differentiator' of *The Logic of Sense*.
3. Mumford, 'The First Megamachine'. Cited in *Anti-Oedipus*, 141. Deleuze and Guattari also cite Mumford's classic work, *The City in History*, but they do not refer to his earlier work, *Technics and Civilization*.
4. Cited in Mumford, 'The First Megamachine', 3. On Reuleaux, see Chapter 11, n. 2.
5. Mumford, 'The First Megamachine', 6. See also Deleuze and Guattari, *Anti-Oedipus*, 141 and 222, and *A Thousand Plateaus*, 427–8 and 457.
6. Mumford, 'The First Megamachine', 2. Mumford takes up the classic analysis denigrating human muscular energy in favour of more powerful, inorganic sources of energy (water, wind, steam, electricity, etc.). 'Non-human form' implies that in making the transition from industry to automation, the human servo-motor, a relay that makes the machine work, also becomes obsolete in the sense that his nervous system is integrated into the

machine itself (sensors, computer programs, etc.). Leroi-Gourhan sees in the same sequence an exteriorisation of human functions, both the skeletal-muscular and then the neurosensory systems (*Le Geste et la parole*). In the sense that he understands this as a 'liberation' (an 'extraniation') from the corporeal organic structure, Leroi-Gourhan becomes an important source for the concept of deterritorialisation in *A Thousand Plateaus*. But Deleuze and Guattari refuse the teleological aspect suggested by the notion of 'liberation', which assumes an organic unity, and turns technics into the extension of biology. With the concept of deterritorialisation, they substitute for 'liberation' the idea of a biological indetermination that forms with social technics a metamorphic assemblage that does not fall into line with a unitary development, which is palpable in Leroi-Gourhan's inspired reading of human history.

7. The Marxist vocabulary of 'class difference' does not belong to Mumford's repertory, but rather to that of Guattari, and of Deleuze, who specifies in one of his interviews with Negri that the class question remains current, even if the 'class struggle' is marked by Stalinist dogmatism. In the present example, it is clear that human material is distributed at different levels of the social machine: the raw reserves of muscular energy (slaves), the transmitters of order (order words and soldiers), and the sovereign.

8. This conception is also flawed in that it presents an evolutionary time-line that discerns the appearance of the machine at a specific moment in the mechanical lineage of the tool. This is the case in Leroi-Gourhan's *L'homme et la matière*.

9. This is the analysis of so-called 'primitive' societies that Deleuze and Guattari initiate with the analysis of 'savages' in *Anti-Oedipus* and develop by means of the antithesis nomadic/sedentary in *A Thousand Plateaus*. What is at stake is a meditation on the opposition between Statist societies, characterised by writing and history, and societies 'without a State'. See Clastres, *La société contre l'État*, and the commentary in *Anti-Oedipus*, Part 3, Chapter 10.

10. Gilles Deleuze and Félix Guattari, *L'Anti-Oedipe: Capitalisme et schizophrénie* (Paris: Minuit, 1972), 482. My translation.

11. See the interview conducted with Deleuze, Guattari and Foucault in September 1972 in *Recherches* 13 (December 1973): 183–6; reedited under the title, 'Chapitre IV: Formation des équipements collectifs', in *Les équipements du pouvoir*, 212–20, and as 'Arrachés par d'énergiques interventions à notre euphorique séjour dans l'histoire, nous mettons laborieusement en chantier des «categories logiques»', in Foucault, *Dits et écrits*, vol. 1, 1320–3. This text has been incomprehensibly excluded from *Desert Islands*.

12. Foucault, *Discipline and Punish*, 237.

13. Foucault, *Discipline and Punish*, 153; Deleuze, *Foucault*, 40.

14. Leroi-Gourhan, *L'homme et la matière* and *Le Geste et la parole*; Simondon, *Du mode d'existence des objets techniques*.

15. Vernant, *Mythe et pensée chez les Grecs*, 2 vols.
16. Braudel, *Civilisation matérielle, économie et capitalisme*, 3 vols; White, *Medieval Technology and Social Change*.
17. Braudel, *Civilisation matérielle*, vol. 1, 128. Deleuze cites Braudel in *Foucault*, 40 n. 28, and White in *A Thousand Plateaus*, 399.
18. Détienne, 'La phalange: problèmes et controverses', in *Problèmes de la guerre en Grèce ancienne*, 119–42; Deleuze and Guattari, *A Thousand Plateaus*, 398ff.
19. Simondon, *Du mode d'existence des objets techniques*. Simondon indeed demonstrates that technical 'essence' is indissociable from its technical milieu, but his work is positioned on a different axis in that he is first and foremost concerned with theorising the criteria of individuation of the technical object in its lineage (its machinic phylum, as Deleuze would put it). He does contribute to the theory of assemblages, but on a different level: that of materials of expression, important for art. For that very reason, he cannot contribute to the level of theorisation by which Deleuze and Guattari, in the first moment of the analysis, dissolve the 'technical individual' into its social assemblage. But he contributes to the second moment, which deals with the material traits that characterise an assemblage *in concreto* (earth or stone for architecture, or iron or steel for metallurgy).
20. Détienne, 'La phalange: problèmes et controverses', 134. My translation.
21. Foucault, *Discipline and Punish*, 224–5.
22. Foucault, *Discipline and Punish*, 225.
23. 'Perhaps also the concept of arrangement (*assemblage*), put forward by Félix and myself, may have helped him with his own analysis of "apparatuses." But he thoroughly transformed everything he used.' Deleuze, *Negotiations*, 89.
24. See Foucault et al., *Les machines à guérir (aux origines de la hôpital moderne)*, which contains this epigraph by Tenon: 'Hospitals are of course tools, or, if you prefer, machines for economically treating sick people *en masse*; the art of healing has never presided over their form or their distribution.'
25. 'One can of course see how each kind of society corresponds to a particular kind of machine – with simple mechanical machines corresponding to sovereign societies, thermo-dynamic machines to disciplinary societies, cybernetic machines and computers to control societies. But the machines don't explain anything, you have to analyse the collective apparatuses of which the machines are just one component.' Deleuze, *Negotiations*, 175.
26. This Foucauldian duality, which Deleuze understands as a neo-Kantianism (the form of intuition of visibilities and the categorical form of knowledges), is taken up by Deleuze starting with the distinction, which he adopts from Hjelmslev, between the form of expression and forms of content (*Foucault*, 59–60; 66–9; 81) and developed within the frame of the theory of capture, to which we shall return. There is a disjunction between

seeing and saying, and 'if there's a gap between them, an irreducible distance, it only means you can't solve the problem of knowledge (or rather of
"knowledges") by invoking a correspondence or conformity of terms. You
have to look elsewhere for what links and weaves them together. It's as
though the archive's riven by a great fault dividing visible form on one side
from the form of what can be uttered on the other, each irreducible to the
other. And the thread that knits them together and runs between them lies
outside these forms, in another dimension' (Deleuze, *Negotiations*, 96–7).
What Deleuze calls the 'diagrammaticism' in Foucault is the 'analogue of
Kantian schematism' (*Foucault*, 82). This Kantian reading of Foucault
provides us with a valuable index for measuring the importance that
Deleuze attributes to Kant.

27. The same considerations are applicable to the 'diagram'. See *Foucault*,
    chapter 2; Foucault, *Discipline and Punish*, 205.

28. See *Foucault*, 38 n. 24, where Deleuze compares Bergson to the way
    Foucault treats relations of power as 'internal conditions of differencia-
    tion'. Foucault, *Histoire de la sexualité, vol. 1: La volonté de savoir*, 124.

29. The example of the yams and rice comes from Haudricourt's analy-
    ses, which Deleuze and Guattari use in *Rhizome* (see Haudricourt,
    'Domestication des animaux, culture de plantes et traitement d'autrui',
    and 'Nature et culture dans la civilisation de l'igname: l'origine des clones
    et des clans'); Deleuze and Guattari, *A Thousand Plateaus*, 18.

30. Just as the forces of life enter into contact with carbon, the era of control is
    in a relation with the forces of silicon (Deleuze, *Negotiations*, 90).

31. Foucault, *Discipline and Punish*, 28.

32. Even while every assemblage includes a 'pathic' stage and is characterised
    by specific affects. In *A Thousand Plateaus*, Deleuze and Guattari treat the
    assemblage on a much more collective and 'transhuman' level, if we can
    use this latter term by referring to Simondon's notion of 'transindividual',
    while the analyses in *Anti-Oedipus* are situated on a level that is more
    infra-individual and sub-human. For example, in *A Thousand Plateaus*,
    'assemblages are passional, they are compositions of desire' (399), in the
    sense, of course, of a machinic construction. This does not mean that the
    analysis concerns the plane of desire, but rather that of the assemblage.

33. This analysis depends on the elegant analysis of Leroi-Gourhan in *Milieu
    et techniques*, and adopts from Simondon the concept of a 'technical
    essence' characterising a given 'technical lineage'. Simondon, *Du mode
    d'existence des objets techniques*, 41. Deleuze and Guattari, *A Thousand
    Plateaus*, 398–9; 406–7.

34. Francastel, *Peinture et société, naissance et destruction d'un espace plas-
    tique, de la Renaissance au cubism*; *La figure et le lieu: l'ordre visual du
    Quattrocento*.

35. See also Foucault, *Discipline and Punish*, Part 3.

36. Deleuze and Guattari, *A Thousand Plateaus*, '1837: Of the Refrain', and
    Deleuze, *The Fold*. Art is the 'first' of arts not in the Hegelian sense of a

'first' art, the most primitive art, the most engaged with matter (symbolic art), but in the sense that it is the clearest example of the articulation of the vital, the social, the technical and the arts, and indubitably indicates the contribution of the arts to the human ethos. Art first has to do with dwelling and the expressive resources that produce a territory. Architecture poses the question of the consistency of the milieu of expression.

37. Leibniz, *Monadology*, §64.

38. This Leibnizian analysis of the machine also relies upon the profound analysis of the machine proposed by Samuel Butler in *Erewhon* (1872). See also the appendix to the French edition of *Anti-Oedipus*, 'Bilan-programme pour machines désirantes'.

39. Raymond Ruyer, not cited on these pages from *Anti-Oedipus*, is nevertheless subjacent to them. It is Ruyer who drew Deleuze and Guattari's attention to the fruitfulness of Markov chains for theories of culture, as well as for theories of the evolution of living forms: he uses them in the frame of a cultural vitalism. See Ruyer, *La genèse des formes vivantes*, chapter 8, 'Formations ouvertes and jargons markoviens'. Even if Ruyer is not cited on this decisive page, the argument of *La genèse des formes vivantes* is summarised in *Anti-Oedipus* on pages 286 and 289, where Ruyer *is* cited: 'On the Markov chains and their applications to the living species as well as to cultural formations, see Ruyer, *La genèse des formes vivantes*, chapter 8. The phenomena of surplus value of code are clearly explained in this perspective of "semifortuitous sequences." Several times Ruyer compares this with the language of schizophrenia' (AO 289). Ruyer's theory of jargon is also important for the theory of creative stuttering and of literature as minor language. It is obvious that such 'jargon' suits the syntactic disorganisation that we recognise in Artaud, but also the jargonistic texts that Michaux and Réquichot create. It also clarifies the theory of suitcase-words elaborated by Deleuze in his comparison between Artaud and Carroll in *The Logic of Sense*.

40. Ruyer, *La genèse des formes vivantes*, 171.

41. 'Thematism' (*thématisme*) is a concept typical of Ruyer, designating a formative power proper to the living being and, more accurately, proper to any form. This power is irreducible to structural mechanism or to finalism. Inspired by Jakob von Uexküll and Bergson, Ruyer compares this mode of 'survey' (*survol*) formation, a being anticipating its own development, to a musical theme. He thereby rediscovers the Bergsonian relation between duration (*durée*) and melody, as well as Uexküll's developments in *Mondes animaux et monde humain* (Berlin, 1921). Uexküll insisted on 'the great richness of the musical analogy on the biological plane' (150), positing that 'the melody of development obeys a score (*une partition*)' (11), and that it is the task of ethology to reconstitute 'nature's score'. With Bergsonian overtones, Uexküll specified that 'corporeal substance can be cut with a knife, but not a melody' (156). It is from Uexküll that Ruyer gets his concept of 'thematism', a 'verticalism' opposed to causal

horizontal linkages that allows him to posit a proto-subjectivity at the level of real form, irreducible to its functioning, elaborating its melody. This is an important notion for Deleuze, which he in turn develops in *The Fold* and *What is Philosophy?* For Ruyer, form in every domain is the product of activity endowed with its own rhythm (*La genèse des formes vivantes*, 140). With the concept of 'thematism', Ruyer made himself vulnerable to attack on two fronts: on the first, the ethologists reproached him for intruding into their discipline in the guise of a philosopher of aesthetics, and so incapable of scientific rigour; on the second, philosophers chastised him for his positivist reliance on the vital domain in a fashion they deemed naïve and, in the end, mystical. Haldane, an ethologist who nevertheless supported the idea that there is a consistency proper to animal behaviour, which he compared to human rituals and held to be irreducible to simple mechanism, judged that thematism remained an illogical aesthetic notion and reproached Ruyer for 'speaking the language of metaphysics'. See Haldane's objections after Ruyer's presentation, 'Finality and Instinct', at the June 1954 colloquium, *Instinct in Animal Behaviour and in Humans* (*L'instinct dans le comportement des animaux et de l'homme*), Actes du colloque organisé par la fondation Singer-Polignac (Paris: Masson, 1956), 745–83; 781; as well as his response to Benveniste's well-known article (Émile Benveniste, 'Communication animal et langage humaine', *Diogène* 1 [1952]; J.B.S. Haldane, 'Rituel humaine et communication animale', *Diogène* 4 [1953]: 77–93). Despite the fact that Ruyer's vitalism recalled the thought of Whitehead, whom Jean Wahl admired and knew well, it drew the ire of the latter, who brought Ruyer's presentation at the Société française de philosophie to an abrupt close with the following dry remark: 'I had understood that it is difficult to admit physics as a reality, that the psychological is difficult to grasp, and that leaves the vital. It does not seem that we have progressed very far.' Ruyer, 'Le psychologique et le vital', *Bulletin de la Société Française de Philosophie* 39.1 (1939): 184.

42. Ruyer, *La genèse des formes vivantes*, 173.

43. Ruyer, *La genèse des formes vivantes*, 174.

44. This recalls Deleuze's analysis of the eternal return, elaborated in *Nietzsche and Philosophy*, and which, in *Difference and Repetition*, he turns into the third achronological synthesis, the Mallarméan 'throw of the dice', a response to the Nietzschean eternal return to indicate the achronological and intensive fulguration of individuations (of thought and of life). Deleuze insists that thinking 'involves throwing the dice' (*Foucault*, 87). This emission of singularities that responds to a semi-aleatory draw thus assembles, in a complex montage, the Mallarméan throw of the dice, Nietzsche's eternal return, the relation between God and nature in Wahl's reading of Whitehead (Jean Wahl, *Vers le concret: études d'histoire de la philosophie contemporaine* [Paris: Vrin, 1932]), and Markov's semi-aleatory drawing of lots.

45. Thus, Foucault's notion of the diagram can be understood in terms of the Markov chain and of the Nietzschean formula, 'the iron hands of necessity

that shake the dice box of chance'. We need to think the diagram in history and to connect historical necessity to the unpredictability of becoming: the diagram is not historical; it relates to becoming (Deleuze, *Foucault*, 85–7).

46. Lacan, 'Seminar on "The Purloined Letter"', *Écrits*, 6–48; Deleuze and Guattari, *Anti-Oedipus*, 38.

47. Ruyer, *La genèse des formes vivantes*, 174.

48. Monod, *Le hasard et la nécessité*.

49. Leroi-Gourhan's influence is important here as well. His theories are discussed twice in *A Thousand Plateaus*: once, in 'The Geology of Morals', when it is a question of connecting the technical to the biological, and again in 'The Treatise on Nomadology', when it is a question of extricating the machinic phylum from the lineage of evolutionary biology.

50. Monod, *Le hasard et la nécessité*, 91. See also Keith Ansell Pearson, ed., *Deleuze and Philosophy: The Difference Engineer* (London and New York: Routledge, 1997). On engineering, see Deleuze and Guattari, *A Thousand Plateaus*, 328 n. 30.

51. Samuel Butler, *Erewhon*, Chapter 24.

52. A virus is remarkable in that it contains the threshold of life below the level of the cell since it is nothing other than a piece of code that survives thanks to its parasitical ability to duplicate its code within other chromosomal chains, without being capable of reproducing itself. Ruyer insists upon Stanley's discovery of crystallisable viruses that demonstrate 'the perfect continuity between chemistry and life', which Ruyer interprets as the triumph of biology, not materialism. See Ruyer, 'La conscience et la vie', 56.

13. Faciality

The analysis of the face, which Guattari initiates in *The Machinic Unconscious* (1979) and pursues with Deleuze in *A Thousand Plateaus* (1980), develops a new philosophy of the sign in its experimental and political reality, a concrete semiotics that replaces and dismisses abstract doctrines of interpretation. For Deleuze and Guattari, in effect, signs are not sequestered in the separate linguistic or mental – psychic and individual – sphere of the human brain, but rather are diffused in concrete universes, producing complex, pragmatic effects, conjugating segments of codes and states of things, regimes of signs in their political and social assemblages. If in a bold stroke, the face enables the integration of a political critique of the human sciences and a new philosophy of the sign, this is because it functions as a concrete system whose reference is historical – labelled 'Year Zero, the birth of Christ' – and as a power that gave birth to the face as the order word of a specific civilisation: our own.

This allows us to explain the overall apparatus of *A Thousand Plateaus* and to discuss the position of the face in this exceptional book, which puts an end to the scheme of interpretation that plagues the human sciences. The title of the seventh of the *Thousand Plateaus*, 'Year Zero: Faciality', opens the chronology of the face in the Christian regime, marking its beginning from the birth of Christ, 'Year Zero' of Western subjectivity.

The face is thus neither a spiritual marker of a humanity that has extracted itself from biological animality nor a cultural universal. It is a historical power that is exercised in some societies as opposed to others and initiates a specific history of the pre-eminence of the face, whose universalising pretension we can, following Deleuze and Guattari, ascribe to this history and summarily call the history of the Western subject. If the face acts as a sign that codes a portion of the body, this is because it is itself the product of a social assemblage, of a complex of forces that we cannot be satisfied to describe as a representation or an act of consciousness. Thus, the concrete example of the face exhibits the political and pragmatic character of the sign as an assemblage. The face is thus not body, but sign. As such, it is neither a natural indicator nor an individual essence, but rather a social formation (*mise en forme sociale*).

SEMIOTICS

The first principle proposed by Deleuze and Guattari is striking and must be developed in all its rigour: the face is not an anthropomorphic constant. There is no human nature. Doubtless, all hominids have a head, an extension of the body and top end of the bust, but all do not have a face in the sense that we understand it, as a normative power and personal instance. The face is linked to the history of the subject, to the pragmatic installation of the individual, to the normative constitution of the person, which cannot be reduced to a natural history of Reason, but must instead be constructed as a singular, historical process. In opposition to any anthropological idealism, Deleuze and Guattari thus relativise and historicise the face. The human shape does not necessarily assume this form, and in those contexts in which the face is produced, this does not depend on a universal history of humanity. The face no more marks the humanity of the body than it reveals the universality of the Western subject. A Spinozist consequence follows from this: there is no separate human essence that the face is supposed to represent. On the contrary, different cultural semiotics exist, and have existed, and the face only actualises one mode. This is the news that needs to be disseminated into the human sciences.

Of course, this modification of the status of the face does not change anything about its existence in our societies. In accordance with one of Deleuze and Guattari's preferred strategies, the polemical transformation of a notion does not invalidate the reality of its existence; it only changes the determination of its status. Deleuze and Guattari thus do not question the existence of the face: they purport to present a coherent explanation of it, while transforming the human sciences at the same time.

The face is not a universal. It is not explanatory; instead, it is the face that must be explained. As a cultural form, the face results from a semiotic formation of bodies, and it is in this sense that it engages a new logic of the human sciences. In effect, the face is a sign. But a sign of this type is not a distinct entity, subject to a meaning in a logic of interpretation. It is necessary to completely revise the articulation of signs and meaning, forms and matter, signifieds and signifiers. Doubtless, it is always a question of explaining signs, but according to a logic of experimentation that replaces signifying and subjective interpretation. This is exactly what the analysis of the face gives us an opportunity to do.

Regimes of Signs

This kind of semiotic is defined in *Rhizome*, the explicit aim of which is to liberate the theory of the sign from the linguistic primacy of signification and structure. In a rhizome, the semiotic trait is not 'necessarily linked to a linguistic feature', but rather 'semiotic chains of every nature' are 'connected to very diverse modes of coding (biological, political, economic, etc.) that bring into play not only different regimes of signs but also states of things of differing status' (TP 7). Of course, the sign is never isolated, and is indeed given in a plurality of signs, as Saussure argued. However, this plurality does not form a system closed upon itself, or composed uniquely of linguistic signs, but is an open connection, functioning, as the principles of the rhizome indicate, through 'connection and heterogeneity'. That is to say that first, the connection is realised between heterogeneous elements, that is, between semiotic chains of different natures, for example, between biological codes, political contents or linguistic signs. Semiotics, as Deleuze and Guattari demonstrate in *Rhizome*, and as Guattari explains in the superb *Machinic Unconscious*, is not limited to linguistic signifiers. It opens discursive linguistics to its concrete assemblages of enunciation – its political and social context – and demonstrates that codings coexist and include any effective organisation, any individuation at whatever scale, without there being a need to introduce qualitative, transcendent leaps separating matter and life, animal and human, signal and sign. The result of this is an extension of semiotics to the whole philosophy of nature and the positing of a continuity between nature and society.

Second, the connection is not only produced between heterogeneous elements (*hétérogènes*), it produces the heterogeneous (*hétérogène*) within itself by creating the new, by introducing difference, as we will see in the case of territoriality. It thus no longer functions to unify differences; on the contrary, it is the connection that, in connecting, produces the heterogeneous.

Under these conditions, it is clear that signs do not form a closed and homogeneous system, in conformity with the lesson of structuralism, but rather that they compose different, open, connected and disparate regimes. In choosing the expression 'regimes of signs' in the plural, Deleuze and Guattari take a distance from the structuralism dominant at the time of *A Thousand Plateaus*. If signs form plural regimes, and not a unique and unitary system, it is because it is necessary to substitute a pragmatic conception of a system for its structural version. Regimes of signs thus compose open systems, in accordance with the functionalist model of a connected, open, historical machine, which replaces structure, characterised by a mental ideality that is abstract and symbolic.

According to this first *principle of machinic production*, the face is not a human structure but rather a machine produced in a specific assemblage. It is necessary, therefore, to stop taking the face as a given of nature and rather to seek out the transcendental conditions of its appearance. Given a concrete face – black holes, white screen – we need to ask to what assemblage it corresponds. We shall see that the face serves to define a determinate mode of domination that corresponds to the historical inscription of capitalism, to the coming of a universal history with its primacy of the signifier and of subjectivity.

The second consequence that leads to the rupture with structuralism is that regimes of signs can no longer be explained through reduction to series of signifiers and signifieds. In place of Saussure's renowned couple, dominant in French thought from Lévi-Strauss to Lacan, Deleuze and Guattari substitute a distinction borrowed from Hjelmslev and reread through Foucault, that of contents (or states of bodies) and expressions (or regimes of signs). This is the second *principle of assemblage*, which transforms the semiotic relation. Instead of putting a signifier into relation with a signified, according to a relation of representation, semiotics functions through assembling (*agençant*) states of bodies (contents) and regimes of signs (expressions) in accordance with a connection through heterogeneity. This is why the face does not express the eternal human subject. On the contrary, the existence of concrete faces assumes a complex process by which a body deterritorialises its uppermost segment and recodes its head onto a face.

At this point, the face is not only a sign; it is the result of a historic assemblage for which it is necessary to trace the intensive map, or diagram, that is, the transcendental condition of its possibility, which Deleuze and Guattari call an abstract machine. Here, also, it is necessary to conduct an analysis on two planes: that of the logic of signs and that of material history.

The Assemblage of the Face

With the concept of the assemblage, Deleuze and Guattari extricate semiotics from its structural, signifying interpretation. The effects of coding link expressions and content by arranging them on the pragmatic plane of territory. There is no coding without territory. It is in this way that the semiotic connection creates the heterogeneous (*de l'hétérogène*), difference. Any semiotic assemblage possesses an effective power of transformation and composes a new reality. With this, Deleuze and Guattari prove Marx right: what is at stake is never interpreting the world, but transforming it.

We take leave of the symbolic plane of structure in order to enter pragmatic semiotics, as Deleuze and Guattari understand it. The face is not
only a structuring percept, symbolically producing a human subject, and
the sign cannot be reduced to a signifying algebra on the symbolic plane.
Semiotics attains the pragmatic plane of the real. It is this dynamic reality
that takes the concept of territory into account.

Territory should not be confused with a given segment of space or be
understood to pre-exist the assemblage. It is instead an act, one produced
in accordance with the vital rhythm of individualising territorialisations
and intensive deterritorialisations. Territory consists in a dynamic of
territorialisation, a vital appropriation that rhythmically coordinates
heterogeneous forces, some tending toward the stratification of organised
forms, others toward the informal becoming of forces. Thus, coding
always produces a mobile and transitory territory with its double valance
of deterritorialising and reterritorialising. Any assemblage, including that
of the face, thus 'has both *territorial* sides, or reterritorialized sides, which
stabilize it, and *cutting edges of deterritorialization*, which carry it away'
(TP 88). Such is the 'tetravalence' of the assemblage. Any assemblage connects, on the one hand, differenciating series of content and expression, a
first pincer (*pince*) that is traversed, on the other hand, by a new dynamic
pincer, opening up an axis of becomings and taking into account relative
movements (reterritorialisation and deterritorialisation), intensive vectors that affect content and expression. Deleuze and Guattari explain this
with a sober definition that applies to the face as well as to any semiotic
assemblage.

The Tetravalence of the Assemblage: 1) Content and Expression; 2) Territoriality and Deterritorialisation (TP 504–5)

In order to explain the face, it is thus necessary to return to the contents
and expressions that it causes to resonate, as well as to the centrifugal and
centripetal forces that it requires, that is, to the intensive dynamisms that
traverse it. Closed in upon its territorialising, molar assemblage (to become
a person, to look like . . .), the face is also traversed by intensive, deterritorialising forces. With that, everything has been said: the face assemblage is
not only composed of territorial movements that organise and individualise
corporeal contents and expressions in forming molar concretions, those
thick bands that Deleuze and Guattari call strata, but regimes of signs and
states of things are immersed at the same time in an intensive dynamic,
one that doubles the static state of contents and expressions with lines of
deterritorialisation and intensive diagrams that reintroduce becoming into
stratified assemblages.

Territorialisations, Deterritorialisations

It is always necessary to think of the coding of signs by taking into account its territorial dynamism from the kinetic perspective of becoming. Concrete faces arise from that kind of intensive phenomenon, one that creates territory, through movements of concretion and territorialising organisation said to be molar, but which also includes destratifying powers and molecular forces of deterritorialisation. The face imposes a rigid territorialisation, which recodes and overcodes the head, but which at the same time contains a power of transformation, of becoming and of molecular virtuality. Not only is the face not re-territorialising with respect to the head, which it overcodes without at the same time de-territorialising with the body that it decodes, but in itself, it is limited to performing one mode of territorialisation among others, one which does not exhaust in any way the potentials of human becoming.

Thus, the deterritorialised head reterritorialises on the face, just as in the mother-child relation, the breast-mouth relation, constituted through nursing, deterritorialises the internal mucus membrane onto the external lips, and the mouth into an organ of speech, while the animal teat is reterritorialised onto the maternal breast, according to a coupling that 'already leads onto the plane of faciality'. In the eye-to-eye contact between child and mother, maternal interaction effectively makes a face for the child, at the same time introducing the child to the percept of the face of the mother – the black hole of the gaze, the white surface of the face – in a correlative relation. The face is neither a natural entity nor an erroneously constructed concept, but a singular reality, the semiotic production of which has not to this point received the explanation that it requires. Such a dynamic process of *territorialisation* engages 'a whole history'. It is produced as concretely as possible in accordance with the phylogenetic axis of an anthropological history of the face, and with the ontogenetic axis of the psychology of the child. This is why the question of the face renews the human sciences. Rather than seeing the face as a transcendent node teleologically orienting the history of hominisation and the development of the child, anthropology and psychology would be better off exploring the complex and concrete movements by which faciality operates. Deleuze and Guattari attempt to formalise these relations in their 'theorems of deterritorialisation'.

POLITICS

Strata and the Emergence of the Face

Like any assemblage, the face is formed through coding and territorialisation, and proceeds through the assignation of differences that are 'small, unconnected or free-floating' into differences that are 'appreciable, connected and fixed' (DR 248). But how precisely is the face formed?

The third plateau, the 'Geology of Morals', distinguishes three principal modes of organisation called *strata*. The main strata at our scale are the organic, the signifying and the subjective, which submit us, respectively, to the principles of organisation of the individuated body, of the psychic signifier and of the social subject. The face does not refer to the organic strata but rather depends upon social stratifications, and precisely, it forms at the junction of the signifying strata and the subjective strata, which it joins together in forming a mixed semiotic.

Concrete faces are thus linked to a social and historic process of formation involving components that are doubtless present to different degrees in all cultures. All cultures privilege one or the other of these strata, and they always implicate one another, at least to a certain extent. There is never significance without subjectivity, or subjectivity without significance. But what defines the mixed semiotic of faciality is this very specific assemblage, which binds, above the organic strata of bodies, the signifying strata of the symbolic and the subjective strata of subjectification.

In order for the face to form, it is necessary for significance and subjectification to enter into a coupling that mutually reinforces them. This coupling, which Deleuze and Guattari call the abstract machine of faciality, provides the signifier with its surface of inscription – the white wall – and subjectivity with the introspective force of its gaze: black holes. Thus, this singular, abstract machine forms by chance in history: the 'black hole-white wall' system, gaze piercing the screen of the surface, the abstract sketch of all faces, the machine according to which empirical faces become realised (TP 168).

The difficulty of these analyses comes from the fact that Deleuze and Guattari simultaneously operate on the terrain of a logic of forces – strata, assemblages, coding and territories, movements of deterritorialisation and reterritorialisation answering to a general semiotics – and on the terrain of a sociology of empirical history. Signifying strata, subjective strata and faciality correspond to segments of universal history, which Deleuze and Guattari strive to connect in accordance with a nonlinear, non-teleological model. The signifying stratum, with its emphasis on the marking of bodies, tends to materialise in despotic societies throughout history. The subjective stratum, with its taste for the *mise-en-abîme* of a point of transcendence, of which the purest form appears without doubt in the destiny of the Jewish people, furnishes the empirical conditions for a history of the subject. Significance and subjectivity converge and reinforce one another in faciality, the system that ensures 'the almightiness of the signifier as well as the autonomy of the subject' (TP 181). The assemblage of faciality thus serves to describe an empirically determined mode of domination that corresponds to the historical inscription of capitalism, to the contingent event of its universal history, with its Christian point of departure and the primacy it accords to the signifier and to subjectivity. The study of the faciality assemblage claims to provide nothing less than an exposition of the development of capitalism.

From the perspective of the logic of forces, as we saw with the alternation of territorialisations and deterritorialisations, stratification manifests itself as a 'very important, inevitable phenomenon, that is beneficial in many respects, and unfortunate in many others'. Strata give 'form to matter' and produce preferential nodes of forces; they 'imprison intensities' and 'lock singularities' (TP 40, with modification). In short, they establish a pragmatic and semiotic order composed of movements of territorialisation and coding. It is in this sense that the face can be said to be an 'organisation': it presents an assemblage on its stratified, actualised, molar, rigid surface, and, like all individuated forms, it is limiting, rigid and constraining. This is why 'you don't so much have a face as slide into one' (TP 177). 'The organization of the face is a strong one', a 'sovereign organization' (TP 188), a principle of order and of normalisation that Deleuze and Guattari counter – in a mode that is both Bergsonian and Marxist – to vital becoming. They present a political critique of the face by refusing the model of centred, unitary and sovereign power upon which it in fact depends. The face imposes its normative order; it is an agent of social normalisation.

The analysis of the face thus coincides with that of the body without organs conducted in the preceding chapter of *A Thousand Plateaus*, and it retrospectively clarifies the impeccable sequencing that orchestrates the succession of the thousand plateaus. The semiotic of the rhizome (first plateau) makes possible the disqualification of psychoanalysis (second plateau), for the coding of the unconscious and of subjectivity depend on an ethology and not a morality (third plateau); this entails a dispensing with the postulates of linguistics (fourth plateau), in order to explain how regimes of signs actually function (fifth plateau) in the intensive mode of deterritorialisation (sixth plateau), but also in the stratifying mode of an assemblage, like that of the face, which rules over the history of capitalism in the West (seventh plateau).

Deleuze and Guattari contest the organic vision of the body centred on its organs and instead insist upon becomings that are virtual, inorganic and informal. This is precisely the polemical function of the analysis of the face, when Deleuze and Guattari proclaim: 'undo your face!' But the following sections of the book also indicate their interest in stratified formations: subsequent plateaus examine the logic of strata (8 and 9) on their intensive side (10), then on their territorialising side (11), and then shift to a concrete analysis of the history of capitalism with 'The Treatise

on Nomadology' (12) and 'The Apparatus of Capture' (13). The logic of
A Thousand Plateaus thus reaches a turning point with the analysis of the
face: the first concrete effort to analyse an assemblage that is decisive for
the history of capitalism.

Signifying and Subjective Strata

From the point of view of a sociology of the face, the production of concrete
faces depends on a history of formations of power, at the intersection of the
signifying and subjectifying strata. The face is not a strata, strictly speaking, but rather a form that is actualised between two pre-capitalist strata
of significance and subjectivity. The whole question '*then becomes what
circumstances trigger the machine* that produces the face and facialization'
(TP 170).

In taking up the analyses of political anthropology conducted in *Anti-
Oedipus* and pursued in *A Thousand Plateaus*, Deleuze and Guattari
distinguish different formations of power that correspond to the large
socialising strata: the stratum of significance and the subjective stratum.
Becoming actualised in the forms of the primitive socius and of imperial,
despotic formations, the signifying semiotic has no need for faces. Rather,
it operates through the marking of bodies. The signifier is inscribed in the
flesh and submits the body's surface of inscription to the abstract machine
of primitive despotism. This semiotics of inscription corresponds to the
shift from the primitive, territorial coding of segmentary and acephalous
societies, those lacking in central agencies of power, to archaic, despotic
– that is, pre-capitalist – States. In their consideration of societies without
States, in particular certain African societies analysed by Evans-Pritchard
and Meyer Fortes, or Amerindians studied by Pierre Clastres, Deleuze and
Guattari insist on the fact that masks and tattoos constitute heads without
faces. These cultures have no reason to envy ours and they 'have no face
and need none' (TP 176).

Faciality does not exist in the great despotic empires either, those that
privilege signifying inscription. Deleuze and Guattari examine the archaic
State formations labelled 'imperialist barbarian', which are defined by State
overcoding, centralisation and castes of functionaries, as in the Egyptian or
Chinese empires (AO 152–3). The signifying, social semiotic is inscribed on
the surface of bodies and not in the interiority of souls. These regimes of
power use signifying marks and, like the primitive territorial regime, have
no need to erect a machine of faciality.

In order for the conditions of faciality to appear, the formation of
an entirely different semiotic is required, that of the subjective stratum,
which Deleuze and Guattari examine in the preceding plateau, 'On Several

Regimes of Signs'. Its point of crystallisation in history appears with monotheism and the history of the Jewish people, whose formation of power sets itself completely apart from the Egyptian and Middle Eastern empires. Deleuze and Guattari see in the formation of this first monotheism the interiorisation of a point of subjectivity, a hidden God, turning aside his gaze, being inscribed in a passional way in the cult of the faithful. In a remarkable apparatus, Deleuze and Guattari connect a datum from the history of philosophy that has become proverbial since Hegel – substance that becomes subject – with a sociology of the formations of power and a nonlinear history of societies. We are not saying that a people creates a regime of signs and that the Hebrews invented subjectivity. Rather, it is that the theocratic regime of power established between the Egyptian and Middle Eastern empires and the Nomads of the desert belongs mostly to a regime of subjective signs. The dominance of a semiotic is always relative. But it is necessary to pursue the analysis of despotic and signifying, authoritative and subjective regimes of signs further to explain how they reinforce one another with the appearance of Christianity.

The face is produced by an entwining and reciprocal amplification of signifying and subjective strata. These two strata are always present, in all social organisations, but their entwining is typical of a formation that corresponds to the figure of Western domination, from the Christian origin it assigns to itself to the cult of the person that corresponds to its recent individualism: Christ, the great master. It is this figure of domination, localised in a spatiotemporal way, that Deleuze and Guattari call faciality.

Christ Faciality

The face thus does not concern the organic strata – even though it naturally puts it in play – because it is not a part of the body. Rather, the face occurs to the body when the body is submitted to a social marking. This does not involve just any kind of marking, but a fully determinate, localised and datable social formation whose coordinates are given on the plateau: 'Year Zero: Faciality'. 'The face is not a universal. It is not even that of the white man; it is White Man himself, with his broad white cheeks and the black hole of his eyes. The face is Christ. The face is the typical European . . .' (TP 176). The face finds its point of application in the development of a history of subjectivity that corresponds to the inscription of Christianity and its European development. As opposed to ancient empires, Jewish monotheism proposed a passional regime of subjectivation: 'God withdraws his face, becoming a point of subjectification for the drawing of a line of flight or deterritorialization' (TP 128). Deleuze and Guattari specify that once again, we are not, of course, doing history: we are not saying that a people invents this regime of signs, only that at a given moment a people effectuates the assemblage that assures the relative dominance of that regime under certain historical conditions (and that regime, that dominance, . . . may be assured under other conditions . . .). (TP 121)

Christianity carried the point of subjectivation to infinity, developing consciousness by redoubling it, separating the subject of the enunciation (the *cogito*, the transcendental *I think*) and the subject of the statement (the empirical self). With subjective semiotics, 'the paradox of the legislator-subject replac[es] the signifying despot' (TP 130).

From monotheism to the coming of the subject – the *cogito*, the transcendental subject – the question of the face engages the critical history of the constitution of the subject, such that the history of philosophy and that of the subject must be read within the concrete realisation of social relations. Through a bold and provocative operation, Deleuze and Guattari graft the philosophical history of the subject to Althusser's Marxist critique. The subject is not given but rather produced by means of a semiotic process 'of interpellation', one that concerns linguistics as much as psychology and sociology. Here we encounter the logic of the social sciences. The subject is produced by a collective assemblage of enunciation, which renders linguistic expression possible. However, no teleology or necessity – whether transcendent or economic – presides over this becoming of the subject, which is neither 'a condition interior to language' nor a production necessary to social relations. Nevertheless, it is necessary to retain the following from the Marxist critique: 'Capital is a point of subjectification par excellence' (TP 130). 'Our semiotic of modern White Men, the semiotic of capitalism, has attained this state of mixture in which significance and subjectification effectively interpenetrate' (TP 182).

CLINIC

The Assemblage of Faciality and the Abstract Machine

We can now assess to what degree the face is not a universal but 'a politics' (TP 181). The face answers to a process that is nothing other than that of Western history. The ambition of this proposal is enormous: Deleuze and Guattari propose to renew the philosophy of history and reform the human sciences by means of a transcendental critique. Unlike the process of the becoming-subject of Spirit in Hegel, or the development of the contradiction between the relations and forces of production of capitalism in Marx, this history of faciality remains an aleatory, nonlinear history.

The methodological revision of the human sciences that this ushers in can be summarised in three principles. First principle: the referral of empirical faces to their transcendental condition. All positive doctrines, from psychoanalysis to palaeontology, from child psychology to art history, misrecognise this critical moment and assume the face to be a fact. However, it is necessary to refer empirical faces to the semiotic assemblages from which they emerge: as an effect of a process of formation (*mise en forme*), of a cultural process of subjectification, the face answers to the dual objective of constitution and normalisation. This is why it is not given but rather produced by a cultural mode of domination that Deleuze and Guattari pinpoint as the emergence of capitalism. In the same way, there is no original human nature that the face would cover up, and it is vain or politically naïve to wish to rip it off or to cover it with a better mask that would elude power. This does not prohibit the transformation of one's faciality traits and the deterritorialisation of faces: the art of the novel, the joyful and gay becomings of faces in the history of painting, and the cinematic close-up, all attest to this.

Second principle: the transcendental condition of an assemblage is virtual and immanent. This condition is not identified with the stratified and territorialised assemblage, but rather with its points of deterritorialisation, which Deleuze and Guattari call the 'abstract machine' or 'diagram' of the assemblage. A given empirical face thus refers to an assemblage of faciality, which entails a whole history, that of Christianity and of the formation of European capitalism. To explain this empirical assemblage without resorting to causal determinism, it is necessary to extract the relations of forces that constitute it. Deleuze and Guattari call such an exposition a 'diagram', in homage to Foucault. The diagram is a map of relations of forces that correspond to what Deleuze and Guattari call an 'abstract machine'. 'The abstract machine' is like 'the diagram of the assemblage' (TP 109; see also F 34, 37).

To explain empirical faces, it is thus necessary to relate them to the abstract machine of faciality, the 'black hole-white wall system'. Nevertheless, the diagram and machine do not constitute structures that would represent historical reality, nor antecedent material causes that would generate the relation of forces. The abstract machine of faciality is neither anterior, nor superior, to concrete faces, but rather constitutes the virtual, unstable, informal, intensive map of them. Where a specific assemblage occurs, it is always possible to extract the diagram of forces from it through an epistemological operation that detects points of deterritorialisation at work in the stratified assemblage.

Third principle: it is necessary to avoid universalising the diagram, or the abstract machine, as if it involved an explanatory, transcendent reality. The diagram concerns neither a transcendent Idea, nor an ideological superstructure, nor an economic infrastructure, but rather a virtual map. It is here that Deleuze's transcendental empiricism stakes a claim to its empirical character. It is necessary to explain what sets the abstract machine in motion. As such, the abstract machine is not explanatory. It depends upon an aleatory history that is only retrospectively necessary. Most importantly, it does not answer to any historical teleology. But, once it is engaged, precisely because it 'is not in operation all the time or in just any social formation' (TP 180), we establish its conditions of determinations.

The virtual map of the diagram is thus necessarily implied by a given form of assemblage, but its determination operates through empirical encounters, in a semi-aleatory mode. It is first necessary that the empirical existence of a concrete assemblage be given in the facts. It is not the abstract machine of faciality that determines the existence of concrete faces, as an essence would determine an existence, but we cannot explain the existence of concrete faces without extracting from their actual reality the virtual (but no less real) map of the relations of forces and the becomings that it includes.

Becoming of Forces and the History of Forms

To conclude, Deleuze and Guattari distinguish three modalities that coexist in each face. An empirical face refers to a collective assemblage, a precise historic formation, and assumes a determined, stratified organisation whose mode of domination produces a specific type of territoriality. A given, singular face (first mode) must thus be related to a social assemblage that it actualises in a determinate form (second mode). But, to identify the assemblage of faciality, it is necessary to view it from the point of view of its becoming, its points of deterritorialisation (third mode). Now – and with this Deleuze and Guattari intend to free themselves from the Marxist hypothesis (of a linear determination of the superstructure by the infra-structure) without renouncing a critique of capitalism – the necessity is not of the order of causal factuality, but of a virtual determination. We cannot relate the element of the face to the assemblage that determines it without using the informal map, diagram or abstract machine, which gets extracted from the assemblage. Because it is the same face that we view from the perspective of its actualisation or from that of its becoming. The informal diagram (or abstract machine) and the historical assemblage coexist in the empirical face, just as the virtual and actual, the becoming of forces and the history of forms, coexist.

Bibliography

Alliez, Éric, *La signature du monde, ou, Qu'est-ce que la philosophie de Deleuze et Guattari*, Paris: Cerf, 1993.

Alliez, Éric, *The Signature of the World, or, What is Deleuze and Guattari's Philosophy?* trans. Eliot Ross Albert and Alberto Toscano, New York and London: Continuum, 2004 (1993).

Ansell Pearson, Keith (ed.), *Deleuze and Philosophy: The Difference Engineer*, London and New York: Routledge, 1997.

Bakhtin, Mikhail, *Le marxisme et la philosophie du langage: essai d'application de la méthode sociologique en linguistique*, trans. Marina Yaguello, Paris: Minuit, 1977.

Barbaras, René, 'La puissance du visible: Le sentir chez Merleau-Ponty et Aristote', in *Le tournant de l'expérience: Recherches sur la philosophie de Merleau-Ponty*, Paris: Vrin, 1988, 15–21.

Bene, Carmelo and Gilles Deleuze, *Superpositions*, Paris: Minuit, 1979 (1978).

Bergson, Henri, *Oeuvres*, Paris: Presses Universitaires de France, 1984 (1959).

Bergson, Henri, *Matter and Memory*, trans. N. M. Paul and W. S. Palmer, New York: Zone, 1991.

Blanchot, Maurice, *La part du feu*, Paris: Gallimard, 1949.

Braudel, Fernand, *Civilisation matérielle, économie et capitalisme*, 3 vols, Paris: Livre de Poche, 1967.

Bréhier, Émile, *La théorie des incorporels dans l'ancien stoïcisme*, Paris: Vrin, 1982 (1907).

Cassin, Barbara, *L'effet sophistique*, Paris: Gallimard, 1995.

Clastres, Pierre, *La société contre l'État*, Paris: Minuit, 1974.

Collège Internationale de la Philosophie, *Gilbert Simondon, Une pensée de l'individuation et de la technique*, Paris: Albin Michel, 1994.

Combes, Muriel, *Simondon, Individu et Collectivité: Pour une philosophie transindividual*, Paris: Presses Universitaires de France, 1999.

Deleuze, Gilles, *Empiricism and Subjectivity: An Essay on Hume's Theory of Human Nature*, trans. Constantin V. Boundas, New York: Columbia University Press, 1991 (1953).

Deleuze, Gilles, 'Bergson, 1859–1941', in *Les philosophes célèbres*, ed. Maurice Merleau-Ponty, Paris: Éditions d'Art Lucien Mazenod, 1956, 292–9.

Deleuze, Gilles, 'La conception de la différence chez Bergson', in *Études bergsoniennes*, Paris: Albin Michel, 1956, 79–112.

Deleuze, Gilles, *Nietzsche and Philosophy*, trans. Hugh Tomlinson, New York: Columbia University Press, 1983 (1962).

Deleuze, Gilles, 'Mystère d'Ariane (sur Nietzsche)', *Bulletin de la Société française d'études nietzschéennes*, March 1963, 12–15.

Deleuze, Gilles, *Proust and Signs: The Complete Text*, trans. Richard Howard, London: Athlone, 2000 (1964/1972).

Deleuze, Gilles, 'Gilbert Simondon: L'individuation et sa génèse physico-biologique (Review)', *Revue philosophique de la France et de l'étranger*, 156: 1–3, 1966, 115–18.

Deleuze, Gilles, 'On Gilbert Simondon', in *Desert Islands and Other Texts, 1953–1974*, ed. David Lapoujade, trans. Michael Taorima, Los Angeles: Semiotext(e), 2004 (1966), 86–9.

Deleuze, Gilles, 'Renverser le Platonisme', *Revue de Métaphysique et de Morale*, 71:4, 1966, 426–38.

Deleuze, Gilles, *Différence et Répétition*, Paris: Presses Universitaires de France, 1968.

Deleuze, Gilles, *Difference and Repetition*, trans. Paul Patton, New York: Columbia University Press, 1994 (1968).

Deleuze, Gilles, *Expressionism in Philosophy: Spinoza*, trans. Martin Joughin, New York: Zone, 1990 (1968).

Deleuze, Gilles, 'Sur Nietzsche et l'image de la pensée', *Les lettres françaises*, 1223, 1968, 5, 7, 9.

Deleuze, Gilles, *The Logic of Sense*, ed. Constantin V. Boundas, trans. Mark Lester and Charles Stivale, New York: Columbia University Press, 1990 (1969).

Deleuze, Gilles, *Spinoza: Practical Philosophy*, trans. Robert Hurley, San Francisco: City Lights, 1988 (1970).

Deleuze, Gilles, *Francis Bacon: The Logic of Sensation*, trans. Daniel W. Smith, Minneapolis: University of Minnesota Press, 2003 (1981).

Deleuze, Gilles, *Cinema 1: The Movement-Image*, trans. Hugh Tomlinson and Barbara Habberjam, Minneapolis: University of Minnesota Press, 1991 (1983).

Deleuze, Gilles, *Cinema 2: The Time-Image*, trans. Hugh Tomlinson and Robert Galeta, Minneapolis: University of Minnesota Press, 1991 (1985).

Deleuze, Gilles, *Foucault*, trans. Seán Hand, Minneapolis: University of Minnesota Press, 1988 (1986).

Deleuze, Gilles, *The Fold: Leibniz and the Baroque*, trans. Tom Conley, Minneapolis: University of Minnesota Press, 1992 (1988).

Deleuze, Gilles, *Negotiations: 1972–1990*, trans. Martin Joughin, New York: Columbia University Press, 1995 (1990).

Deleuze, Gilles, *Essays Critical and Clinical*, trans. Daniel W. Smith and Michael A. Greco, Minneapolis: University of Minnesota Press, 1997 (1993).

Deleuze, Gilles, 'L'immanence: une vie . . .', *Philosophie*, 47, 1995, 3–7.

Deleuze, Gilles, *Pure Immanence: Essays on A Life*, trans. Anne Boyman, New York: Zone, 2001.

Deleuze, Gilles, *Two Regimes of Madness: Texts and Interviews, 1975–1995*, ed. David Lapoujade, trans. Ames Hodges and Mike Taormina, New York: Semiotext(e), 2007 (2001).

Deleuze, Gilles, *Desert Islands*, ed. David Lapoujade, trans. Michael Taormina, Los Angeles: Semiotext(e), 2004 (2002).

Deleuze, Gilles and Félix Guattari, 'La synthèse disjunctive', *L'Arc*, 43, 1970 (Special issue on Klossowski), 54–62.

Deleuze, Gilles and Félix Guattari, *Anti-Oedipus: Capitalism and Schizophrenia*, trans. Robert Hurley, Mark Seem and Helen R. Lane, Minneapolis: University of Minnesota Press, 1983 (1972).

Deleuze, Gilles and Félix Guattari, *Kafka: Toward a Minor Literature*, trans. Dana Polan, Minneapolis: University of Minnesota Press, 1986 (1975).

Deleuze, Gilles, and Félix Guattari, *Rhizome: Introduction*, Paris: Minuit, 1976.

Deleuze, Gilles and Félix Guattari, *A Thousand Plateaus: Capitalism and Schizophrenia*, *Volume 2*, trans. Brian Massumi, Minneapolis: University of Minnesota Press, 1988 (1980).

Deleuze, Gilles and Félix Guattari, *What Is Philosophy?*, trans. Hugh Tomlinson and Graham Burchell, New York: Columbia University Press, 1994 (1991).

Deleuze, Gilles, Félix Guattari and Michel Foucault, 'Chapitre V: Le discours du plan', in François Fourquet and Lion Murard (eds), *Recherches*, 13, 1973 (*Les équipements de pouvoir*), 183–6.

Deleuze, Gilles and Claire Parnet, *Dialogues*, trans. Hugh Tomlinson and Barbara Habberjam, London: Continuum, 2002 (1977).

Deligny, Fernand, *Oeuvres*, ed. Sandra Alvarez de Toledo, Paris: L'Arachnéen, 2007.

Deligny, Fernand, *L'Arachnéen et autres textes*, ed. Sandra Alvarez de Toledo, Paris: L'Arachnéen, 2008.

Détienne, Marcel, 'La phalange: problèmes et controverses', in Jean-Pierre Vernant (ed.), *Problèmes de la guerre en Grèce ancienne*, Paris: La Haye, 1968, 119–42.

Flaxman, Gregory, *Gilles Deleuze and the Fabulation of Philosophy: Powers of the False*, vol. 1, Minneapolis: University of Minnesota Press, 2012.

Foucault, Michel, 'Le «non» du père', *Critique*, 178, 1962, 195–209. Reprinted in Foucault, *Dits et écrits*, vol. 1, ed. Daniel Defert and François Ewald, Paris: Gallimard, 2001, 217–31.

Foucault, Michel, *Maurice Blanchot: The Thought from Outside*, trans. Jeffrey Mehlman, New York: Zone, 1987 (1966).

Foucault, Michel, 'La pensée du dehors' (1966), in *Dits et écrits*, vol. 1, ed. Daniel Defert and François Ewald, Paris: Gallimard, 2001, 546–67.

Foucault, Michel, 'Qu'est-ce qu'un auteur?', *Bulletin de la Société française de la philosophie*, 63:3, 1969, 73–104. Reprinted in *Dits et écrits*, vol. 1, ed. Daniel Denfert and François Ewald, Paris: Gallimard, 2001, 817–49.

Foucault, Michel, 'What is an Author?', in *Aesthetics, Method, and Epistemology*, ed. James D. Faubion, New York: New Press, 1998 (1969), 205–22.

Foucault, Michel, 'What is an Author?', in *The Essential Foucault*, ed. Paul Rabinow and Mark Seem, New York: New Press, 2003 (1969), 377–91.

Foucault, Michel, *L'ordre du discours*, Paris: Gallimard, 1970.

Foucault, Michel, *The History of Madness*, ed. Jean Khalfa, trans. Jonathan Murphy and Jean Khalfa, London and New York: Routledge, 2006 (1972).

Foucault, Michel, *Discipline and Punish: The Birth of the Prison*, trans. Alan Sheridan, New York: Vintage, 1995 (1975).

Foucault, Michel, *Histoire de la sexualité, vol. 1: La volonté de savoir*, Paris: Gallimard, 1976.

Foucault, Michel, 'The Thought of the Outside', in *Aesthetics, Method, and Epistemology*, ed. James D. Faubion, trans. Robert Hurley et al., New York: New Press, 1998, 147–69.

Foucault, Michel, *Dits et Écrits*, 2 vols, ed. Daniel Defert and François Ewald, Paris: Gallimard, 2001.

Foucault, Michel, Blandine Kriegel, Anne Thalmy, François Beguin and Bruno Fortier, *Les machines à guérir (aux origines de la hôpital moderne)*, Paris: Institut de l'environnement, 1976.

Francastel, Pierre, *Peinture et société, naissance et destruction d'un espace plastique, de la Renaissance au cubisme*, Paris: Gallimard, 1965 (1951).

Francastel, Pierre, *La Figure et le lieu: l'ordre visuel du Quattrocento*, Paris: Gallimard, 1967.

Guattari, Félix, 'La transversalité', *Psychothérapie institutionnelle*, 1, 1965, 91–106.

Guattari, Félix, *Psychanalyse et transversalité: essais d'analyse institutionnelle*, Paris: Maspero, 1972.

Guattari, Félix, *La révolution moléculaire*, Fontenay-sous-Bois: Recherches, 1977.

Guattari, Félix, *The Machinic Unconscious: Essays in Schizoanalysis*, trans. Taylor Adkins, Los Angeles: Semiotext(e), 2011 (1979).

Guattari, Félix, *Les années d'hiver*, Paris: Barrault, 1986.

Guattari, Félix, *Schizoanalytic Cartographies*, trans. Andrew Goffey, London: Bloomsbury, 2012 (1989).

Guattari, Félix, *The Three Ecologies*, London: Athlone, 2000 (1989).

Guattari, Félix, *Chaosmosis: An Ethico-Aesthetic Paradigm*, trans. Ian Pindar and Paul Sutton, London and New York: Bloomsbury, 2014 (1992).

Guattari, Félix and Suely Rolnik, *Molecular Revolution in Brazil*, trans. Carel Clapshow and Brian Holmes, Los Angeles: Semiotext(e) and Cambridge, MA: MIT Press, 2008.

Guillaume, Gustave, *Temps et Verbe*, Paris: Champion, 1965.

Haudricourt, André-Georges, 'Domestication des animaux, culture de plantes et traitement d'autrui', *L'Homme: Revue française d'anthropologie*, 2:1, 1962, 40–50.

Haudricourt, André-Georges, 'Nature et culture dans la civilisation de l'igname: l'origine des clones et des clans', *L'Homme: Revue française d'anthropologie*, 4:1, 1964, 93–104.

Hottois, Gilbert, *Simondon et la philosophie de la 'culture technique'*, Brussels: de Boeck, 1993.

Jakobson, Roman and Claude Lévi-Strauss, '"Les Chats" de Charles Baudelaire', *L'Homme: Revue française d'anthropologie*, 2:1, 1962, 5–21.

Kisser, Thomas, 'Visualität, Virtualität, Temporalität', in Thomas Kisser (ed.), *Bild und Zeit: Temporalität in Kunst und Kunsttheorie seit 1800*, Munich: Wilhelm Fink, 2011, 87–136.

Kisser, Thomas, 'Carnation et incarnation: Logique picturale et logique religieuse dans l'oeuvre tardive du Titien', in Audrey Rieber (ed.), *Penser l'art, penser l'histoire*, Paris: L'Harmattan, 2014.

Lacan, Jacques, *The Seminar of Jacques Lacan, Book III: The Psychoses*, trans. Russell Grigg, New York: Norton, 1997 (1958).

Lacan, Jacques, *Écrits*, trans. Bruce Fink, New York: Norton, 2006 (1966).

Laplanche, Jean, *Hölderlin and the Question of the Father*, trans. Luke Carson, Victoria, British Columbia: ELS Editions, 2007 (1961).

Leroi-Gourhan, André, *L'homme et la matière*, 2 vols, Paris: Albin Michel, 1971 (1943).

Leroi-Gourhan, André, *Milieu et techniques*, Paris: Albin Michel, 1973 (1945).

Leroi-Gourhan, André, *Le Geste et la parole*, Paris: Albin Michel, 1964.

Lévi-Strauss, Claude, *Preface to the Work of Marcel Mauss*, trans. Felicity Baker, London: Routledge, 2002 (1950).

Marker, Chris, 'Fernand Deligny: Les vagabonds efficaces', *Esprit*, 148, 1948, 434–5.

Merleau-Ponty, Maurice, *La phénomenologie de la perception*, Paris: Gallimard, 1985 (1945).

Monod, Jacques, *Le hasard et la nécessité*, Paris: Seuil, 1970.

Moreau, Pierre-François, *Fernand Deligny et les idéologies de l'enfance*, Paris: Éditions Retz, 1978.

Moreau, Pierre-François, 'Quand la psychologie passe l'arme à gauche', *Quinzaine Littéraire*, 332, 1980, 23.

Mumford, Louis, *Technics and Civilization*, New York: Harcourt, Brace & World, 1934.

Mumford, Lewis, *The City in History: Its Origins, Transformations, Prospects*, New York: Harcourt, Brace & World, 1961.

Mumford, Louis, 'The First Megamachine', *Diogenes*, 14, 1966, 1–15.

Nietzsche, Friedrich, *The Gay Science*, trans. Walter Kaufmann, New York: Vintage, 1974.

Oury, Jean, Félix Guattari and François Tosquelles, *Pratique de l'institutionnel et politique*, Vigneux: Matrice, 1985.

Pasolini, Pier Paolo, *Heretical Empiricism*, trans. Ben Lawton and Louise K. Barnett, Bloomington: Indiana University Press, 1985 (1972).

Pearson, Keith Ansell (ed.), *Deleuze and Philosophy: The Difference Engineer*, London and New York: Routledge, 1997.

Polack, Jean-Claude and Danielle Sivadon-Sabourin, *La Borde, ou, la droit à la folie*, Paris: Calmann-Lévy, 1976.

Reuleaux, Franz, *Cinématique: principes fondamentaux d'une théorie générale des machines*, Paris: Savy, 1877.

Ruyer, Raymond, 'La conscience et la vie', *Cahiers de la philosophie*, 32, 1951, 37–57.

Ruyer, Raymond, *La génèse des formes vivantes*, Paris: Flammarion, 1958.

Sauvagnargues, Anne, *Deleuze: L'empirisme transcendental*, Paris: Presses Universitaires de France, 2010.

Sauvagnargues, Anne, *Deleuze and Art*, trans. Samantha Bankston, London: Bloomsbury, 2013.

Sauvagnargues, Anne, François Zourabichvili and Paola Marrati, *La philosophie de Deleuze*, Paris: Presses Universitaires de France, 2004.

Simondon, Gilbert, 'L'amplification dans les processus d'information', in *Cahiers de Royaumont* 5, Paris: Minuit, 1962.

Simondon, Gilbert, *Individuation psychique et collective: à la lumière des notions de forme, information, potential, et métastatique*, Paris: Aubier, 1989.

Simondon, Gilbert, *L'individuation et sa genèse physico-biologique*, Grenoble: Millon, 1995.

Simondon, Gilbert, *L'individuation à la lumière des notions de forme et d'information*, Grenoble: Millon, 2005.

Vernant, Jean Pierre, *Mythe et pensée chez les Grecs*, 2 vols, Paris: Maspero, 1974.

White Jr., Lynn, *Medieval Technology and Social Change*, Oxford: Clarendon Press, 1962.

Worringer, Wilhelm, *Form in Gothic*, trans. Herbert Read, London: G. P. Putnam's Sons, 1927.

Zourabichvili, François, *Le vocabulaire de Deleuze*, Paris: Ellipses, 2003.

Zourabichvili, François, 'La question de la littéralité', in Bruno Gelas and Hervé Micolet (eds), *Deleuze et les écrivains: littérature et philosophie*, Nantes: Éditions Cécile, 2007.

Zourabichvili, François, *La littéralité et autres écrits sur l'art*, Paris: Presses Universitaires de France, 2011.

Index

EU Authorised Representative:

Easy Access System Europe Mustamäe tee 50, 10621 Tallinn, Estonia

gpsr.requests@easproject.com

Printed and bound by CPI Group (UK) Ltd, Croydon, CR0 4YY

16/09/2025

01956800-0007